German Baroque Drama

Twayne's World Authors Series

Ulrich Weisstein, Editor of German Literature

Indiana University

TWAS 634

Sophonisbe accepts the poison sent her by Masinissa, engraved frontispiece by J. Sandrart from Daniel Casper von Lohenstein's Sophonisbe, Trauerspiel *(Breslau: J. Fellgibel, 1689). Reproduced courtesy of the Special Collections Department of the Milton S. Eisenhower Library, The Johns Hopkins University, Baltimore, Maryland.*

German Baroque Drama

By Judith Popovich Aikin

The University of Iowa

Twayne Publishers • *Boston*

German Baroque Drama

Judith Popovich Aikin

Copyright © 1982 by G.K. Hall & Company
All Rights Reserved
Published by Twayne Publishers
A Division of G. K. Hall & Company
70 Lincoln Street
Boston, Massachusetts 02111

Book Production by Marne B. Sultz

Book Design by Barbara Anderson

Printed on permanent/durable acid-free
paper and bound in the United States of
America.

**Library of Congress Cataloging in
Publication Data**

Aikin, Judith Popovich, 1946–
    German baroque drama.

(Twayne's world author series; TWAS 634)
Bibliography: p. 169
Includes index.
1. German   drama—Early   modern,
1500–1700—   History and Criticism
I. Title.   II. Series.
PT636.A35 1982   832'.4'09   82-9270
ISBN 0-8057-6477-1   AACR2

To my parents,
Milosh Popovich and Jeanne Hartman Popovich,
with love and gratitude

Contents

About the Author

Judith Popovich Aikin received the M.A. degree at the University of Oregon in 1969 and the Ph.D. degree at the University of California at Berkeley in 1974. She is an associate professor at the University of Iowa, where she has been teaching since 1975. Publications in the field of this study include a book on Lohenstein's dramas (*The Mission of Rome in the Dramas of Daniel Casper von Lohenstein: Historical Tragedy as Prophecy and Polemic*, Stuttgart, 1976) and articles and papers on Lohenstein's *Cleopatra*, Hofmannswaldau's *Pastor fido* translation, Stieler's *Der Vermeinte Printz*, Baroque "catharsis," the play-within-the-play motif, and Gryphius's tragedy *cum* satyr play. She is preparing a facsimile edition of the complete dramas of Caspar Stieler with extensive introductory material for the Nachdrucke deutscher Literatur des 17. Jahrhunderts series.

Preface

Drama was far more important during the Baroque Age than in any subsequent period in Germany, for theater—the true medium of expression for the dramatic text—was the major form of entertainment for all social classes at the time. Theatrical performances punctuated the liturgical year with appropriate dramatizations of biblical events, accompanied market days and seasonal festivals, were the pedagogically sound culmination of the school year, and added luster to courtly festivities and occasions of state. As various theaters or troupes vied with one another for recognition and popularity, the entertainment value was enhanced: theatricality was born. And the most creative and clever dramatists took advantage of their power over their enthralled audiences by using the plays to promote their religious or philosophical perceptions of the world, to alter behavior of princes and subjects alike, and to influence personages and events in the lesser and greater political arenas of Germany.

This study of German Baroque drama, the first attempt at a complete survey of the subject, is designed to acquaint the English-speaking reader with a body of literary texts, none of which has been translated into English, and many of which are even difficult to locate in the original German (some exist only in one or two copies in Eastern Europe). Even the specialist in the German Baroque, however, should find much of interest in this study, for the interpretations provided for the plays (stressing religious and political allegory, effect upon the audience, political theory, and the "life is a stage" theme) are usually original and occasionally in direct opposition to established scholarship.

This volume is intended as a partner to two other genre surveys in the Twayne World Authors Series, *German Baroque Poetry* and *The German Baroque Novel.* Due to the limits of the format, it was neither possible nor desirable to aspire to absolute completeness. The selection of plays to be examined here was based on my perception of their importance, aesthetically and as a contribution to a balanced overview of the period, and (in the minor genres) on availability. As a bulky footnote apparatus was to be avoided, it would not have been possible to give credit to others wherever it was due, even if it were feasible to track down the origins of what has become general knowledge in the field. For these reasons, there is no clear division in this study between my own contributions and generally accepted views. I can only acknowledge my great debt to past and present Baroque scholarship here and in the selected bibliography. Several of the most recent items in the bibliography were available to me too late to be included in the text.

Since the purpose of the series is to present foreign literatures to English-speaking readers, I have provided an English translation for each quotation and for each German term at its first appearance. In transcribing the seventeenth-century German, I have modernized only to the extent of following modern usage for j/i and v/u and placing an umlaut instead of an "e" over certain vowels. Wherever possible I have used recent editions of the texts. Complete critical editions exist only for the plays of Lohenstein and Gryphius at present, but many others are generally available in collections, facsimile editions, or the microfilm series of the Yale University Library. I have resorted to the rare original seventeenth-century editions only in the absence of such modern multiple copies for particular authors or plays I considered indispensable to the study.

Judith Popovich Aikin

The University of Iowa

Acknowledgments

I would like to acknowledge my debt of gratitude to the American Philosophical Society for a travel grant which enabled me to finish my research for *German Baroque Drama* and to the University of Iowa for its support of the project in the form of a research assistant, research office space, excellent library holdings and services, typing funds, computer time, and a leave of absence. The following individuals contributed in some major way to the project, and therefore also deserve my heartfelt thanks: Professor Ulrich Weisstein for his helpful editorial comments and criticisms; Professors Blake Lee Spahr, John D. Lindberg, and Edward Dvoretzky for their support in my quest for funding; my colleague Professor James Pusack for introducing me to the text editor on the university computer and for offering corrections for the notes and references and bibliography; Dr. Sue Otto, for her help with the computerized text; the students of my Baroque Seminar, fall 1979, whose ideas and reactions always stimulated and often influenced my writing; my mother-in-law, Professor Marian Carlin, for her companionship and child care during the European research trip; and, above all, my husband, Roger, for his patience and love, and my son Tom, who had to forgo many hours of his mother's time, if none of her love, for the sake of this project.

Chronology

1653   Lohenstein's *Ibrahim Bassa* appears in print.

1657   Gryphius's original dramas to date appear in print.

1659   Gryphius's *Papinianus*; Avancini's *Pietas Victrix*.

1660   Lohenstein's *Cleopatra* (first version).

1660–1661   Gryphius's *Verlibtes Gespenste/Die Gelibte Dornrose*.

1664   Gryphius dies.

1665   Lohenstein's *Epicharis* and *Agrippina*.

1665–1667   Rudolstädter Festpiele (comedies by Filidor = Caspar Stieler).

1666   Lohenstein's *Sophonisbe* written and performed; Hallmann's *Theodoricus*.

1662–1667   Johann Mitternacht's dramas appear in print.

1670   Hallmann's *Mariamne*.

1673   Lohenstein's *Ibrahim Sultan*.

1679   Christian Weise begins his dramatic production with *Der Bäurische Machiavellus* (published 1681).

1680   Lohenstein's *Sophonisbe* and revised *Cleopatra* published. Stieler's *Bellemperie* and *Willmut* written and published.

1682–1683   Weise's *Masaniello*.

1683   Lohenstein dies.

1688–1702   Weise's "pause" in dramatic production.

1695–1700   Christian Reuter's dramatic production.

1707   Stieler dies.

1708   Weise dies.

Chapter One
Introduction

All the world's a stage,
And all the men and women merely players:
They have their exits and their entrances;
And one man in his time plays many parts.
(*As You Like It,* II, vii, 139ff.)

The cynical philosophy of Shakespeare's melancholic Jaques, pronounced at the threshold of the seventeenth century, reveals not only the character's own skepticism about the value and uniqueness of human life, but can also speak for the predominant *Weltanschauung* of Germany during the entire century as well. The theatrical metaphor for life expresses the transitoriness and vanity of earthly existence, and points out that the basis for these negative qualities is the dichotomy between appearance and reality, between role and actor, that is inherent in all human endeavor. Human actions, rather than deriving from individual decisions or even circumstances, merely follow a preextant "script" (destiny or the Divine Plan for history). The role played by any individual in this "script" is assigned independently of worth or talent—on the basis of such arbitrary categories as social caste, age, sex, or nationality. The importance of theater in the seventeenth century in Germany may lie in part in the fact that the metaphor was also capable of inversion: not only was life a stage, but the theater was life, distilled and represented on a higher and more abstract plane. Its function was to present the essence of life and of human experience in a form understandable to a wide audience. The very existence of the metaphor as a commonplace made theater exceptionally effective as a vehicle for such thought.

This survey of seventeenth-century German drama is intended to complement the two other monographs in the Twayne World Authors Series on literature of the seventeenth century in Germany—*The German Baroque Novel* and *German Baroque Poetry*. In spite of the objections

1

raised against the term "Baroque" by such scholars as Curtius and Hartmann,[1] it continues to be used to denote the artistic and literary production of the seventeenth (and often the early eighteenth) century. Objections to the term usually point to the varying definitions and resultant lack of clarity of the word. To some, "Baroque" is an ornate style of art of a particular epoch; to others, it is a recurring stylistic phenomenon which reappears cyclically as a reaction to "classical" artistic production; others, leery of any definition based on style, have limited its use to the label for an historical period.[2] Persistent utilization of the term in the face of its problematical meaning is probably indicative of its ultimate usefulness—it is a less bulky adjective than "seventeenth-century," and it seems to identify the wide variety of included literary and artistic phenomena better than such suggested alternatives as "Mannerist,"[3] "Counter-Reform,"[4] or "Jesuitical."[5] As it is used in the title of this study, it is to be taken to mean, following Wellek,[6] the historical period, but one which I believe exhibits some kind of underlying unity of style and *Weltanschauung* which crosses national and class boundaries. As Brauneck has said,[7] further argument concerning the term would constitute an anachronism; the task ahead in seventeenth-century studies is to examine common or distinct traditions of the European Baroque era and their reception and use by literary figures. This study of the German Baroque drama may aid scholars in fields outside German to embark on such an effort by providing a survey of a difficult and often unprocurable body of literature; on the other hand, since it is the first to attempt a synthetic presentation of the drama of the period, it should prove to be of interest to students and scholars of the specialized field as well.

Because of its nature, drama presents more problems as a genre than narrative or lyric literature. Drama—even so-called "Lesedrama"—cannot be separated from at least hypothetical theatrical presentation. Theater presupposes not a number of isolated readers, each reacting individually to a work, but rather a composite audience of viewers interacting with one another as they interact individually with the presentation. It also presumes actual visual and audial stimuli, rather than those merely imagined by a reader. In other words, drama is the literary genre ideally suited for strongly influencing the minds of a group. For this reason, it, more than other literary genres, can be seen to have a social purpose. It has the potential to be an organ for polemical stances on politics, morality, and religion, and in seventeenth-century Germany the realization of this generic potential became a primary goal for dramatists.

On the other hand, the dramatic genre provides more opportunity for the manipulations of *homo ludens* than any other literary genre. A drama presented in a theater can attempt, as no other kind of literary creation can, to produce a total illusion of reality. In seventeenth-century Germany, stage sets were elaborate perspectival devices designed to trick the eye into thinking it saw a vast landscape or cityscape in which the actors, dressed in period costume, acted out their roles in imitation of real personages. But accompanying this elaborate illusion in the mind and eye of the audience is always its opposite and counterpart: the knowledge that what is seen and heard is illusory, that it takes place on a small stage, and that the emotional speeches of the characters are merely lines memorized by the skilled professional actors, courtiers, or even schoolboys. This paradox underlying the aesthetic appreciation of drama was, on the one hand, an opportunity for humor and lighthearted fun, but since it was also perceived as an analogy to the nature of earthly existence, it had a more serious and metaphysical side as well. When Lohenstein modestly introduces his tragedy *Sophonisbe* with the phrase, "Ich liefer' nur ein Spiel" (I offer a mere play), the result is ironic, for he has just expounded at great length that *Spiel*—in the sense of "playfulness"—is the underlying force behind the inner workings of the cosmos and all human endeavors within it. Drama itself, then, is a prevalent metaphor for the existential crisis of seventeenth-century man, caught in the net of paradoxes involving appearance and reality, time and eternity, life and death. What it has to offer is not only social, political, and practical in nature, but also metaphysical and religious.

Drama in seventeenth-century Germany also is a major sphere of activity for the tendency to try to concretize abstract concepts. This tendency finds its most intriguing manifestations in the love of emblem and allegory, in the use of personification, in the manufacture of colorful, concrete compound nouns to substitute for Latin abstractions, and in the creation of a story or reuse of a story for its ability to express an abstract moral or religious truth. All such concretizations are to be found in the other literary genres of the German Baroque, but find in the dramatic form their culmination, since drama by its nature is a concretization of abstractions, a presentation and acting out on stage of words. This tendency for concretization has led the eighteenth-century literary theorist and critic Herder, and more recently Albrecht Schöne,[8] to term the period the "Emblematic Age" and Herbert Cysarz, among others,[9] to see allegory as the determining structure of the period. Both concepts make reference to the tendency of literary works of the period to have a twofold structure composed of the concrete representation and its underlying abstraction—in emblematic jargon, a *pictura* and a *subscriptio*; in the terms of allegorists, a literal and a mystic sense. This theory of a twofold structure of representation and hidden meaning will be the basis of interpretation used in this survey. The allegorical, rather than emblematic, perspective will predominate; the result will be, in most cases, a Christian, religious interpretation.

Previous attempts to discuss seventeenth-century drama adopted various categorizations to organize the presentation of the material. The major types of categorization that have been applied in the past include geographical centers, confessional differences, class, and genre divisions. It should be understood that "Germany," in the seventeenth century, did not exist. The German-speaking area of Europe, shrunken to the south and west since the Middle Ages, but greatly expanded to the east, was composed of an old power which ruled more of Europe on paper and in its polemic than in actuality (the Holy Roman Empire), a rising power ("der große Kurfürst," or Great Elector of Brandenburg), and dozens of large and small principalities and free cities. Much of the "German" literature to be discussed in this book was actually written in areas to the east of present-day West Germany—in what is now East Germany, Poland, Russia, Czechoslovakia, and Austria. Many surveys of German seventeenth-century literature divide the material by geographical centers, of which the most important were Königsberg, Nürnberg, and Breslau, but such categories are perhaps less important for the development of drama than for other genres. While geographical location of major dramatists will be mentioned, it will not be stressed in this study. Easy distribution of manuscript and printed copies, and increased opportunities for travel, after all, meant that geography had become less important as a determinant of influences.

Religious divisions during the Thirty Years War and in the decades following it would seem to be important. One might imagine that the confessional differences, which usually provided the stated reason for the war and which were not entirely resolved as a result of it, would have determined the easy categorization of dramatists into Protestant and Catholic. Instead, major German dramas in the second half of the seventeenth century are typically aconfessional. Jesuit dramas not only provided models for Protestant dramatists, but were even translated by them on occasion. The historical dramas of the Catholic convert Hallmann do not differ enough in confessional content from those of his fellow Breslau dramatists Gryphius and Lohenstein, both Protestants, to constitute a separate category. In fact, drama between 1640 and 1680 (the high point of seventeenth-century German drama and the period to be stressed in this study) tends to present an ideal of Christianity which rises above confessional differences. Its appeal, whether from the pen of a Protestant or a Catholic, was to all German-speaking Christians. Even Jesuit drama created during this period seems rarely to have a strictly Catholic perspective on the histories it presents.

The seventeenth century in Germany has been termed the transitional phase in which feudal and folk art coexist or the bourgeois emancipatory period,[10] but class distinctions are probably not the best way to distinguish dramatists or their audiences, either. While folk drama certainly continued to be created and performed, it was not of a literary quality or nature. A few princes dabbled in theater, but it would make little sense to create a category for them. Courtly drama, that is, drama written for and often produced at the many courts, was created in most instances by members of the educated middle class who filled the ministries and civil service positions in various governments. Some of these "courtly" dramatists dedicated their entire production to pieces intended for performance at court, while others apparently wrote their plays for performance by schoolboys of their own social class, but also sent copies to court complete with dedications to courtiers or princes. In the period under discussion, there seem to be few class-oriented distinctions in those historical dramas written for middle-class school production and those for performance at court. This fact may reflect the desire for upward mobility of these middle-class servants of nobility (a real possibility—many such talented officials were made government advisers and were elevated to the minor nobility) or it may indicate that the concept of drama transcended class boundaries. The rhetorical school drama culminating in Christian Weise, however, represents a deviation from this elevated "classless" drama.

German drama in the period can be divided into two major types and a host of minor ones. Most important and of highest status was the *Trauerspiel* (literally, "sadness play"), nearly always with a plot based on historical events. The *Lustspiel* ("happiness play"), *Scherzspiel* ("joke play"), and *Schäferspiel* ("pastoral play") were various manifestations of comic drama. Although the terms of Greek origin, *Tragödie* and *Komödie,* are often used interchangeably with these German terms, both by seventeenth-century sources and by modern scholars, it should be recognized that the German plays of the period fit neither the Aristotelian definitions nor the practice of classical Greek and Roman drama. Other dramatic forms important in the seventeenth century defy all attempts at classical categorization: *Festspiel* (festive play), *Singspiel* (musical comedy), *Oratorio* (sacred musical drama), and early opera were more popular genres of theater for the courts and patrician audiences than were the tragedies and comedies, while folk theater— consisting of *Fastnachtspiele* and *Schwänke* ("Shrovetide plays" and "burlesques") and liturgical plays and augmented in the seventeenth century by the political plays and love stories of the itinerant stage— continued to entertain not only the lower social class audiences, but those of towns and courts as well. The system of categorization by dramatic form, with chronological development within each, has been chosen as that most appropriate for this study. This choice will allow stress to be placed on exploration of aesthetic norms in dramatic theory and practice. If the chapter on tragedy seems to dominate this study in terms of allotted space, let it be known that *Trauerspiel* likewise monopolizes both theory and practice of the period in terms of assessed valuation and quality of product.

The drama and dramatic theory of seventeenth-century Germany are not isolated phenomena, but have interconnections with other European literatures, albeit not with major currents. While Shakespeare's plays seem not to have been accessible to German authors directly, many of their plots and some of their theatrical devices entered German literature through the intermediary of itinerant English theater troupes. Late Renaissance and early seventeenth-century tragedy and comedy from Spain, Italy, and France had a more direct effect on

Germany, but most of the acknowledged great figures among romanic dramatists—Calderón de la Barca, Lope de Vega, Pierre Corneille, and Racine—probably had no influence at all. Molière's comedies entered Germany via translation as early as 1670, but cannot be shown to have altered German dramatic practice until at least the end of the century. While many of the theorists pay lip service to Scaliger, their own theories tend to describe dramatic practice in Germany rather than promote the neo-classical principles of French theory. Seventeenth-century Germany tended, much like England, to create a drama out of whole cloth to fit its own needs, often turning to the same gold-mines of plot sources—the Italian novella and the various universal chronicles. Perhaps only in opera, as practiced in the great southern German courts of Vienna and Munich (usually created entirely by Italians), did German Baroque theater participate in a homogeneous pan-European movement. What makes German Baroque drama unique will become apparent in the course of this study.

Chapter Two
Origins of German Baroque Drama

While it would be tempting to construct a theory of development in a straight line from the earliest known dramas of antiquity to the theatrical creations of seventeenth-century Germany, such an organic and logical growth does not seem to have occurred. The roots of German Baroque drama can be traced to classical Greek and Roman plays, but the influence is direct, not one of gradual transition and change through the centuries. As a matter of fact, the history of the sources of inspiration and influence for German Baroque drama is a long series of discontinuities, rediscoveries, reinterpretations, and totally new and naive creations.

Medieval Drama

Roman civilization in the outposts of transalpine Europe seems to have had a theatrical tradition of wandering theater troupes, perhaps not at the level of Seneca, Terence, or Plautus, but at least as an activity of professional entertainers. Likewise, the Germanic inhabitants of the area in pre-Christian centuries have been shown to have had some kind of semidramatic traditions associated with pagan rites.[1] In spite of the attempts of scholarship to link these two pre-Christian traditions to the German liturgical drama of the Middle Ages, however, no such relationship has been conclusively shown; indeed, even the likelihood is remote. Instead, it seems that Christian drama arose spontaneously, a fresh reinvention of the dramatic genre, after a break in the tradition of the theater in the period of decline of classical civilization.[2]

Christian or liturgical drama seems to have originated during the Carolingian Renaissance from passages called "tropes," which were unsanctioned literary additions to the authorized liturgical text. Such tropes had dramatic potential because they were usually in the form of dialogue, perhaps itself a reflection of the structure of much of the liturgy (which consisted of a dialoguelike statement and response—antiphony—by priest and choir or priest and congregation). The tropes also tended to select events, often on the periphery of the religious milestones, which most effectively dramatized and humanized the biblical history.

Three major tropes of the Easter week liturgy developed into dramatic performances: the *depositio* (burial of a crucifix and/or host, in a ceremony symbolic of the burial of Christ, on Good Friday), the *elevatio* (raising of same at dawn on Easter Sunday), and the *visitatio* (visit of the three Marys to the tomb at dawn of the third day to discover the empty sepulcher guarded by an angel who tells them of the risen Christ and commands them to announce the resurrection). The last of these, since it involves not just a symbolic ceremony or rite, but a plot involving impersonation, realistic dialogue, and a modicum of insight into the human side of biblical events of cosmic importance, remained the most popular through the centuries, and underwent seemingly endless variations and elaborations.

The Christmas story also received dramatization, and once again peripheral events, rather than the central story of Christ's birth in Bethlehem, were those chosen for development as tropes and (eventually) as dramas: stories of the shepherds, the three kings, and the jealousy of Herod culminating in the slaughter of the innocents. Other topics evolved from biblical readings, rather than from the liturgical text: plays of the Last Judgment and the Antichrist, or Old Testament stories thought to prefigure events of the New Testament. Still others had no connection to the liturgy or to the Bible: the so-called "miracle" and "martyr" plays, which told the stories of the saints and their relics.

In the later Middle Ages, the liturgical and other spiritual plays began to be separated from the liturgical text and church service for a number of reasons. Their expanded length no longer allowed their production within the framework of the liturgy; they showed increasing tendencies toward adding secular, often comic episodes; they required a large performance area to accommodate the multiple scenes, more elaborate sets, and casts of dozens. This process of secularization, which caused the plays to be moved out of the apse and eventually outside the church to the marketplace, was also characterized by a turn to the vernacular. At first the German appeared side by side with the

Latin, alternating with it. Gradually, however, the vernacular took over, leaving only a few lines of Latin—the traditional core of the original trope—as in the famous *Innsbrucker Osterspiel* [Innsbruck Easter Play] of 1391. Freed of the spatial and temporal confines of the church and its liturgy, the plays continued to expand until they became those pageants commonly known as "Passion Plays" or "Mystery Plays," which involved hundreds of participants and required several days for performance. These plays, exemplified to modern audiences and students of theater by the Oberammergau Passion Play, tried to encapsulate the entire history of salvation (*Heilsgeschichte*) from the Creation to the Last Judgment, the focal point being the sacrifice of Christ's passion.

At this time another type of religious play also arose. A "Morality Play" presents the salvation or damnation of the soul through the dialogue and actions of personifications of good and evil, the human soul, the virtues and vices, etc.[3] Instead of being imitation of historical or biblical events and personages, these plays present a typical, universal struggle in abstracted form—the allegorical significance or "moral" behind each individual's specific life story.

The religious drama of the Middle Ages, whether attached to the liturgy or separated from it, had a clear purpose: to educate the members of the Christian audience about their faith in order to strengthen their beliefs, and to convert the skeptical and heretical. Like the frescos which decorated church walls, these plays formed a kind of "Pauper's Bible" for the illiterate. They helped to bring the historical events which formed the core of Christian dogma to life by imitating them. The performers' involvement was seen to constitute giving honor to God, an action contributing to their salvation. Some plays also had a semipolitical function, in that they urged support of political entities, particularly the Holy Roman Empire, albeit for religious reasons.

In order to accomplish this spiritual improvement of the audience, the religious drama of the Middle Ages employed theatrical techniques which, as many modern scholars have pointed out, show similarities to the anti-illusionistic Brechtian or "Epic" theater of this century.[4] Those plays with more than one scene, instead of changing sets, used a device termed the simultaneous stage (*Simultanbühne*)—a playing space with a series of sets all seen simultaneously, but used one at a time. When outdoor performance permitted spatial expansiveness, it was often necessary for the audience, too, to move to the next set when the actors did so, thus giving the audience a feeling of participation in a kind of religious procession from set to set. Elements of folk entertainment such as song, dance, and clowning were often interspersed in serious religious works. Many plays, to underscore their didactic or polemical intent, used a commentator of some kind—a prologue or epilogue speaker, or even a "rector ludi" who provided a running commentary on the portrayed events.

The actors were often low-level clerics or even, in the case of a production by a convent, nuns, but more often boys (even for the women's roles) from a monastic school. In the later Middle Ages, lay brotherhoods and craftsmen's guilds often provided the performers, as well as the technical personnel, props, and costumes. In other words, the performance of a medieval religious play was not a product of a professional troupe of trained actors, nor had the authors any literary ambitions. The plays of the nun Roswitha von Gandersheim may have been an exception, but these constituted an isolated phenomenon, neither part of the mainstream medieval tradition nor even influential until rediscovered by the Humanists in the early sixteenth century.

As the Middle Ages were drawing to a close, there arose a new, secular theater and body of theatrical works called *Fastnachtspiele* (plays for the pre-Lenten season) which existed side by side with the religious drama. In attempting to trace the origins of this worldly and comic theatrical genre, scholars have tried to connect it to the pre-Christian dramalike rites of the Germanic peoples, to the performances (recitations) of heroic narrative works filled with dialogue in both Germanic and Courtly times, to the popular dialogue presentations of philosophical or theological themes (*Streitgespräche*), or to the ever-expanding secular comic scenes which were to be found in the religious plays (e. g., the purchase of unguents by the three Marys in the *visitatio*).[5] But none of these possible sources can be shown to constitute a true secular dramatic tradition, and the *Fastnachtspiel* itself seems to be an original product of the early fifteenth century. Indeed, the *Fastnachtspiel* (often called in English "carnival farce" or "Shrovetide play") seems to have evolved spontaneously from the customs of *Fastnacht* (*Karneval,* the period of "letting go" before Lenten fasting) and to have remained bound to its original function as contribution to the festivities until the Reformation. These short dramatic entertainments (they were rarely over 300 lines of *Knittelvers*) tended to express the central ideas of *Karneval*—the animality of man's nature which will then be overcome in the Lenten fasting to follow. The coarse humor relies on obscene and scatological subject matter.

The *Fastnachtspiel* is an interesting episode in the history of theater, for its relationship to the audience is unique. The play created no illusions and established no reality in its own right but remained integrated in the festivities. The acted reality did not separate itself from its audience—the actors materialized from the crowd and reentered it at the play's end. Often the play ended with a dance in which actors chose partners from the audience, thus purposely erasing any temporary separation created by the play. The "stage" was merely a cleared space in the room where the celebration took place, and there were generally few props and no scenery. The play was usually introduced by the "Praecursor"—the director/author—whose speech stressed the integration of reality represented by the play into the reality of the audience and thus eliminated any possibility of the creation of illusion. The entire production was done by amateurs.

The early *Fastnachtspiele,* exemplified particularly in the works of Hans Rosenplüt (ca. 1400 to ca. 1470) of Nuremberg, were primarily a series of monologues on a theme (*Reihenspiel*); gradually, a new type of *Fastnachtspiel* developed which revolved around a plot in the modern sense (*Handlungsspiel*). This tendency appeared in the works of Hans Folz (who arrived in Nuremberg in 1479 and died in the early sixteenth century) and continued to be the dominant configuration of sixteenth-century *Fastnachtspiele,* although the *Reihenspiel* form did not totally die out.

The greatest writer of *Fastnachtspiele,* Hans Sachs (1494–1576), was actually a participant in a revival of the genre after it essentially died out during the chaotic early years of the Reformation. His eighty-five *Fastnachtspiele,* however, deviate from the traditional format due to the changes in religious practices and society brought about by the Reformation. Although coarseness continues to be cultivated as a source of humor, obscenity is no longer allowed on stage; instead of participating in the temporary freedom from restraint promoted by the old Catholic *Karneval,* these post-Reformation *Fastnachtspiele* serve the functions of moral didacticism and social satire. And in these plays by Hans Sachs (as well as by others of his generation) the theatrical goals of the fifteenth-century writers are thus altered as well. Although still not illusionistic theater, the theater of Sachs precludes integration of play and audience. The action on stage is autonomous, monologues directed at the audience are eliminated except in a moralizing epilogue, and the actors do not merge with the crowd following the performance.

After a renewed blossoming of the *Fastnachtspiel* under Sachs and others, its original function lost (the Protestants generally eliminated *Fastnacht*), this native dramatic product gave way to a new comic theater indebted to theater traditions of Italy *(commedia dell' arte)* and England (the English Comedians) by the turn of the century. The only native German comic tradition seems to have died out without progeny.

Sixteenth-Century Drama

But the *Fastnachtspiel* was not the only secular dramatic genre by the beginning of the sixteenth century. With the rise of Humanism in the late fifteenth century and with the particular interest in drama on the part of prominent German Humanists like Reuchlin, Celtis, and Wimpfeling, a secular neo-Latin theater for the educated elite arose.[6] The tragedies and comedies of antiquity (especially the Roman comedy writer Terence, but also Plautus, Seneca, and the Greek dramatists), as well as the Latin dramas of the medieval nuns Roswitha von Gandersheim and Hildegard von Bingen, constituted its inspiration, while its subject matter came from contemporary events and the popular stage, as well as classical antiquity. The Humanist theater was not created in one climactic moment, in spite of these models, however. It underwent a gradual development toward theatricality, and can be shown to have been related in its early stages more closely to the Humanist dialogue (an outgrowth of the late medieval *Streitgespräch* and/or such classical dialogues as Plato's *Symposium*) than to modern conceptions of stage drama.

Several kinds of Humanist drama predominate: the school drama designed with pedagogical purposes in mind (the student actors and audience will practice speaking and hearing fine Latin style), and the *Festspiel* ("festival play"), designed for performance at court, which contained either panegyric or polemic in favor of its royal audience. But both types, unlike the earlier theater of the Middle Ages, allow for an additional purpose: the aesthetic pleasures of *homo ludens*. Theater becomes a pedagogical institution for the ethical improvement of the state and mankind and teaches the use of elegant style and effective rhetoric while it provides entertainment for the audience.

Although without fully understanding ancient theater's division into tragic and comic genres, the Humanist dramatists did produce both "tragedies" and "comedies"—the division being determined by social class of the characters and the outcome of the play, as it was to continue to be even in the seventeenth century. Another type, the "tragicomedia" or "comicotragedia" or mixture of the above, was likewise introduced. In addition to genre designations, the Humanists also initiated some major innovations in format. Following the pattern of Roman theater (particularly Seneca), they divided their plays into acts and scenes, observed the unities of time, place, and action, added an explanatory chorus at the end of each act, and used a monologue of one of the characters, rather than a "praecursor" or narrator, for purposes of exposition. They began to explore the use of Aristotelian structure— rising and falling action, moments of retardation—to create suspense. They replaced the stress on gesture, mime, and tableau characteristic of medieval drama with the central significance of the text, as when verbal humor (puns, witty exchanges) replaces humor of gesture and situation. And the stage itself is new. Modeled on the Terentian set, it is a raised platform (which provides separation from the audience) with a backdrop containing two doors. The stage of the Middle Ages, with its simultaneously depicted areas for the various scenes (*Simultanbühne*) on which the actors move from one area to another to signify a new scene, is replaced by a predecessor of the modern stage, on which the scenes successively use a single area (*Sukzessivbühne*), although still without change of set.

With the advent of the Reformation, the Humanists turned their attention to additional functions for the drama: polemic for the confessional struggle, the presentation of major tenets of the respective faiths, and the teaching of religious morality.[7] The struggle of the individual in ancient tragedy becomes in their hands the format for structuring the new Reformation biblical drama, which instead of duplicating events from *Heilsgeschichte* (the life of Christ and the progress of universal salvation in history), selects short biblical stories about a single individual (e.g., Judith, Susanna, Tobias, Joseph) or New Testament parables which illustrate a particular dogma or provide a model for ideal Christian behavior. Since the Humanists were primarily employed as teachers in the Latin schools or mushrooming universities, this "biblical drama" was also "school drama"—performed by and for schoolboys and university students. But as an educated class emerged and became the merchants and bureaucrats of the new society of post-Reformation Germany, they also formed an eager audience for these Latin-language plays. Increasingly, too, these school plays were translated into German or written originally in that language, and were thus accessible to an even larger audience. The purpose of theater, in addition to the pedagogical one of teaching style and rhetoric, was now identical with that of the sermon delivered from the Protestant pulpit. But the form and language derive from Humanist endeavors: the plays contain prologue, epilogue, and choruses; are divided into acts and scenes; have an "Argument" (a prose description of the plot); use the raised podium stage with its several doors to represent a succession of different scenes. Some of these school plays follow the other type of Humanist play, the allegorical *Festspiel,* combining it with the late medieval tradition of the Morality Play. A prominent theme is the "Everyman" story of the worldly man who, when he learns he must die, repents of his secular desires and recognizes the vanity of human existence. This type of play and this theme became particularly popular in the imitative Catholic school drama.

The resurgence of drama after an initial hiatus during the early years of the Reformation has been attributed to Luther's attitude toward theater.[8] His statements in his translation of the biblical stories of Judith and Tobias indicate his belief that the Jews themselves dramatized these Old Testament tales. In response to a direct question in 1537 concerning the suitability of theater in the schools, Luther's Table Talk reveals that he felt that performance of comedies (in this case, those of Terence) not only provided excellent stylistic and rhetorical practice, but also that comedy taught proper and moral behavior.

Meanwhile, the medieval religious theater—liturgical drama, Passion Plays, Mystery Plays—had essentially died out, in Protestant areas, at least, due to Protestant attacks upon it. Some such performances continued in Catholic areas, and there were some revivals of the traditions in the later sixteenth century in Protestant areas as well, but for the most part the new biblical drama had to replace a long and beloved tradition. The stress on the word or text initiated both by the Humanists and by Luther himself at the expense of the traditional visual delights of the medieval stage did, however, find an outlet which continued the medieval traditions intact well into the eighteenth century even in Protestant areas, although transformed into a new medium: the Oratorio or choral passion. Instead of acting out the events of *Heilsgeschichte* or the Passion, the performers recited, usually to music, the great monologues and dialogues of the Passion Plays. As influences from Italian secular opera combined with the liturgical *recitativ* in the late seventeenth century, the genre was on its way to a climax in the first half of the eighteenth century in the hands of the masters of German Baroque music, Johann Sebastian Bach and Friedrich Händel.

Jesuit Drama

The opposite possibility—drama as a primarily visual and sensual experience—was the one initiated in Germany by the fathers of the Jesuit order in their school theaters.[9] Although they followed the pre-Reformation Humanist schoolmasters in designing Latin plays for their students to perform as an exercise in rhetoric, they quickly discovered the value of the performances as a method of *propaganda fides*—strengthening the audience in, or converting it back to, the Catholic faith. And because they used a Latin text, the fathers had to exploit the purely theatrical arts of mime and visual effects, in addition to German-language program notes, in order to make their plays intelligible to an audience composed not only of the educated, but of the uneducated "masses" as well. Thus their plays were veritable feasts for the eyes and ears, combining declamation, mime, instrumental and choral music, dance, elaborate costumes, props, painted scenery, and all sorts of special effects made possible by the new advances in science of the sixteenth and seventeenth centuries. The value of the plays as pure entertainment attracted the audiences, but those audiences left the theater perhaps wiser and more moral than when they entered, firmer in their faith or even converts to Catholicism or to a monastic life.[10]

Various attempts have been made to define Jesuit drama as an entity, but in fact it seems to follow the same stylistic development as contemporary secular literature: Humanistic, Confessional, Mannerist,

Early Baroque, High Baroque, Late Baroque, and Enlightenment periods have been identified in the history of Jesuit drama from its start in the mid-sixteenth century to its end in 1773.[11] Various divisions into periods that are specifically those of Jesuit drama have been attempted, based on a supposed progression in the choice of dramatized material or in the central ideas to be promoted by the plays. Most scholars agree that the central theme of all Jesuit plays is the vanity and transience of human existence; a recent theory holds, however, that instead the common theme of all Jesuit plays is the sureness of Divine Retribution.[12] All scholars agree that the distinguishing feature of Jesuit theater is its ideological function, its clear connection to the primary purpose of the Jesuit order, propagation of the Faith. Many have pointed to the tendency of Jesuit dramas to have a dualistic structure: the representation and its allegorical significance.[13] This dualism is apparent even in the titles of many Jesuit plays, which display a twofold structure—the name of the protagonist and the moral of his story (e.g., *Pietas Victrix, sive: Flavius Constantinus Magnus de Maxentio Tyranno Victor*) or the event and a biblical event to which it bears an analogy (e.g., *Servus Abrahami Rebeccam Isaaco ex Mesopotamia deducens seu Franciscus Xaverius Sponsam Christi in India magno labore adducens*).

Jesuit plays usually retain the basic outline of Humanist drama: prologue, division into acts (usually three or five) and scenes, choruses after each act, and epilogue. The choruses, at first merely commentary on the action, often set to music, quickly become interludes which take on a life of their own. These entre'acts might contain mythological or allegorical figures who would elucidate the events in the acts through their words or through an analogous action. Tableaux or pantomimes which further the plot, rather than commenting on it, also frequently appear in these interludes (e.g., a shipwreck). Such elaborate operatic interludes already appear in plays performed in Munich in the second half of the sixteenth century. Their origin probably lies in the *intermezzi* of contemporary Italian courts, rather than in any German secular dramatic tradition.

The subject matter of Jesuit plays can be categorized into a number of major varieties, although attempts to arrange such categories chronologically have not been entirely successful.[14] Early Jesuit plays tend to be morality plays, biblical plays, or historical *Festspiele* (festival plays which glorify a historical figure), although these types continue to reappear throughout the history of Jesuit drama. In the seventeenth century the legends of saints, allegorical plays (e.g., Masen's *Androfilo*), and historical tragedies tend to predominate, but were not entirely absent earlier. In the later seventeenth century, family conflicts become extremely popular, but they, too, were well represented even in the sixteenth century. All of these types will prove to be important in the discussions of seventeenth-century secular drama to come.

The most famous and influential of the German Jesuit dramatists were Jakob Bidermann (1578–1639, primarily active in Munich; works published 1666, but often performed in the first half of the seventeenth century)[15] and Nikolaus von Avancini (1612–1686, dramatist for the imperial court in Vienna; works published 1655ff.)[16] Jakob Masen (1606–1681) wrote several plays, but is perhaps more important for his theoretical treatise (*Palaestra eloquentiae ligatae dramatica,* 1657). Avancini and Masen will be discussed in the context of similar secular works in a later chapter. Foreign Jesuits whose plays were influential in Germany, not only on German Jesuit drama but on secular dramatists as well, were Joseph Simon or Simeons (ca. 1595–1671; English, dramas published 1656) and Nicolaus Caussinus (1580–1651; French, dramas published 1620).

The Jesuits took over the Humanist designations for dramatic genres—tragoedia, comoedia, and tragicomoedia—but did not use them in quite the same way. Although there was much variation, in fact, in their usage, it was common practice to term martyr plays comedies, plays about guilty persons who were punished by God tragedies, and tragedies with comic scenes interspersed tragicomedies. Even the Jesuit stage was not new. The early Jesuit plays used a version of the medieval *Simultanbühne,* which has been dubbed the "kubische Simultanbühne" because of its use of cubicles—interior sets—on the *postscenium (Hinterbühne),* while the proscenium (*Vorderbühne*) was a neutral zone, perhaps representing the street, in which many of the scenes took place. With the move to an indoor theater, which took place during the period in which Bidermann wrote (ca. 1600), this stage was compressed, and the number of cubicle sets on the *postscenium* limited to three, shut off by curtains except when in use. The central cubicle soon became a changeable set, in which the scene was changed while the curtain was shut. Since the curtains between *postscenium* and *proscenium* represented doors and walls, it could be maintained that this *kubische Simultanbühne* was a combination of the medieval stage on which the actors moved spacially from scene to scene and the Humanist stage on which all interacting was done in a neutral area—the street in front of a backdrop representing buildings with doors and windows.

Before the middle of the seventeenth century, probably under the influence of Italian theater and opera, the Jesuit variant of the native *Simultanbühne* gave way to the *Sukzessivbühne,* a stage which made possible not only illusionistic sets, but quick changes of scene. While the earlier stage used curtains only for the *postscenium* and set changes occurred only in the middle cubicle, the new stage used a variety of curtains for backdrops, on which perspectivally illusionistic scenes were painted. Soon it added the front curtain—to hide scene changes and thereby add to the illusionism and suspense—and movable stage flats. Even then, the *postscenium* did not disappear. It remained a curtained-off area now used for special effects—shipwrecks and sea voyages, gruesome martyrdoms and executions, tableaux and pantomimes—especially during the entr'acts.

At its pinnacle, exemplified best perhaps in Avancini's *Pietas Victrix* of 1659, the new Jesuit stage provided amply for the special effects so beloved by the audience: holes in the stage for sudden appearances and disappearances of ghosts and apparitions, space below the stage for the setting off of fireworks and the running of machinery (e.g., to move waves and the ship traversing them), space above the set to hang painted backdrops which would be lowered for miraculously fast scene changes and for the flying machines used for clouds, angels, demons, and flying beasts, not to mention apotheoses. Oil lamps were placed variously above stage for spectacular lighting effects, and the magic lantern which projected mysterious images (e.g., for apparitions and comets) was probably used by around 1675 on German stages. In front of the stage was a large orchestra pit for the musicians. It was this stage which provided the culmination of Jesuit desires for the ultimate in the spectacular and marvelous for their plays, and which helps to explain the latter's tremendous popularity with the courts, as well as with the masses. And it was this stage which enabled the Jesuit theater to continue to compete with the growing popularity of the Italian opera in courts north of the Alps.[17] The Jesuit drama certainly has to be given some of the credit for the success of the Counter-Reformation in Southern Germany and Austria.

The German Humanists, like their Italian counterparts, had found themselves composing dramatic *Festspiele,* as well as plays for their students; and the Jesuits followed their example. In fact, Jesuit theater quickly became the court theater, most notably in Munich in the late sixteenth century and in Vienna under Leopold I in the second half of the seventeenth century. As such, it is not surprising to find that it promulgated not only theological or moral concerns of the Church, but the political concerns of its secular allies, the absolutistic princes, as well. Thus the historical figures who crossed their stages provided not only a moral for the general audience, but a good or bad model for the prince and his heir as well. The model ruler of the Jesuit stage (e.g., Constantine, Theodosius, Charlemagne) typically furthered the interests of the Faith through partnership with the Church, conversion of the Heathen and Heretic, or military protection of Christians from non-Christian attackers. One of the most popular polemical stances, whether direct or disguised in analogous events from the past, was the call to arms against the Turks. To the Jesuits history, far from our modern conceptions of it as development of secular society or a series of secular causes and effects, was the realization of God's plan for the world—specifically the Divine Plan for universal salvation *(Heilsgeschichte)*—and Jesuit drama served to demonstrate the truth of this view.

Foreign Itinerant Theater

Along with the new theatricality initiated by Jesuit drama in the late sixteenth century a similar stress on the specifically theatrical arts of mime and spectacle entered Germany from another source: the itinerant stage *(Wanderbühne)* of the English Comedians and their German successors. Their portable stages and impoverished coffers did not allow them the extravaganzas proffered by the Jesuit court theaters, but what they lacked in extravagance they more than made up for in professionalism. For they brought a theater to Germany which, for the first time in the history of the German stage, was not directed and performed by amateurs. The English Comedians and their German successors were professional actors who traveled from town to town, market to market, and court to court, setting up their stages and performing their plays to an audience which had paid for admission.[18] The theatrical skills of the actors apparently reflected the fact that they were professionals for whom acting was the primary occupation, for the amateur actors— schoolboys—of the Jesuit theater could not stand up to a comparison.[19]

The most important role in almost every play, which was usually played by the director of the troupe, was not that of the protagonist, however; it was the clown, usually called Pickelhering (after whom the English troupes were frequently called "the Pickelherings"), whose partly extemporaneous lines kept the audience well entertained. In other guises he was called Hans Wurst, Johan Bouset, or other names usually denoting food or drink. The plays themselves, as Willi Flemming has described them, had in common an abundance of adventuresome events, full of pomp and circumstance, which took place in the court of a far and exotic land.[20]

The stress on mime, spectacle, and entertainment in the itinerant theater probably stems from a characteristic it shares in its early years with Jesuit theater: the use of a foreign language in the productions. In this case the native English, instead of school Latin, was the impetus, but the results were the same—theatrical effects were necessary to make the plays understood by the audience. While the Jesuits used these methods in order to propagate the Faith, the professional theater troupes did so in order to make money. Their success was measured in profits, not in conversions.[21]

While there were English troupes of entertainers in Germany perhaps as early as 1560, their performances do not seem to have been dramatic in nature until the arrival in 1592 at the court in Wolfenbüttel of a troupe invited by Duke Heinrich Julius von Braunschweig (Brunswick) after he had apparently seen its members act in Copenhagen two years earlier.[22] In the same year another troupe gave its first public performance in a German town. The early performances of these troupes seem to have been in English, as noted, but apparently that same year there were German translations of their plays performed, and two German playwrights indicate their inspiration from the plays of the English Comedians already in 1593–95: Duke Heinrich Julius himself, whose plays will be discussed below, and Jakob Ayrer, a writer of *Fastnachtspiele* in the tradition of Hans Sachs, whose plays of this period, while they claim to be "in the English manner" and include some of the exterior trappings of the plays of the English itinerant theater, remain otherwise essentially within the older German tradition.[23]

By 1600 all the troupes of English Comedians used German on their stages, albeit in rough translations by Englishmen, whose incomplete knowledge of German resulted in an awkward combination of the language of "the man on the street" and the stilted language of courtiers, rather than in a high literary style. After 1620, with the influx of German actors in the troupes, the German translations became at least correct and fluent, if still not of literary quality. So popular and numerous had the "English" Comedians become that in 1605 the first standing theater in Germany, the Ottonianum or Ottoneum, in Kassel, was built by Landgraf (Count) Moritz von Hessen to house performances of itinerant theater troupes.[24] During the Thirty Years War the *Wanderbühne* continued to roam Germany, primarily in the North and East, where there was less chaos, but apparently did not undergo much development until the end of the war in 1648. The end of the war saw the last English troupe arrive in Germany—the *Wanderbühne* was to become a totally German institution—but this last troupe, led by Joris Joliphus, also initiated some drastic changes in performance practice. By 1652 Joliphus's troupe was performing pastoral plays and *Singspiele* ("musicals") "nach Italienischer Manier" and Dutch tragedies, plus simplified prose versions of the "high-art" tragedies *(Kunsttragödien)* of the important contemporary German dramatist Andreas Gryphius.

The *Wanderbühne* continued to provide popular theater in Germany throughout the second half of the seventeenth century, and indeed was still powerful enough late in the century to cause Christian Weise to attack it explicitly, then go about using many of its devices in writing and producing plays which would successfully challenge it. Eventually, the *Wanderbühne* traditions were to find their culmination in the Viennese folk theater of Joseph Stranitzky (1676–1726) and his successors, who include such notables as Mozart-Schikaneder *(The Magic Flute)*, Grillparzer, Nestroy, Raimund, and Hofmannsthal. And even the "cleansing" of German theater of Hans Wurst/Pickelhering by Gottsched in the eighteenth century was carried out within the itinerant theater troupe of Neuber and his wife.

The plays often derived from English and Romance language plays of literary merit (including Marlowe's *Faust* and eleven plays by Shakespeare) which were rewritten for performance on the popular stage. In the process they lost much of their literary quality, but they did become more easily understood by the audience. The principle followed by the revisers was to simplify the plot into a single, easily followed, and dramatic train of action. Most popular were those about political intrigue (*Staatsaktionen*) and romantic love, both essentially new themes to the German stage. Scholars have identified two different (and conflicting) causes for the events portrayed. One view insists that, as true Renaissance drama, these plays are herocentric; that is, men fall victim to their passions (generally desire for power—*Ehrgeiz*—or love in these two types of plot), and fall due to them. The other maintains that characters are not central; rather, it is *Fortuna*—chance, or impersonal Fate—which causes the events to storm upon the protagonists, regardless of their own actions.[25] But both agree that the *Wanderbühne* represented a theater essentially without religious or political intentions, usually without even the excuse of didacticism for its existence—in short, the first theater in Germany existing entirely for the sake of entertainment and the love of play-acting.

Although most of the plays were performed from scripts which have long since disappeared, many were preserved in three published collections of the seventeenth century: the *Englische Comedien und Tragedien . . . samt dem Pickelhering* of 1620; the *Liebeskampf, oder Ander Theil der Englischen Comoedien und Tragoedien* of 1630; and the *Schaubühne, Englischer und Französischer Comödianten* of 1670. Prominent among them and easily accessible in modern editions are *Niemand und Jemand* (from English folk theater) and *Der Jude von Venedig* (derived from Shakespeare's *Merchant of Venice,* but considerably changed, as were the other Shakespearean plays).[26]

The stage which the English Comedians brought with them was similar to that developed by the Jesuit fathers in that it was a raised platform divided into a *proscenium* which was generally the street or large antechamber used for the majority of the scenes and a *postscenium* which was a curtained-off area—in this case, a single room which represented throne room and/or bedroom. Above this room there was often a gallery used to represent a second-story window or even heaven. It was a portable stage with simple sets which could be quickly erected in a market square, town hall, or other large room. They also carried with them a limited number of props and costumes which could be used in a repertoire which might number thirty plays. Each troupe numbered from twelve to eighteen players, so that the number of characters in each play was necessarily limited, and, as in Jesuit plays, female roles were acted by boys or young men.[27]

The *Wanderbühne* fostered a distance between audience and performers that was new to German drama, at first due to the fact that the troupes were made up of foreigners, but later because the actors were considered to be outsiders who did not fit into any class of society and who were therefore lumped together with vagabonds. Certainly they were strangers to the audience, unlike the amateur actors of the medieval pageant plays, the *Fastnachtspiele,* or the various school theaters of earlier German theater. Their plots, too, were new. No longer could the audience depend on prior knowledge of biblical stories or well known events of Continental history to help sustain their interest and understanding of the dramatized events. Instead, the *Wanderbühne* involved the audience through the creation of illusion and suspense. The dramatic (as opposed to epic or narrative) theater, which was to dominate in the seventeenth, eighteenth, and nineteenth centuries in Germany, was born.

Duke Heinrich Julius von Braunschweig

The English Comedians created a sensation in Germany, and their impact on German literature was immediate. In 1593–94 Duke Heinrich Julius von Braunschweig (1564–1613), who had invited a troupe to his court at Wolfenbüttel in 1592, as mentioned above, was already able to publish ten plays he had written for their stage. The lead role in each (in all but two the clown, usually called Johan Bouset) was undoubtedly designed to be played by the actor Thomas Sackeville, whose troupe was engaged there on a long-term basis. The duke's interest in theater predates the English Comedians, however. His education, along Humanist lines, reportedly included the study of the comedies of Terence and Plautus. In 1585 he composed and played the leading role in two *Festspiele,* probably similar to those written earlier in the century by Humanists, for his own marriage festivities. One celebrated an illustrious ancestor (*Triumph Heinrich des Löwen*) while the other was a mythological masque (*Jagdzug der Diana*).[28] And Heinrich Julius was not alone among princes of the period to dabble in playwriting. The Catholic Archduke Ferdinand of Tirol (1529–1594), under the influence of Jesuit drama, wrote a prose drama in German called *Speculum vitae humanae* in 1584. Heinrich Julius's Protestant contemporary Landgraf Moritz von Hessen (1572–1632, famous for founding the first standing theater in Germany, as mentioned above) wrote (or provided sketches which others finished for) a series of biblical dramas under the influence of the English Comedians, as well as several reworkings of Roman comedies and several original plays.[29] But among them only the plays of Heinrich Julius merit consideration as the introduction of a new type of drama never before seen in Germany. Even his earliest plays—including two versions of the biblical story of Susanna—demonstrate this distinction in their attempt to enhance theatrical performance, in their realistic treatment of human emotions, and above all in their use of colloquial prose and even dialect in place of the stilted *Knittelvers* ubiquitous in earlier German drama.

While the use of prose, the stress on the dramatic value of human passions, and the knowledge of the workings of the theater undoubtedly derive from his contact with the English Comedians, Heinrich Julius did not slavishly follow their lead, but instead merged what he perceived most valuable in their productions with native German traditions. Thus his sources are not foreign plays or novellas, but collections of *Schwänke* ("anecdotes") published in Germany in the sixteenth century.[30] His characters, with several exceptions, were bourgeois people with petty but rather universal sins—cheating, deception, adultery—rather than kings and courtiers from some exotic land whose failings fell them together with their kingdoms.[31] Even the fool or clown in Heinrich Julius's plays, in spite of his obvious origins in the Pickelhering of the English Comedians, may have been modeled on his counterpart from German narrative literature, Till Eulenspiegel. For Johan Bouset is neither witty nor obscene, nor even uncannily clever, but is rather an honorable, loyal servant whose very straightforwardness allows him to see through the deceptions of his social betters and to comment upon them for the benefit of the audience.

Heinrich Julius, following the Humanist tradition, divided his plays into three genres: tragedy, comedy, and tragicomedy. But unlike the classical definitions, and like the plays of the Jesuits, his tragedies involve the Divine Punishment of sinners (devils carry off the protagonists, who have previously judged themselves guilty and committed suicide), while the characters in the comedies either elude the waiting devils or do not concern themselves with eternal judgments. The tragicomedies (e.g., *Susanna*) begin ominously, but have a happy ending.

While most of his plays seem to belong to the sixteenth century in terms of style and content (similarities to school drama or late *Fastnachtspiele* can be discerned), three have elicited scholarly attention as progressive and even influential for the seventeenth-century drama to come. *Buler und Bulerin* [The Lover and His Mistress], in spite of its clumsy, inarticulate style and its warning against adultery, has been seen as the first expression in Germany since the Middle Ages of the power and beauty of the love between man and woman, a theme which will continue to dominate theater for centuries thereafter. *Von einem ungeratenen Sohn* [The Son Who Turned Out Badly], the story of a second son named Nero who murdered father, brother, and brother's family in order to succeed to the throne, has been seen as the first Baroque tragedy in the sense that, like the later tragedies of Gryphius and others, it heaps horror upon horror with grisly morbidity. Nero has been likened to the tyrants Chach Abbas, Bassianus, and Ibrahim Sultan of High Baroque tragedy. But it is the comedy *Vincentius Ladislaus* which has universally won approval as marking the onset of a new era for drama in Germany. It is a play on the *miles gloriosus* theme—the soldier whose sense of his importance and deeds far exceeds reality—which dates back to Plautus. In this play linguistic dexterity and stylistic elegance of the later period do indeed make their first appearance in a typical Baroque plot on the theme of the disparity between appearance and reality. In the protagonist (whose role undoubtedly demanded the skill of Thomas Sackeville himself, relegating the clown Johan Bouset to secondary importance), Heinrich Julius was ridiculing and criticizing a type of person who would become ever more numerous in the coming decades during and after the Thirty Years War, in a sense the self-styled "Baroque Man." And it is in this play, and in the *Sohn* tragedy, that Heinrich Julius switches his interest from the sins of the bourgeoisie to those of the members of the great courts—a pattern which the Baroque dramatists were to follow.

The English Comedians were not the first foreign theater troupes to perform in Germany, and in fact their influence on the dramatic accomplishments of seventeenth-century German writers has probably been overemphasized, insofar as it has been stressed to the exclusion of that of other nationalities. While professional French and Dutch troupes performed in Germany during the seventeenth century, and probably had some effect on the German *Wanderbühne,* Italian theater troupes in the *commedia dell'arte* tradition had been performing, at least in southern areas, since the late fifteenth century. In 1568, for example, the famous troupe who called themselves *comici gelosi* performed in Vienna for the imperial court.[32] Landgraf Moritz von Hessen, mentioned above in context with his own plays and his contact with the English Comedians, was one of many German princes who invited leading Italian literati to their courts, bringing the literature and theater of Italy to popularity in the North. Moritz was particularly interested in furthering the Italian language, and also sponsored translations from the Italian and works modeled on famous Italian works.[33] Even Heinrich Julius, always linked to the English Comedians in scholarship, probably derives his *Vincentio Ladislaus* from current *commedia dell'arte* renditions rather than from Humanist forebears, for "Capitano Spavento da Valle Inferno" was a popular stock figure on the Italian itinerant stage in the late sixteenth century. For the southern courts of Munich and Vienna, Italian opera became ever more popular, and its theatrical effects made their way into nonmusical theater as well. From this direction, rather than from the English Comedians, the great female roles of the German Baroque probably derived, for the itinerant Italian theater as well as the opera utilized actresses and female singers, and their works could therefore be designed with this fact in mind. Italian literary tragedies of the sixteenth century were dominated by female protagonists of strong character, as any list of titles shows. The play usually given credit as the first Italian tragedy, Trissino's *Sofonisba* (1515), begins the tradition which includes Dolce's *Marianna,* Ricellai's *Rosmunda,* Giraldi's *Orbecche, Cleopatra,* and *Didone,* Groto's *Dalida,* Decio's *Acripanda,* and Aretino's *Orazia.* The *commedia dell'arte* players, who, like the English Comedians, used diluted versions of literary dramas for their performances, undoubtedly introduced plays from this tradition to their German audiences. The imperial court under Leopold I in the second half of the seventeenth century was, by all accounts, more Italian than German. And the "romanesque" or romance-language drama, whether Italian or Spanish, entered Germany indirectly through the English troupes and through collections of novellas, as well as directly through the productions of the *commedia dell'arte* troupes. The action of this type of play generally takes place at an exotic foreign court and has a convoluted plot full of intrigue, near-disaster, disguise, deception, and romance. It is well represented already in the *Liebeskampf* collection of 1630 and finds its way into German works of literary quality in the 1650s and 1660s. Under Italian influence another type of play which became extremely popular in the second half of the seventeenth century in Germany was the Pastoral play, modeled on Tasso's *Aminta* and Guarini's *Il Pastor fido*. French influence in the seventeenth century was limited to the comedy in the Spanish ("romanesque") tradition, until around 1670, when Molière's comedies began to arouse interest. But the classical French tragedy of Corneille and Racine had no impact until the early eighteenth century, when the efforts of Gottsched brought it to the attention of the German theater.

Chapter Three

The Creation of a New Drama: First Attempts

In spite of the efforts of Duke Heinrich Julius von Braunschweig, German drama at the turn of the century remained trapped in the moribund traditions of *Fastnachtspiel* and school drama. The language of the amateur theater, incapable of carrying the lofty ideas of literature, doomed folk theater to an activity of uneducated craftsmen of the lower classes—*Reimschmiede* ("rhyme-smiths"), as they were sarcastically called. School drama, while it found Luther's German adequate for the expression of simple religious and moral lessons, likewise labored under the disadvantages of a language incapable of higher purposes. Only in Latin did there exist a language suitable for literary discourse, and thus the poetry written for and by persons of high social class—the courtiers and the educated elite of the middle class—was in an elegant and epigonal neo-Latin. Theaters of the courts, except when they invited an English troupe of comedians to perform their crudely translated foreign dramas, depended on the Latin drama of the Jesuits or the Italian-language opera and *Singspiel*. Attempts to write poetry in German relied either on *Knittelvers* or on the Latin method of versification—both of which involved counting the total number of syllables, an approach unsuitable for the German language. The terms "tragedy," "comedy," and "tragicomedy" were applied to a variety of dramatic manifestations with little or no understanding of their meanings.

Martin Opitz

It was this sorry state of vernacular literature which Martin Opitz (1597–1639),[1] then only twenty years old, deplored in his *Aristarchus, sive de contemptu linguae teutonicae* of 1617. This essay, ironically written in Latin, was a manifesto for a new German literature worthy of respect as a national literature, equal to those of contemporary Italy, Spain, France, or England. The young man, well educated and already adept at writing poetry in Latin, began instead to write poems with literary pretensions in his native tongue. By 1624, when a collection of these early attempts appeared, he had turned away from neo-Latin-style syllable-counting to the more applicable versification he found in the Netherlands: a pattern of alternating stressed and unstressed syllables which coincided with the natural stress patterns of German words. To repudiate his earlier German poetry he published that same year his poetical treatise: *Buch von der deutschen Poeterey*. In this slim volume he not only explained his new method of versification and provided examples, but also contributed to the development of a German literary language by attacking the use of foreign words, providing rules and examples for building new German words to expand the vocabulary, and propounding the use of images, rhetorical constructions, and onomatopoeia. He clarified and defined the literary genres, enumerated the various subtypes of poems and dramas, and addressed himself to the nature and value of literature. It is not an exaggeration to say that this book, supported by Opitz's continuing output of models for the new verbal art form, changed the course of German literature.

As models for the dramatic genre for which he had supplied definitions in the *Poeterey*, he soon began to translate tragedies (Sophocles's *Antigone* and Seneca's *Trojan Women*) and the libretti of Italian operas (Rinuccini's *Dafne* and Salvadori's *Judith*). The first of these, *Die Trojanerinnen* (1625), provided a true turning point in the history of German drama. Opitz decided to translate Seneca's hexameters into the rhymed alexandrine[2] lines that were to be the chosen verse for German tragedy until the mid-eighteenth century, and his songlike free-verse choruses likewise influenced all later usage. Other techniques apparent in this play also continued to dominate German tragedy until Gottsched: the division into five acts, the use of extensive notes to explain obscurities in the text, the use of reports by messengers as a substitute for the direct portrayal of some events. The language is uniformly elevated and elegant and the verse flows easily, with little stiffness or apparent effort. The choice of a plot which portrays human beings pushed to the limits of mental suffering and which enumerates the gory details of horribly painful deaths leads to the establishment of a vocabulary well equipped to express such suffering and horror. His purpose in selecting this play for translation is, as he says in the preface, to inure the reader/audience to life's misfortunes by depicting historical misfortunes far worse than any that can befall one in the present—in other words, to instill a stoic attitude in the audience. As many scholars have pointed out, it was no accident that Opitz chose this play (as well as *Antigone* and *Judith*), since its wartime setting and theme made it particularly relevant during this period in the middle of the Thirty Years War.

The year 1627 saw the production of his *Dafne,* a translation of the first Italian opera libretto (Florence, 1597) for which the famous composer Heinrich Schütz wrote a new score (now lost). The sun god Apollo answers the prayers of shepherds and kills a dragon with his great bow, proving his heroism and prowess; but then he laughs at the puniness of the bow of the love god Cupid, who punishes him by causing him to be crazed with love for the nymph Dafne, who flees him. As Apollo gives chase, she prays to be saved, and the river god answers her prayer by changing her into a laurel tree. Apollo has to be satisfied with a wreath from her foliage. This mythological masque based on a tale in Ovid's *Metamorphoses* is a far cry from the *Festspiele* of the sixteenth-century Humanists, and not just because it is entirely set to music. Two contemporary Italian elements have made it fashionable: the inclusion of shepherds with all their pastoral trappings, and the use of the madrigal[3] verse form. Thus Opitz's translation not only constitutes the first German opera, but also introduces pastoral poetry and its usual verse form, the madrigal, into German literature.

Opitz published a translation of a second opera libretto, Salvadori's *Judith,* in 1635, although probably not for performance as an opera in this case:[4] he calls it a "Tragoedie." And indeed, some of the basic elements of later German tragedy of the seventeenth century make their appearance here: the boastful speech (*Prahlrede*) of the tyrant that opens the play, the Christian stoicism of the female protagonist (not unlike the martyr type, although she does not undergo martyrdom), the prayer for the defeat of all heathens at the end. But it lacks psychological depth and insight into human passions, and in general fails to create the great central personage which will dominate the tragedies of Gryphius and Lohenstein in the next generation. Its brevity (only twenty-five pages in the edition of 1638) surely accounts, in part, for the lack of depth and breadth.

The translation of Sophocles's *Antigone* in 1636 provided a pendant to *Die Trojanerinnen* and continued many of the contributions of the earlier translation of the Senecan tragedy to German drama: the alexandrine verse (this time to replace the Greek trimeter), the language of mental anguish, the use of messengers to further the plot. The Christian martyr play makes its appearance here in secular form: Antigone chooses the tenets of her religion (albeit pagan) over the orders of a tyrant, and is condemned to death for her actions—a death which she, like her Christian sisters in Jesuit drama, comes to desire. Instead of the tragedy of a person—Antigone—who is caught between two contradictory requirements, it becomes, in Opitz's hands, the tragedy of Creon, whose pride and disregard for the gods lead to his fall. In other words, it has become the typical Baroque tragedy of the tyrant-martyr configuration. Two formal elements of this translation which did not appear in the Senecan play will also become part of the canon of norms for Baroque tragedy: the use of stichomythia[5] during climactic moments in the dialogue, and the division of the chorus into *Satz* and *Gegen-Satz* ("strophe" and "antistrophe").

The difference in tone, style, and structure between these dramatic translations and all earlier dramas written in German could not be more extreme, and while Optiz's primacy as the father of Baroque poetry has been doubted in recent years, his position of importance as catalyst for the new German drama cannot be denied. Opitz created no original German drama himself, having merely mediated between German literature and the established drama of antiquity and of contemporary foreign literatures, while he was creating an elevated, versatile, emotive German literary language. His drama translations may be "neoclassical" rather than Baroque in style, as Alewyn (see note 1) and others insist, but they constituted a model for the dramas of the High Baroque to which Gryphius and Lohenstein only needed to add a density of imagery, an augmented psychology of the passions—and the creative spark.

While a translation is not an original work, it can and should be interpreted like one, since the translator's own ideas about the original and his reasons for translating it affect the final text. In addition to wishing to develop a literary language and style for German and to provide a model for the literary genre, "tragedy," Opitz sees *The Trojan Women, Antigone,* and *Judith* as plays in which moral and ethical lessons are demonstrated by their pagan and biblical protagonists. This interpretation is apparent both in his prefaces and in commentary within the plays. In the case of *Dafne,* two features can provide clues to Opitz's intentions: the dedication and prologue of the play, which indicate its meaning in the context of the performance for which it was designed; and traditional interpretations of the myth of Apollo and Daphne. The former are vague. Both claim that the story demonstrates love's potentially demonic power, yet hint at some unspecified positive meaning for the depicted love. After all, the *Singspiel* is designed for performance in honor of a state marriage, and the marital love of the bridal pair, tempered by duty, presumably makes them immune to the dangers of demonic passion. Although Apollo is foolish in love, Dafne will provide for him a fame (laurel wreath) that will never wilt, as long as his love lives on:

> Ihm machet Dafne selbst von ihren frischen Zweygen
> Den Krantz der nicht verwelckt; sein Nachklang wird nicht schweigen
> So lange Liebe wehrt.
> (Dafne herself makes for him from her fresh twigs
> The garland that doesn't wilt; his [its] reverberation will not fade
> As long as love lasts.)[6]

This laurel wreath, signifying eternal fame, will then pass to the bridal pair and will last forever, while their own deeds and selves will pass away. On one level, Dafne's gift is the reward for loving well. Yet the traditional interpretation of the myth in Christian times, as espoused in dozens of "moralized Ovids" from the late Middle Ages to the seventeenth century,[7] offers another possible answer. In this tradition, Dafne is the human soul pursued by Christ, who, at the moment he touches her, gives her immortality. Her gift, the laurel wreath, thus stands for immortality achieved through divine love—the love of Christ for mankind, for which human marriage was considered a "postfiguration."[8] Such allegorization was an appropriate way to lend significance to the marriage being celebrated, and will continue to be used for marriage plays throughout the century. Considering the strength of these two traditions, there was little need for Opitz to be more explicit; his audience would have been aware of their applicability whether he wished them to or not. While Opitz's other plays, not "engaged" or attached to any particular event or personage, merely stress moral and ethical lessons demonstrated by the actions of the characters, *Dafne* can be seen to represent a tendency of seventeenth-century "occasional" literature (that is, literature written to honor, or dedicated to, a contemporary personage on an auspicious occasion) to use traditional allegorization of myth, legend, or history to connect the present occasion with the content of the literary work. Thus occasional literature of seventeenth-century Germany, rather than being so specific that it becomes time-bound and irrelevant once the occasion for which it was written has passed, attains a kind of universality through its relation to a metaphysical or religious truth. Recognition of this tendency will aid in approaching many dramas of the High Baroque, not just those intended as *Festspiele.*

Other Translations

Opitz's pen was not the only one busied with drama translations from foreign-language literatures; in his wake some of the best talents of the age were to follow, and their translations, too, provided examples and models for the new German drama. Like Opitz, they used translation to learn the craft from foreign writers, but unlike him, some of them went on to create original dramas of considerable merit. The greatest of these, and probably the best dramatist of the age, was Andreas Gryphius (1618–1664). But other prominent poets of the period— Christian Hofmann von Hofmannswaldau, Sigmund von Birken, Caspar Stieler, and Hans Assmann von Abschatz—also tried their hands at drama translation. Although many *Knittelvers* and nonliterary prose translations also introduced the materials of foreign drama to Germany, this analysis will limit itself to those having literary merit in their own right.

Two translations of Jesuit dramas provided prototypes for important dramatic genres in German-language literature. Andreas Gryphius translated Nicolaus Caussin's *Felicitas* (he owned Caussin's collected works) at some point between 1634 and 1646, and although he did not publish it until 1657 (first performed 1658), it was influential at least for his own dramatic production by 1646. *Felicitas* is the quintessential martyr drama. In this play a tyrant (Marcus Aurelius), who wavers between good and evil but is surrounded by evil advisers who prod him to choose the evil course, persecutes a Christian widow (Felicitas) who refuses to renounce her religion. She and her seven sons, who are

tortured and executed before her eyes, stoically accept their martyrdom, and even desire it as a certain path to eternal glory. In the
choruses, the dialogues between the Church Militant and angels comment on the place of martyrdom in the growth of the Church and
foresee the eventual victory of the Church and its union with the Roman
Empire under the Christian emperor Constantine.

The type of the martyr drama, varied but not abandoned in German
literature until Lessing, is thus canonized: a hero or heroine, constant in
his or her belief in religion or virtue, passively resists the demands of a
tyrant to abandon the chosen belief and accepts torture and death
stoically or even enthusiastically. The chorus comforts the persecuted
martyrs with the promise of heavenly reward for themselves, Divine
Retribution for the guilty tyrant, and eventual victory for the Church
or for virtue. As in *Felicitas,* the idea that the female martyr will be
received in glory into Heaven is often phrased, following the common
exegesis of the Song of Songs, as a marriage with Christ. The double
title common to many Jesuit dramas of the seventeenth century here
enters German literature (*Beständige Mutter/Oder Die Heilige Felicitas*),
and indicates that German drama, like its Jesuit counterpart, has two
levels of meaning—one literal or historical and the other moral or
allegorical.

Another type, the allegorical drama, is likewise established in German literature by a translation of a Jesuit play, in this case Jakob
Masen's *Androfilo* (1648), translated by Sigmund von Birken and
published and performed in 1656. While it was not actually the first of
the genre, as Birken indicates in the prologue (he cites his own
unpublished *Psyche* as a predecessor), it was certainly the most highly
developed example of the genre to date. Andropater (= God the
Father), after the rebellion and banishment of the courtier Andromiso
(= Enemy of God), takes a foster son (Antropo = Man) from one of the
lowliest families of his folk and commands his own son (Androfilo =
Son of God) to love him like a brother. A vengeful Andromiso thwarts
Andropater's intention to educate Antropo to virtue, and Andropater
sentences his erring foster son to lifelong punishment as a galley slave.
But Androfilo loves his foster brother so well that he risks his own life to
rescue Antropo and return him to his father's good graces. The Enemy
of God is thus defeated by the Son of God, who takes Mankind's sins
and punishment upon himself in order to reconcile God and Man.

The allegory, alluded to in the use of names and hinted at in the prologue, where Birken notes that truth is often hidden in fiction when circumstances prevent its overt revelation, is not directly explicated until the epilogue. In fact, the play seems to be of the *Staatsaktionen* type so favored by the itinerant stage, and contains fairly realistic dialogue and depiction of political conflicts. But the choruses, although they do not reveal the underlying plot typology to be that of *Heilsgeschichte,* provide additional clues. They offer religious lessons for the audience. At the end of the first act, the chorus (*Zwischenlied*) states that it is the nature of mankind to sin; the second chorus comments on man's blindness to evil; the third discusses the fall of Adam into sin and its results—Original Sin; but the fourth proclaims the salvation offered by Divine Love. This play, too, has a double title, *Androfilo/ Oder Die Wunderliebe* [Androfilo, or Miraculous Love], denoting its dual nature. Thus the typology of the allegorical play, too, is established for German literature: a plot which seems, on the surface, to be for entertainment and perhaps moral edification is revealed, through the use of significant nomenclature for character names, the double titles, and the commentary in the choruses and epilogue, to be a disguised portrayal of the events of the salvation of mankind through Christ.

Another source for German Baroque drama was the Dutch tragedy, particularly that produced by Joost van den Vondel (1587–1679). Although Gryphius's translation of Vondel's *De Gebroeders* (1640) was not published until 1698 as *Die Sieben Brüder/Oder Die Gibeoniter* [The Seven Brothers or the Gibeonites], it was probably finished during Gryphius's years in Leiden (1638–1644) and was performed in 1652 in Breslau. It certainly influenced Gryphius's own works,[9] and it may have had an impact on later Silesian *Kunsttragödien* through its performance. The plot concerning the execution of seven brothers derives from the Old Testament (2 Samuel) and the Jewish historian Josephus, but it is not (as some scholars have claimed) a parallel to the martyr drama *Felicitas,* but rather constitutes a contrast. For in this play the seven brothers are executed for the illicit behavior of their parent—the tyrant Saul, whose crimes are punished by the extinction of his family line—at the command of God himself. Instead of being a martyr play, this drama depicts the fall of a high personage due to Divine Retribution and the establishment of a new, moral ruling house (that of King David) in his place. This play is thus the model for a third type of

Baroque drama in Germany: the historical tragedy (a literary relative of the *Staatsaktionen* of the itinerant theater). While Gryphius himself did not produce an original finished tragedy of this type, a Silesian dramatist of the next generation, Daniel Casper von Lohenstein (1635–1683), brought this dramatic type to its highest form in Germany.[10]

Various comic genres, too, entered German literature through the medium of translation by prominent poets. Opitz's *Dafne* of 1627, as noted above, introduced pastoral motifs and the madrigal verse into German drama for the first time, and the *Liebeskampf* collection of plays of 1630 from the itinerant theater contained a poor translation of Torquato Tasso's *Aminta*.[11] The first literary translation of a major pastoral drama, however, was Christian Hofmann von Hofmannswaldau's rendition of Giovanni Battista Guarini's *Il Pastor fido* (1587).[12] *Der Getreue Schäfer* [The Faithful Shepherd] was probably complete by 1652 and circulated in manuscript by 1659, although it was not published until 1678 and 1679. The faithful shepherd, Mirtillo, a stranger to Arcadia, loves Amarillis, who is betrothed to Silvio, son of the highpriest, who does not love her. Their marriage, however, is thought to be the only remedy for a curse laid on the land long before. Due to a supposed transgression (she is caught alone with Mirtillo), Amarillis is to be sacrificed to the gods, but Mirtillo demands to be sacrificed in her place. At the last minute tragedy is averted when the highpriest learns that Mirtillo is his eldest son, supposed dead in a flood in his infancy. The marriage of Mirtillo and Amarillis lifts the ancient curse, and Arcadia returns to its original blissful state. Hofmannswaldau has skillfully imitated Guarini's madrigal verse, albeit in the more flowery "Marinistic" (from the Italian poet Marini, 1569–1625) style popular after 1650 in Germany.

Thus the type of the pastoral drama is determined for German literature, and will be imitated frequently in the 1660s and 1670s: a shepherd and shepherdess whose love is thwarted by an intricate network of circumstance and intrigue are finally joined in marriage, while their companions are likewise paired off. Onto this superficial plot a variety of social, philosophical, and religious themes are imposed: satire of life at court, the "cure" of antisocial characters, the power of human and divine love, even the *Heilsgeschichte* schema of the allegorical drama discussed above. Two episodes in the Guarini play reappear in most later pastoral drama: the echo poem, in which the queries of the despairing lover are "answered" by an echo (either Providence speaking through echo or another person supplying the significant rebounding sound) and the game of blindfolded lovers. The variations of these two elements, as well as the plot, give interest and individuality to the imitations.

The continuing popularity of Guarini's pastoral play was demonstrated both by a new translation, less mannered in style, by Hans Assmann von Abschatz (1646–1699) published in 1672, and by the publication of Hofmannswaldau's version not only in his collected works in 1679, but also in the unauthorized pirate version of 1678. In fact, the play underwent yet another translation late in the seventeenth century, this one by August Bohse in 1699. But the reaction against excessive use of pastoral trappings has already set in by 1661, when Andreas Gryphius (who had little use for the frivolities often associated with this genre) translated Thomas Corneille's parody of the pastoral, *Le berger extravagant*. An extract of Gryphius's *Schwermender Schäffer* [The Rapturous Shepherd] was performed as a *Festspiel* and published in 1661, and the play appeared in its entirety in 1663. He translates Corneille's French alexandrine verse into its German counterpart—the dramatic verse with which he is most familiar—rather than using the madrigals introduced into German for pastoral drama by Opitz and Hofmannswaldau, but his ridiculous shepherd speaks as if he were a true *Pegnitz-Schäfer* (member of the literary society of Harsdörffer, Birken, and Klaj—all ardent lovers of pastoral lyric—in Nuremberg).

While the italianate romantic comedy practiced throughout Europe since the middle of the sixteenth century had already made its appearance in Germany in the mutilated versions represented in the repertoire of the itinerant theater, translations of literary merit did not appear in print until the 1660s, although Gryphius's *Seug-Amme, Oder Untreues Hausgesinde* [The Wet-Nurse, or Disloyal Servants, from Girolamo Razzi's *Balia*], published in 1663, was written very early in his career, possibly before 1644. This comedy contains the requisite disguises, intrigues, and complications of the genre. Lesbia, a slave, is stolen from her owner by the young nobleman Gismondo, who is enamored of her. His uncle, Girolamo, upon whom he calls for money with which to purchase Lesbia, likewise becomes besotted with passion for her, as does his friend Livio, whose sister Silvia loves Gismondo. Through intrigue

Livio manages to spend the night with Lesbia, as he thinks, but due to a counterplot by Silvia, ends up in bed with his sister, who believes she is with Gismondo. The complications are resolved with the discovery of the true identity of Lesbia—Silvia's sister—and Livio—Girolamo's lost son. No incest had taken place, since Livio and Silvia are actually unrelated, and they marry; Gismondo marries Lesbia, whose virtue had protected her from incest with her (then unknown) father, Girolamo, who now marries the widow who is mother to his nephew Gismondo. Humor is introduced both through the release of nervousness brought about by the near catastrophes in the intrigues of the lovers and by the stupidity and wit of the servants. Razzi's play, and Gryphius's translation of it, are exceptional in their heavy moral and religious content, as one scholar has shown.[13]

Interestingly enough, the other literary translation of an italianate comedy published in this decade, Caspar Stieler's *Ernelinde/ Oder die Viermahl Braut* [Ernelinde, or The Four-Time Bride, 1665], also deals with supposed and real near instances of incest. Ernelinde, an orphan, lives at a royal court under the protection of the king. Due to misinformation about her parentage and that of her suitors, she is affianced first to the king (who is actually her father), then to Ferramond (who is then falsely discovered to be her brother), then to Filander (who is actually her brother), and finally to Ferramond again (who is the real Filander). Although Stieler does not name his Italian source, it is *La moglie di quattro mariti,* a comedy by Giacinto Andrea Cicognini published in 1659. While this comedy lacks the serious moralizing of Gryphius's *Seug-Amme,* it, too, was not merely for entertainment, even though it was translated specifically to be performed for a marriage at the Schwarzburg court where Stieler was secretary to the count. It is a dramatized *Fürstenspiegel* ("mirror for princes," an educational tool to influence the behavior of princes) which urges princes to marry with sufficient concern for their state and for morality, rather than follow their passions into tyranny, folly, and sin. The opening lines, in a stark, abstracted prose style which reminds us more of Expressionist drama than of Baroque ornateness, convey the problematics:

Heinr[ich].   Ich bin Konig.
Isab[elle].   Ich bin Konigin.
Heinr.   Ich kan und will.

Is.   Ihr kont nicht und must nicht wollen.
Heinr. Wer will mirs wehren?
Isab.   Mein Verboth.
Heinr. Ich bin Konig.
Isab.   Ihr seyd mein Sohn.
Heinr. Ehre ich euch schon als Mutter/ so musset ihr doch wissen/ das ihr
        nur Stiefmutter seyd. Ich will sie haben.
Isab.   Ihr sollt sie nicht haben.
Heinr. Ich sage: Ich will sie haben/ die Ernelinde. (1)

(Heinrich: I am King.
Isabelle: I am Queen.
H.:   I can and I intend to.
I.:   You cannot and must not intend to.
H.:   Who will prevent me?
I.:   My prohibition.
H.:   I am King.
I.:   You are my son.
H.:   Even if I honor you as my mother, don't forget that you are only my
      stepmother. I intend to have her.
I.:   You shall not have her.
H.:   I say: I intend to have her, the woman Ernelinde.)

It is interesting to note that the bride to be honored by the performance
of the play, the orphaned daughter of a neighboring count, was brought
up at the Schwarzburg court as a "sister" to her future bridegroom.
Again, humor is provided by the confusion of the protagonists as well as
by the subplot involving the servants.

Thus literary translations of foreign drama, in addition to the stage
versions of the itinerant theater and direct borrowing from foreign
sources, constituted an important contribution to the creation of most
of the major dramatic types of German Baroque drama: the opera, the
martyr tragedy, the historical tragedy, the allegorical play, the pastoral
play, and the italianate comedy. Only two types remain from the
heritage of the German Humanists (borrowed in turn from Italian
Humanists and Roman comedy), the *Festspiel* or masque, and the
satirical comedy.

Chapter Four

Tragedies of the High Baroque (1640–1680)

Theory of Tragedy

From the hindsight of our own age of manifestos, it might be assumed that a theory of tragedy would precede the creation of tragic dramas during any period. But in fact literary theory has rarely antedated the literary texts it purports to prescribe, instead providing a justification and interpretation of such texts *ipso post facto*. The Baroque age in Germany was no exception. Martin Opitz's *Poeterey,* which did purport to prescribe directions for a new literature, contains only a brief paragraph on drama which is too vague to qualify as theory. It certainly cannot explain the sudden appearance in Germany of two mature tragedians, Gryphius and Lohenstein, in the next generation, nor can it even account for the success of Opitz's own dramatic translations in the several years following its appearance. His foreword to the *Trojanerinnen* is much more specific and enlightening about the nature of the tragic experience, but it, like Aristotle's *Poetics,* is more an attempt to explain why model literary works of the past were effective than a prescription for a totally new approach. Other Baroque treatises,[1] written in most cases after the major works of the High Baroque had been published, were even more apparently descriptions of current literary practices. Yet they are useful for us twentieth-century readers as an aid to understanding the plays.

The dramatic theory of the seventeenth century in Germany (actually beginning at the end of the preceding century with the Latin *Institutio Poetica* of 1594 by the Jesuit Jacobus Pontanus) attempts to address itself to the definition of tragedy and to its function and effect, a necessary reaction to the chaos of genre designations prevalent in the sixteenth century. Four aspects of drama provide the topics of discussion: the subject matter, the outcome, the type of the protagonist, and the effect of the play upon the audience. Each theorist defines tragedy by its subject matter and provides a list of possible plots, for which Opitz's list can stand as an example: *von Königlichem willen/ Todtschlägen/ verzweiffelungen/ Kinder- und Vätermörden/ brande/ blutschanden/ kriege und auffruhr/ klagen/ heulen/ seuffzen und dergleichen* ("about kingly desires, assassinations, despair, infanticides and patricides, fires, incest, wars and rebellions, complaints, howling, sighing, and such subjects," *Poeterey*, 20). As one scholar has pointed out, such a list was not a sign of naiveté, but an indication that the plot was the essence of the Baroque tragedy.[2] Accordingly, German theorists followed Scaliger in preferring a catastrophic ending, although, more timid than their model in this case, they reluctantly allow, with Aristotle, the possibility of a happy ending for a tragedy. But their preference for the German term *Trauerspiel* is indicative of actual practice. And all insist on the high social position of the protagonist. Only Birken addresses himself to the dramatic practice of serious plays with royal protagonists which end happily—a phenomenon which he himself insists is not a tragedy, but a heroic drama (*Helden-Spiel*).[3]

Beginning with Pontanus at the threshold of the Baroque, all German theorists address themselves to Aristotle's discussion of catharsis, tragic pleasure, and the twin emotions fear ($\phi o \beta o \sigma$) and empathy ($\epsilon \lambda \epsilon o \sigma$),[4] and it is this involvement with the effect of tragedy which shows the new concern with theater. Pontanus sees catharsis as the process of purifying the members of the audience of their passions through the arousal of empathy and fear (*misericordia et terrore*) at the sight of the imitation of the catastrophic end of an important person. It is the knowledge that it is an imitation, and that the audience watches from a position of safety and security, which accounts for the sensation of pleasure. Thus tragedy for this early Jesuit theorist is a method of moral dissuasion.

Martin Opitz, following his Dutch model, Daniel Heinsius, and the practice of the Roman tragedian Seneca, provides a new interpretation of Aristotle's catharsis in his preface to the *Trojanerinnen* translation of 1625. He couples pity (*Erbarmen*) with fearlessness or constancy (*Beständigkeit*) in the face of suffering. He explains this effect of tragedy upon the audience:

Solche Beständigkeit aber wird uns durch Beschawung der Mißligkei deß Menschlichen Lebens in den Tragödien zu föderst eingepflantzet: dann in dem wir grosser Leute/ gantzer Stätte und Länder eussersten Untergang zum offtern schawen und betrachten/ tragen wir zwar/ wie es sich gebüret/ erbarmen mit ihnen/ können auch nochmals auß Wehmuth die Thränen kaum zurück halten; wir lernen aber darneben auch durch stetige Besichtigung so vielen Creutzes und Ubels das andern begegnet ist/ das unserige/ welches uns begegnen möchte/ weniger fürchten unnd besser erdulden.[5]

(Such steadfastness is implanted in us through perceiving the vulnerability of human life in tragedies, for, when we often see and contemplate the most extreme falls of great people, and of whole cities and nations, we appropriately feel pity and can hardly hold back tears, but we also learn through viewing so much suffering and evil which befalls others how to better endure and to fear less that which befalls us.)

Engendering a stoic attitude in the audience which will make it more capable of accepting its own sufferings with equanimity is the goal of tragedy, according to Opitz.

Harsdörffer returns to Aristotle's concept, rather than following Opitz, and redefines the terms to produce yet another theory of the effect of tragedy on the audience. According to him, the goal of tragedy is either to arouse astonishment or shock (*Erstaunen*) by confrontation with the portrayal of the sudden punishment of a vice with which we can identify, or else to arouse sorrow and compassion (*Hermen und Mitleid*) through portrayal of undeserved sufferings. Thus he provides for the separation into two kinds of tragedies, or at least two kinds of tragic effects which could perhaps coexist in a single play, by separating Aristotle's pair of tragic emotions. And indeed, since Opitz's theories and translations had been published, a new kind of tragedy, the martyr play inherited from Jesuit theater, has made its appearance in German literature. Harsdörffer is vague as to the purpose of the arousal of *Mitleid* for the martyr (it was probably obvious to an age which saw the value of *imitatio* and *exemplum*), but his explanation of the effect of *Erstaunen* amounts to a theory of catharsis of sorts:

Durch das Erstaunen wird gleichsam ein kalter Angstschweiß verursacht/ und wird von der Furcht unterschieden/ als welche von grosser Gefahr entstehet; dieses aber von einer Unthat und erschröcklichen Grausamkeit/ welche wir hören oder sehen. Solche Gemütsbewegung findet sich/ wann wir ein Laster scheuen ernstlich und plötzlich straffen/ daß wir in unsrem Gewissen auch befinden; und wir werden zu Mitleiden veranlasst/ wann wir einen Unschuldigen viel Ubel leiden sehen.[6]

(Shock causes a cold sweat of anxiety to break out which differs from fear in that the latter arises instead from great danger, but the former from hearing or seeing a deed of shocking horribleness. Such an emotion is created when we see a vice punished severely and suddenly which we also find in our own conscience; and we are aroused to compassion when we see an innocent person suffer greatly.)

Presumably the sight of the punishment of our vice in another allows us to rid ourselves of it through the instrument of the "cold sweat of anxiety" or fear of Hell—a sort of empathy.

If Harsdörffer seems willfully to have misinterpreted Aristotle in order to account for contemporary dramatic practice, Jacob Masen makes yet another attempt to deal with the authority of antiquity while at the same time relating to current phenomena. His *Palaestra Eloquentiae ligatae* of 1664 actually describes two totally different types of drama, one based on a close reading of Aristotle and a good understanding of Sophocles's *Oedipus Rex,* the other on the type of the Jesuit martyr play in contemporary practice. The result is a muddled conception which must be recognized as such and separated into its component parts. Thus when Masen describes the type of play exemplified by *Oedipus,* he follows Aristotle very closely: the goal of tragedy is the purification and moderation in the audience of pity and fear (*misericordia et metus*) through the arousal of these emotions; the hero has a tragic flaw or error which he does not recognize until it is too late, and it causes his fortunes to swing from good to bad. But even in the midst of such classical definitions there appear signposts from his own century. For instance, according to Masen, pity and fear are not the only emotions purged. In addition, the passions and vices of the protagonist are purged from the audience through the fear of their punishment coupled with the empathy with the character who exhibits them and is punished (Pontanus's idea). Elsewhere, a totally nonclassical picture of tragedy emerges. Masen disagrees with Aristotle's view that mixed characters are needed for tragedy, preferring a suffering hero who does not deserve his pain in order to demonstrate for the imitation of the audience the ideal of steadfastness. Indeed, through such theatrical experience, the audience will find itself freed of the fear of such pain and thus will be able to emulate the steadfastness when confronted with a similar situation. He also allows for the opposite type of protagonist, the criminal or tyrant who arouses less empathy but greater horror and fear. And he postulates a tragedy, which he terms "double," in which both protagonist types would confront one another, each earning an appropriate fate at the end. For Masen's concept of the martyr play, empathy verges on emulation, much as the purpose of the imitation of Christ's passion in the Catholic pseudodrama of the stations of the cross is to arouse Christ-like behavior through empathy with His suffering.

Sigmund von Birken, who translated Masen's *Androfilo* and can be assumed to have read his theoretical work, follows the Jesuit in postulating two kinds of heroes and therefore two kinds of tragedies:

Der Held/ welchen man als Hauptperson vorstellet/ muß ein Fürbild aller Tugenden/ und zwar erstlich gekränkt seyn/ aber endlich ergetzet werden. Ist er aber ja ein Tyrann oder Böswicht/ so soll ihm seine Straffe auf dem Fus nachfolgen/ oder er endlich/ wie der König Manasse/ bekehrt werden. Dann wann/ in Schauspielen/ die Tugend nicht belohnt/ und die Laster nicht gestrafft erscheinen/ so ist solches ärgerlich und eine Gottslästerung/ weil es der Göttlichen Regirung zuwider lauffet. Sonsten kan man/ wann man einen Wütrich vor sich hat/ ihm einen Tugendhaften Helden an die Seite setzen/ und also Gutes and Böses zugleich vorstellen. (*Teutsche Rede-Bind*, 330–31)

(The hero whom one introduces as the main character must be the model of all virtues and although mistreated at first, he must eventually be rewarded. However, if he is a tyrant or an evil-doer, then his punishment ought to follow his footsteps, or he should, like King Manasse, be converted at the end. For when, in dramas, virtue isn't rewarded and vice isn't punished, it is annoying and blasphemous since it conflicts with Divine Order. In other plays, when one has a tyrant before him, a virtuous hero can be set beside him, and thus the play can depict good and evil at the same time.)

Like Masen, he also allows the possibility of a double tragedy in which both types of protagonist appear and confront one another. But the core of Birken's concept of drama is Christian and moral, and thus it acknowledges Aristotle's terms only insofar as they might have some applicability to Christian viewers. Thus Birken explains the rationale for showing executions and suicides on stage by referring to the tragic emotions. It is clear that for him the function of the two emotions is to produce penitence and ethical improvement in the viewer. He goes on to state explicitly the Christian function of drama: When they write and perform plays, Christians should, as in all other endeavors, also have as their sole purpose honoring God and moving their fellowman to good (336). In language bordering on that used in medieval criticisms of and apologies for sacred drama, Birken states that a dramatist should avoid material which might corrupt or embarrass the viewer, and should write as if God Himself and all His angels made up the audience (337). The ultimate purposes of drama have nothing to do with the arousal and purification of the Aristotelian tragic emotions, but are essentially rational in nature:

Die Schauspiele sind Spiegel des Menschlichen Lebens/ und ist allen Menschen nützlich/ sowol als das Historien-Lesen/ sich darinn zuweilen ersehen: damit man an den Ausgängen die Vorsicht/ an den Unglücksfällen Gedult und Hoffnung/ an den Lastern dieselben hassen/ und an den Tugenden dieselben lieben und üben lerne. (339)

(Dramas are mirrors of human life and are just as useful to all people as reading history, so that one might learn the ways of Divine Providence from the outcomes, patience and hope from viewing the sad events, hatred of vices, and love and practice of virtues from viewing them on stage.)

As in Opitz's theory, seeing the misfortunes of others acted out on stage leads to a stoic attitude (patience), but in Birken's case also carries a more positive note: hope for a better life in the hereafter. The protagonists provide models or *exempla* for virtuous and evil behavior which the viewer should emulate and eschew, respectively. And central to Birken's theory is a concept not elsewhere stated in theory, but of great importance in practice: the viewer learns from the outcome of the play the nature of Divine Providence and the Divine Plan for history *(die Vorsicht)*. It is Birken in his *Teutsche- Rede-Bind- und Dicht-Kunst* who, alone among German theorists, abandons all pretense of following in the footsteps of Aristotle and the French Renaissance theorists, and who thus produces an original and pertinent theory which corresponds in fact to current practice.

The theorists in their confrontations with Aristotle reveal in spite of themselves that there is not a single type of tragedy in seventeenth-century Germany, but a multiplicity of tragic forms, none of which conforms to classical concepts of tragedy. The martyr play, the most respected in the eyes of all the theorists, can deal with the ideal martyr/saint of legend (e.g., Caussinus's *Felicitas* in Gryphius's translation) or with a more historical martyrdom (e.g., Gryphius's *Catharina von Georgien,* Hallmann's *Mariamne* and *Catharina*) which may have political overtones, but which remains essentially religious. The martyr play may also begin with a protagonist of questionable character who, through suffering and death, rises to a kind of sainthood (Gryphius's *Leo Armenius*) or may even involve a hero whose suffering is brought about rather by adherence to principle than to religion, and whose triumph is the fame of his stoic acceptance rather than the anticipation of any heavenly rewards (Gryphius's *Papinian*). The purest form of the martyr play, theoretically, at least, would portray the suffering and constancy of a Christian martyr who is confronted by a totally evil persecutor. In fact, however, the tyrant/antagonist often arouses the interest of the dramatist as much as does his innocent victim, and involvement with the tyrant's qualms, waverings, and ultimate fall becomes as much a part of the viewer's experience as his sympathy for the martyr. Thus, in reality, the martyr tragedy is a double tragedy, to use Masen's terminology, which utilizes both the sufferings of an ideal figure and the fall of a proud tyrant to achieve the ultimate in audience response. The sympathetic tyrant in the martyr tragedy is probably most clearly exemplified in Chach Abas, the Persian captor of Catharina von Georgien, and in Sultan Soliman of Lohenstein's *Ibrahim Bassa.*

The other main type of tragedy in seventeenth-century Germany, which I will call the "historical tragedy," has no innocent victim. Its two possible kinds of protagonists, which may both appear in any one play, are the sinful tyrant whose guilt causes his or her fall and the heroic positive ruler whose deeds aid the Divine Plan for history. Lohenstein's *Sophonisbe* and *Cleopatra* and Avancini's *Pietas Victrix* are examples in which both sorts appear, while Lohenstein's *Agrippina, Epicharis,* and *Ibrahim Sultan* provide examples of the fall of a guilty tyrant who has no direct, positive counterpart of equal status.

A third type, which generally overlaps with one of the other two, is the conversion play, which may or may not end with the death of the convert, but which certainly ends with his salvation. Examples are Gryphius's *Leo Armenius* (the tyrant who converts to become a martyr) and *Cardenio und Celinde* (the potentially fatal passion is defeated by recognition). In a subplot of *Sophonisbe*, Lohenstein's Masinissa recognizes his folly and is thus rescued from a tragic fall. Birken mentions this type but does not name it (331–32).

Andreas Gryphius

While the purely religious martyrs remained the property of Jesuit drama, one of the secular dramatists, Andreas Gryphius (1616–1664), was particularly interested in the martyr tragedy. It will be remembered that he provided the translation of the Jesuit martyr play *Felicitas* as one of his first dramatic efforts, and his later tragedies, while dealing with historical rulers and politicians rather than religious martyrs, bear some relation to this pure example of the type. Perhaps closest to it in religiosity and intent in his *Catharina von Georgien*, the dramatization of the recent martyrdom of the Christian queen of Georgia at the hands of her Persian captor and suitor, Chach Abas (published 1657; written between 1647 and 1651).[7] The entire play is a series of peripatetic scenes followed by the grisly martyrdom, which occurs mercifully off stage. Catharina steadfastly refuses to marry the Persian king and abandon her religion, and when the last diplomatic attempts to save her fail, she accepts—indeed, embraces—her martyrdom as the ultimate act of Christian worship.

The play opens with a prologue scene which provides the metaphysical backdrop not only for this play but for all serious Baroque drama, however secular it may appear. The personification of Eternity descends from the realm of heavenly bliss at the top of the stage onto a deserted battlefield cluttered with the detritus of war—bodies and severed limbs, broken swords, shattered spears, discarded armor, lost crowns and scepters. Below stage, the flames of Hell glimmer ominously. The middle realm on center stage is the epitome of earthly existence, reeking of vanity and transience, in Eternity's words, *Schauplatz der Sterbligkeit* ("scene of mortality," 1:81). She interprets the entire stage set as the representation of the choice to be made by both actors and audience:

Schmuck/ Bild/ Metall und ein gelehrt Papir/
Ist nichts als Sprew und leichter Staub vor mir.
Hir über euch ist diß waß ewig lacht!
Hir unter euch was ewig brennt und kracht.
Diß ist mein Reich/ wehlt/ was ihr wundtschet zu besitzen. (1:69–73)

(Finery, portraiture, metal, and scholarly writing
Are nothing more than chaff and fine dust to me.
Here above you is that which ever laughs!
Here below you is what ever burns and cracks.
These are my realms, choose which you wish to possess.)

Indeed, the fifth act of the play, while there may be no physical opening of the stage to reveal Heaven above and Hell below, certainly places the action of the tragedy in relation to these two manifestations of eternity. In the final scene Chach Abas is visited by Catharina's triumphant ghost, who announces his fall to the accompaniment of visions of engulfing flames and sulphurous smells.

But the play is not merely a glorification of a Christian martyr and a moral lesson on the vanity of human existence. It also has several allegorical levels of meaning. Like Felicitas, Catharina views her martyrdom as a marriage to Christ in terminology borrowed from the Song of Songs. Gryphius, however, has improved upon the Jesuit martyr play in creating an opposition between the lure of earthly love (the marriage proposals of the amorous Chach Abas, with their promises of earthly pleasure and glory) and Catharina's steadfast divine love for Christ (her Christian faith). The chorus to the fourth act demonstrates the power of divine love over death in a dialogue between personifications of them and thus provides a paean to her choice, while Chach Abas's last despairing words—the final ones of the play—indicate his enduring enslavement to earthly love:

Doch ist wol herber Rach' und die mehr kan betrüben
Als daß Wir/ Feindin/ dich auch Tod stets müssen liben. (5:447–48)

(But is there a more bitter revenge, one that can cause more pain,
Than that we, lovely enemy, must even in death for you feel love?)

The two kinds of love, of course, correspond to the two choices of eternal existence beyond death, Heaven and Hell.

On a more abstract level, it is possible to see the plot as an allegory of the nature of the split between body and soul. In this interpretation of the play, Catharina represents the human soul, suffering in the prison of the body, longing for release from captivity. Death provides the freedom for the soul to enter the bliss of eternal spiritual life, while the painful tortures may represent the difficulty inherent in parting captive from her prison—the final exhibition of the power of the flesh to torment the imprisoned soul. It is also possible to discern an allegorical interpretation which is a commentary on contemporary events—the enduring military conflict between Turks and Christians in the Mediterranean and Balkans. In this version of the allegory, Catharina would represent the captive Eastern Church and her retinue the many faithful Christians imprisoned and enslaved by the Turks, while the Persian king Chach Abas would represent the Muslim conquerors who continue to assault the faithful and who try to separate Christians from their faith wherever possible. The actual historical facts of Catharina's martyrdom—she was martyred by the Muslim Shah of Persia for clinging to her Christian faith in Gryphius's time (1624)—lend force to this interpretation.

Gryphius's other tragedy based on contemporary events, *Ermordete Majestät Oder Carolus Stuardus König von Groß Britannien* [Murdered Majesty, or Charles Stuart, King of Great Britain; first version written in 1649, published 1657; revised version published 1663], is also a martyr drama. In this case, however, there is no tyrant/antagonist, but rather an amalgamation of revolutionaries—*der Pövel* ("the mob")—led by Cromwell. In their conversations we hear that Charles Stuart was a tyrant who was responsible for the loss of freedom, for unjust executions, and for civil war. Although history has tended to agree with the revolutionaries to some extent, Charles himself never appears in this role in the play, nor do we hear a confession of these wrongs from his lips. Indeed, Gryphius wrote the drama in a few weeks in the heat of his horrified reaction to the news of Charles's fate. Thus the play must be regarded not as a conversion play like the earlier drama about revolution, *Leo Armenius* (to be discussed below), but as a straightforward martyr drama.

Charles Stuart (Charles II of England), as the play opens, is a prisoner of the revolutionary forces led by Cromwell. He has been convicted of treason by a court of somewhat dubious constitution and sentenced to be beheaded. In the first scene the chief of staff of the army, Fairfax, is confronted by his wife with a request to attempt to rescue the king before the execution scheduled for the following day. The resultant plot, which fails due to Charles's refusal to consider it, adds suspense and human interest to an otherwise one-dimensional portrayal of the stoic acceptance of his sentence by the king juxtaposed to the heartless revolutionaries discussing plans for the execution. A judgmental framework for the action is provided by a number of appearances of ghosts—of unjustly executed supporters of Charles, of his ancestor Mary Stuart, of other murdered and executed English kings—who lament Charles's fall and promise Divine Retribution.

In order to propagate his strong support for the idea of the divine right of kings, Gryphius utilizes several techniques which separate this drama from his other plays. In general, the play is much more stylized than his other tragedies. There are few real conversations, and these lack dramatic intent and impact. Instead, even in scenes containing two or more characters, long monologues prevail, varied only by passages and scenes made up entirely of single-line interchanges (stichomythia). The individual scenes, rather than providing a continual sequence of exposition, climax, and denouement—the classical dramatic structure—are episodic in nature. Each episode illuminates another aspect of the central theme, but does not necessarily relate to the scenes before and after it. We see no dramatic actions on stage, but only the commentary of the characters in hindsight or in expectation of the momentous events outside the play: civil war, Charles's trial and sentencing, the trip to the gallows, and the execution itself. These characteristics, much criticized by subsequent literary theorists and even scholars, all support Gryphius's purpose in writing the play: to convince his audience of the rightness of his view.

Another aspect of stylization lends support to this purpose on an emotional rather than a strictly rational level. Gryphius, as Albrecht Schöne has shown, has modeled his executed King Charles on the passion and crucifixion of Christ, at times even to the extent of adding fictitious events and footnoting them with fictitious references.[8] This patterning of Charles's death on that of Christ does not merely give him stature as a Christian martyr. Gryphius's use of the *imitatio Christi* imagery, like his departures from strictly dramatic presentation of events, has a polemical purpose—to propagate his conviction that an anointed king is Christ's earthly substitute and therefore above the law and of a class apart from his subjects. This "divine right" of kings is stated in Charles's own utterances when he claims that God alone has the right to judge a king, that it is impossible for those not of kingly birth to rule the nation, and that the difference between king and subject is insurmountable. While such claims may sound like tyranny to our own democratic age, to Gryphius, as to Charles, they were self-evident truths. The concept of the divine right of kings, coupled with the Christian, anti-Machiavellian view of how a prince should behave and rule (prevalent in ideal if not always in practice in the seventeenth century), promoted benevolent, divinely ordained and supported monarchy as the ideal form of government. Charles's execution is modeled on that of Christ because the author felt that any challenge to these ideas was not only shocking, but blasphemous.

Gryphius's other martyr drama, *Großmüttiger Rechts-Gelehrter/ oder Sterbender Aemilius Paulus Papinianus* (1659), on the other hand, probably deserves the appellation often applied to it, secular martyr drama. For Papinian dies not for Christian or even religious principles, nor in order to acquire the glory of a martyr, but to uphold ethical ideas of justice. Papinian is minister and adviser to the half-brothers Bassianus Caracalla and Antoninus Geta, sons of the previous Roman emperor Severus and coheirs to the imperial office. When the elder brother, Bassian, goaded to the deed by the courtier Laetus, murders his brother and thus wrests all the power to himself, he needs the public approbation of Papinian to excuse the deed to the army and the Roman populace. Papinian's ethics and sense of justice do not permit him this apologist role, and his refusal leads to the execution of his son, and subsequently himself, by the outraged tyrant.

Although nominally related to the royal family and thus satisfying the requirement of the theoreticians that he be a high personage whose fall will amaze, Papinian may be seen to represent the class of patrician bureaucrats who served the German princes and city-states as ministers and advisers—the class to which Gryphius himself, along with most other literary figures of the age, belonged. Thus Papinian's tragedy, the fall of a principled courtier, represents a dilemma which could someday be faced by many in the audience for which it was intended—the patrician schoolboys of Breslau—and thus could strike a chord of relevance unequaled by the sad tales of the deaths of kings which provided the usual theatrical fare.

The parallels to the religious martyr drama are manifest. The protagonist is asked to abandon his principles by a Roman Emperor who offers rewards for obedience and death for disobedience. Other modes of escape are offered, in this case by the army, which wishes to put him in power in Bassian's stead, and by the mother of the murdered Geta, who wishes to usurp and share the imperial power with Papinian. His virtue, however, overcomes both temptations and threats, and he insists on upholding justice. He, like many martyrs, must watch as his innocent child is put to death before his eyes, and only then be executed himself. Like the typical martyr, Papinian denigrates the value of earthly glory and sees death as the door to eternal rewards—in this case fame instead of heavenly grace. His ultimate value is a clean conscience: *Diß ist der höchste Sig/ daß mein Gewissen rein* ("This is the highest victory: that my conscience is clear," 5:266). In contrast, his antagonist, the Emperor Bassian, is shown beset by the sufferings of a bad conscience.

Unlike a martyr, Papinian dies not for the glory of God, but out of patriotic motives which ultimately attest to and augment the glory of the Roman Empire. The glory of Rome is no mere secular glory, however, for, in the Christian view of history prevalent in the seventeenth century, Rome is the last and greatest world empire whose task is to become the Holy Roman Empire under Constantine and Charlemagne in later centuries and to spread Christianity to the entire world. This concept of the sacred destiny of Rome is an integral aspect of Birken's concept of *Vorsicht*—Divine Providence and the Divine Plan for History—the revelation of which is one of the purposes of tragic drama. Gryphius's use of the amphibolic term *Heil* (which can signify both well-being or health and salvation) conforms to this interpretation of Papinian's patriotism. Thus even this most secular of martyr dramas has religious import. Papinian's stand for justice will contribute to the ultimate nobility of Rome and to the deservedness of its glorious mission in the Divine Plan. His fame is thus more than a secular parallel to the salvation obtained by Christian martyrs; it is a cipher for it. This use of drama, which appears among Gryphius's works only in his final tragedy, will dominate the entire dramatic output of Lohenstein, as we shall see.

Gryphius's first original tragedy, *Leo Armenius, Oder Fürsten-Mord* [Leo Armenius, or Murder of a Prince; written ca. 1646, published 1650], is a martyr tragedy of a different sort. Like Bidermann's *Philemon*

Martyr, it portrays the saintly Christian martyrdom of someone who at the beginning of the play did not even qualify as a good Christian. In fact, Gryphius's impetus for writing the play, a Jesuit drama by Joseph Simon which he is thought to have seen in Rome in 1646, is the tragedy of the deserved fall of an impious tyrant, not a martyr drama at all. Gryphius, perhaps in part due to his opinions about the sacredness of kingship or to his own religious beliefs,[9] instead provides for the ultimate conversion to Christianity and subsequent martyrdom of the former tyrant.

The Eastern Roman Emperor Leo Armenius (d. 820) is depicted in the opening speech of his general Michael Balbus as a bloodthirsty, greedy, and treacherous tyrant who must be overthrown. The conspiracy is born as the coconspirators agree to an assassination attempt and coup. The plot is discovered before it succeeds, however, and Michael Balbus finds himself imprisoned, accused, convicted of treason, and sentenced to die at the stake that very evening. As it is Christmas Eve, however, Leo's wife, Theodosia, pleads with him to delay the execution until after Christmas, and he finally reluctantly agrees. At dawn Leo's worst fears are realized as the other conspirators carry out their plan to kill him and place the freed Michael on the throne. The play ends with Michael making plans for his own coronation.

The precarious and changeable nature of man's existence, presented in exemplary form in the fall of the emperor and in the high office, imprisonment, and crowning of the usurper, are the subject of commentary in the first three choruses, all of which are sung by courtiers—those supreme examples of the vanity of earthly glory. The first, although ostensibly a commentary on Michael Balbus's mistake—talking too much—uses man's ability to speak to reveal both his superiority over animals and nature and his vulnerability to treachery, error, and vice. The second chorus laments the inconstancy of human life:

> O du wechsel aller dinge
> Immerwehrend' eitelheit/
> Laufft denn in der zeiten ringe
> Nichts alß unbestendigkeit.   (2:597–600)
>
> (O, you vicissitude of all things,
> Everlasting vanity,

> Does nothing but inconstancy
> Run in the track of time?)

And the third admits that the ends planned by Divine Providence are
beyond man's ability to know for certain and to control. This chorus
speaks not of the fickle *Glück* ("Fortuna") addressed in the previous
chorus, but of *Verhängnis*—what God has preordained to happen.
Leo's fall is thus already subtly shifted from the realm of mere bad fortune and
the vanity of human existence to an element in the Divine Plan. The
fourth chorus, on the other hand, is anything but commentary on the
preceding or impending events. It is simply the announcement of
Christ's birth in the Christmas celebration, its joyful words sung by
priests and virgins, not by courtiers—a sharp contrast to the entire
fourth act, which is taken up by the plotting of the conspirators,
goaded on by a "hellish spirit" (*Der Höllische Geist*).

A second overtly religious element enters the play in Leo's murder,
reported at the beginning of the fifth act. The tyrannical emperor is
murdered at the altar as he attends early Mass on Christmas morning,
and as he dies he clings to the actual cross upon which Christ was
crucified—a greatly treasured relic in Constantinople. It is explicitly
stated that the blood of this arch-sinner, this tyrant, mingles with that
of the Son of God on the cross. The messenger who recounts this
circumstance reacts with horror: *O Grewell* ("Oh, abomination!"). But
it is unclear whether this reaction refers to the blasphemy involved in
mixing a sinner's blood with Christ's or at the equally blasphemous
action of murdering a ruler, Christ's earthly substitute. Had Leo been
left in his wickedness, not even his kingship could have called for
martyrdom imagery for his death from Gryphius's pen. Yet since it is
Leo himself who points out that his sinner's blood does not merit being
mixed with that of Christ, it becomes clear that Leo has repented. What
has brought about this change in Leo which warrants for him a death as
symbolically sanctified as that of the innocent Charles Stuart? We see
him, in the third act, careworn, fearful for his safety, insecure, even
paranoid. But we do not see him repent of his past sins or undergo a
conversion. His conversion is instead expressed metaphorically, using
the typology of the biblical account of the salvation of mankind. The
crucial turning point for Leo, as for mankind, is the birth of Christ into
flesh and history in preparation for his ultimate sacrifice on the cross.
Just as Christ's birth marked the end of the historical period ruled by

the Law of Moses (the Old Testament) and the onset of the Age of Grace
(the New Testament), so the announcement of it during the Christmas
service marks the end of the old Leo, whose sense of justice is that of
revenge, and the birth of the new Leo, who can show mercy, confess sin,
imitate Christ. Actual chronology (Leo was a Christian in a Christian
age) becomes secondary as the symbolic time of the typological relationship between the event and its postfiguration is victorious. Even
crucifixion imagery can occur at Christmas, since rational time is
superseded by symbolic significance.

In Gryphius's *Leo Armenius,* alone among the great Baroque dramas,
we see the lingering tradition of the medieval liturgical drama,
elsewhere confined to the oratorio. The fourth chorus, which seems to
be a processional for the Christmas Mass attended by Leo, has an
appropriately liturgical tone and does resemble the Christmas plays. It
certainly has dramatic character, since it announces the birth of Christ
as a present event rather than reciting the story of a past one. But the
most significant usage of liturgical drama is one whose existence is less
apparent, yet crucial for a total understanding of the play. It is the
portion of the Easter play derived from the old *quem queritis* trope of the
three Marys at the tomb. Empress Theodosia's sudden joyful announcement that Leo is alive, following on her passionate laments for
his death, cries for retribution, and a deathwish for herself, is taken by
those present—Michael Balbus and his coconspirators—as madness.
She cries out, delirious with joy:

> . . . Wo sind wir? was für lust
> Empfinden wir an jtzt? Der Fürst ist nicht erblichen:
> O frewd/ er lebt! er lebt! Nun ist diß leid gewichen:
> Er wischt die Thränen selbst uns ab mit linder hand!
> Hier steht er!
> . . . .
> Gefährten trawr't nicht mehr/ er lebt.   (5:438–48)

> (Where are we? What ecstasy
> Do we now feel? The prince is not dead;
> Oh joy, he lives! he lives! Now sorrow has retreated.
> He himself wipes the tears away with gentle hand!
> Here he stands!
> Comrades, mourn no more, he lives.)

If Gryphius had researched the Easter liturgy of the Eastern Church—the one once based in Leo's Constantinople—he would have found the Easter trope of *quem queritis* still dramatized in the midnight Mass of Easter Eve. The congregation gathers outside the Church, anxiously awaiting word of the fate of the crucified savior, as if his death had occurred that very day instead of centuries earlier, as if their own salvation still hinged on the news. At midnight, as if receiving Divine revelation, the priests suddenly announce that Christ has indeed risen from the dead. The congregation expresses its joy with Alleluias and then enters to hear Mass. But it was probably not necessary for Gryphius to turn to the Byzantine liturgy to discover the trope which was the model for Theodosia's words. Similar versions appear to have been used throughout medieval Europe[10] and had not totally disappeared by the seventeenth century. One variant recorded by Young even uses the name "leo," albeit in this case referring to Christ, presumably a reference to Christ as Lion of Judah. The angels tell the women who seek the body of Christ:

> Non est hic, surrexit sicut predixerat; ite,
>   nuntiate quia surrexit, dicentis:
> Alleluia, resurrexit hodie; hodie resurrexit
> leo fortis, Christus, filius Dei; Deo gratias,
> dicite eia![11]

> (He is not here, he has risen again as was prophesied; go,
>   announce that he has risen, saying:
> Alleluia, he rose from the dead today; today he rose from the dead,
> the strong Lion, Christ, son of God; thanks be to God,
> announce it indeed!)

The women then use the latter words to announce the resurrection to the disciples, who use them in turn to tell the clergy, who repeat them to the congregation. Theodosia's use of similar words reveals that she is aware through heavenly revelation that Leo, like Christ, upon whose mercy he has thrown himself at the end, has attained eternal life. His resurrection, like that of Christ, involves the reception into Heaven of the soul now cleansed of all sin, and this resurrection, like Christ's, constitutes a promise of similar salvation for other sinners. The name of the protagonist, Leo, does indeed have connotations which enhance this interpretation. For just as tyrant and martyr, in Benjamin's words, are the *Janushäupter* ("twin faces") of the prince[12] (as Leo is each in turn), so the image of the lion has had a dual nature in Christian symbolism. He is the Old Testament realm of bloodshed and revenge conquered beneath the feet of the Virgin Mary in many depictions, but also the prophesied Lion of Judah, Christ, who will redeem souls. He is the arch enemy but also the king of beasts, the devil and the savior.[13] He is the symbolic beast of the Evangelist Mark and as such can represent the New Testament. Thus in this one traditional Christian symbol with its set of seemingly contradictory meanings we see the significance of Gryphius's story of Leo Armenius: Old Testament superseded by New Testament, vengeance and tyranny converted to mercy and noble kingship, sinfulness redeemed by the sacrifice of Christ and by the martyr's imitation of this sacrifice.

Indeed, in this play, unlike *Carolus Stuardus,* the divine right of kingship alone does not justify use of the *imitatio Christi* imagery, nor is Leo an innocent martyr dying for divinely prescribed principles of kingship. Unlike Charles, Leo does not imitate Christ because of his similarly pure nature, but as a plea for mercy for his sinfulness based on the promise of salvation offered by Christ's action in taking the sins of the world upon himself. Unlike Charles, Leo does not provide us with a postfiguration of Christ, but rather is the representative of sinful mankind that merits damnation, yet, through the grace offered by Christ's sacrifice on the cross, receives undeserved heavenly reward.

Gryphius's other conversion drama, *Cardenio und Celinde, Oder Unglücklich Verliebete* [Cardenio and Celinde, or Unhappy Lovers; published 1657, written perhaps in 1649], is also termed a *Trauer-Spiel.* Subject of the play is an eternal triangle: Cardenio's love for Olympia and Celinde's love for Cardenio. For the entire first act Cardenio confides to a friend the peripatetic history of his unhappy love for Olympia, ending in Olympia's marriage to another suitor, Lysander, and Cardenio's involvement with Celinde, whose previous lover, the Templar knight Marcellus, he had killed in a duel. At the end of the act we learn that Cardenio, no longer interested in Celinde, now plans to murder Lysander in revenge for the theft of Olympia. The next three acts constitute the true action of the play, for which the first act was only the exposition. Celinde attempts to use magic in order to regain Cardenio's attentions, and is instructed by a witch to obtain Marcellus's heart from his corpse for this purpose. We meet Olympia, whose old love for Cardenio has totally disappeared to make room for marital love, a change she attributes not to faithlessness on her part, but to divine will. Cardenio, lying in ambush for Lysander, is distracted by a mysterious apparition in Olympia's form which lures him to a lonely spot where it metamorphoses into the personification of death. He swoons and awakens in a tomb where a terrified Celinde fell when Marcellus's dead body fled at her arrival. The entire fifth act is taken up by a repentant and reformed Cardenio and Celinde telling their tale to a stunned Olympia and Lysander.

It is perhaps easier for us today to appreciate the characters, predicament, and emotions of this play than those of Gryphius's martyr plays. The story is entertaining, and the desperate loves of Cardenio, Olympia, and Celinde more understandable to us than the love of Catharina for Christ or Papinian for his honor. Due to the novella-like tone of the story, we may even be ready to accept the black magic, ghosts, and apparitions. Certainly the passions are convincingly, realistically, and seriously portrayed—a characteristic of the play which reminds us of Shakespeare's *Romeo and Juliet* (of which a much altered stage version had made the rounds in Germany on the itinerant stage). But these lovers do not die for love like Shakespeare's even younger and more foolish protagonists, although the play abounds with death and allusions to death. Instead, they convert from their foolishness and sinfulness, reject their unhappy loves, and vow to orient their future lives toward eternal values.

Unlike the more symbolic conversion in *Leo Armenius,* this conversion is overt, moralistic, and rational. The moral lesson to be learned is revealed by Gryphius's statements in the prologue, by commentary in the choruses, by the words of supernatural figures, and by the characters' self-analyses in the fifth act. The play is, as the author tells us in the prologue, a tale of two loves, one a good model for emulation, the other a bad example to avoid: *Eine keusche/ sitsame und doch inbrünstige in Olympien* ("a chaste, virtuous, and yet powerful love in Olympia"), and *Eine rasende/ tolle und verzweifflende in Celinden* ("a raving, crazed, and despairing one in Celinde"). Gryphius then proceeds to moralize all the actions of the play, saying that one will find in this short drama a summary of all the vanities into which erring youth might fall: Cardenio seeks what he cannot and should not find; Lysander behaves dangerously and unwisely until his follies are replaced by reason, virtue, and understanding; Olympia suffers the inconstancies of fortune and love until she turns to honor as the only proper goal of life; Celinde's black magic is despicable, accursed, and evil (5:100).

The choruses, too, help to reveal the moral fabric of the play, although their connection to the acts they follow is more tenuous than in Gryphius's other plays, and their commentary is less direct. In fact, there has been a great deal of disagreement about the significance of the first (*Der hohe Geist*—"the lofty spirit") and the third (the four seasons) choruses. The first chorus describes the lofty spirit who, like the eagle in the emblem,[14] ignores the lure of earth below to fly toward the heavenly sun above, the only creature unblinded by its magnificence. This is the ideal person whose ties to earthly joys are minimal, whose orientation is rather toward eternal values. Yet his allegiance to these high ideals is threatened by the prince of the underworld (Satan), who sends the vices to try to fetter the wings of the aquiline spirit. The chorus ends with a summary of the state of the mortals in this play, themselves distracted from the lofty goal to which their spirits should aspire by the vices just catalogued:

> Sie reissen (ach!) deß Menschen reine Seel
> Von ihrem Zweck in deß Verterbens Höl
> Und ziehn/ die den Gott gab den Himmel ein
> Auß stiller Ruh/ in jmmer-strenge Pein.   (1:577–80)

> (They tear, alas, man's pure soul
> Away from its purpose and toward hellish destruction,
> And draw the soul, to which God granted Heaven,
> Out of its quiet peace into eternally severe pain.)

The second chorus is more explicit. Those who stray into sin are like the man who ventures out into a swamp, only to find that the apparently firm surface conceals the morass into which he will sink. The singer of the chorus then turns to Celinde's acceptance of black magic, which he deplores. He even calls out a warning to her (and to the audience) to abandon such sinful follies, but realizes the hopelessness of the situation and gloomily forecasts quick punishment for her sins, since no sin can long remain unavenged.

The third chorus, unlike any other produced by Gryphius, is a miniature play within the play, a *Zwischenspiel* ("intermezzo") rather than a chorus in the classic sense. The personification of Time (*Die Zeit*) tells the human being (*Der Mensch*) that he must choose among the female personifications of the four seasons who represent the four stages of life. As he sees each parade by, the man hopes that the next will be even lovelier, and so is confronted at the last by grim Winter, whose visage horrifies him:

> Weh mir! Was seh ich hier! ist diß mein gantz verlangen
> O häßlich Frauen-Bild! was ist die Fackel noth!
> Bist du mir in mein Grab zu leuchten vorgegangen!
> O lebend Sichen-Hauß/ O Muster von dem Tod.
> . . . .
> O allzu späte Rew'/ O höchst-verschertztes Glück.   (3:243–50)

> (Woe is me! What see I here! Is this my whole desire,
> Oh repulsive image of a woman! What is that torch for!
> Did you go ahead of me to light my way into my grave!
> Oh living house of deadly illness, Oh model of Death,
> Oh Regret that came too late, Oh Chance that I passed by.)

This conceit of the four seasons, usually used in the *carpe diem* topos, is here instead a part of Gryphius's *memento mori* imagery. Winter's death's-head features remind him—too late—of the vanity of earthly values. Had he, like the lucky Cardenio in the act to follow, already caught a glimpse of death while yet in his youth and behaved accordingly, his fate could have been different.

Dramatizations of the *memento mori* experience also occur in the action of the play itself, albeit always in words and actions of supernatural source. The apparition in the form of Olympia not only metamorphoses into the symbol of death, like the Medieval *Frau Welt* ("Dame World"), but also, as an instrument of Divine Retribution, threatens Cardenio with punishment for his earthly orientation and sin. Marcellus's ghost, too, lectures Cardenio and Celinde (and the audience):

> Deß Höchsten unerforschliches Gerichte
> Schreckt eure Schuld durch dieses Traur-Gesichte

Die ihr mehr tod denn ich! O selig ist der Geist
Dem eines Todten Grufft den Weg zum Leben weist.   (4:381—84)

(The inscrutable judgment of the Highest
Offers through this mournful apparition fright for your guilt—
You, who are more dead than I! Oh blessed is the spirit
To whom a dead-man's tomb has shown the way to life!)

The ghost's paradoxical use of the concepts "Death" and "Life," of course, are those we have heard from Gryphius's other positive characters.

Cardenio's and Celinde's comments in the fifth act, joined by those of the others at the end, constitute another source of direct moralizing in the play. Cardenio reveals his thoughts upon viewing the apparition:

Zu dencken . . .
Wie alle Pracht der Welt in Eitelkeit vergeh!
Wie schnell ich dieses Fleisch der Erden soll vertrauen/
Und den gerechten Thron deß höchsten Richters schauen. . . .
                                                                        (5:223—26)

(To think . . .
How all the splendor of the world dissolves into mere vanity,
How quickly I shall have to entrust this flesh to the earth,
And look upon the just throne of the highest Judge.)

The play ends with a series of adages offered by all four lovers to teach the audience what they have learned by their experience, advising orientation toward eternal values rather then earthly ones, ending with Cardenio's summation:

Wer hier recht leben wil und jene Kron ererben/
Die uns das Leben gibt: denck jede Stund ans Sterben.   (5:429—30)

(Whoever wishes to live properly on earth and win that crown
Which life offers us: think each hour about dying.)

In the prologue Gryphius had termed this play *Trauer-Spiegel* ("tragic mirror") instead of *Trauer-Spiel* ("tragic play"), and this pun does indeed describe the content of the drama. In seventeenth-century Germany, the popular image of the mirror signified the concept of learning vicariously from history, literature, and theater. The virtues and vices of the protagonists were mirrors in which the readers or audiences would look, see themselves reflected, and change their ways before it was too late. *Cardenio und Celinde* is not only a "mirror of death," a *memento mori* for the audience, but for the characters as well, who learn and undergo conversion as a result of the reminders of death which confront them.

Although Cardenio can hardly be termed a great sinner or titanic personality, echoes of the Faust story emerge in his account of his own fall. The catalog of Faust's errors recurs here in the stories of Cardenio and Celinde: faith in Renaissance learning, lust, murder, use of black magic. Pointing ahead to Goethe's *Faust* and away from the sixteenth-century chapbook version, however, is the conquest of Reformation pessimism about salvation by an act of the Grace of God and by the essential benevolence of Divine Providence. For it is clear that it is the infinite patience of Divine Providence which continues to offer Cardenio yet another chance to reform, yet another experience which may damage his self-sufficiency enough to bring about conversion. That this view of Providence does not restrict man's right to choose freely whether he will do good or evil is clear in Cardenio's admission of sole responsibility for his fall: *Der Mensch fällt nur durch sich* ("Man falls only through his own fault," 5:375). Yet Divine Providence also provides ample opportunity and guidance for making the choice of good over evil, as Olympia's actions and Cardenio's fate reveal. And this benevolence, not only to the virtuous but to sinners as well, is its "amazing Grace." This divine mercy is proffered to a terrified Cardenio and Celinde, left in Marcellus's tomb as the curtain falls at the end of the fourth act, by the chorus, which begins, appropriately, with the word *Dennoch* ("however"). Death does not have the final word over the fate of man, for the soul is eternal.

The title page indicates that Gryphius considered this play a tragedy, but some modern scholars, in the absence of the death of the protagonists and in consideration of a brief comic scene (4:161–67), have preferred to term it a tragicomedy. As a matter of fact, the Jesuits routinely termed their conversion plays comedies. As Gryphius himself, nervous about the play's reception, admitted in the preface, its subject matter was not typically tragic: the characters are not kings and queens whose fates influence historical events and the events were not heroic or political deeds, but young lovers and love affairs. Indeed, were it not for the *memento mori* theme and the renunciation of worldly love at the end, this play might qualify as an italianate comedy.

One criterion for the tragic genre remains: does the play exhibit tragic catharsis (in the Baroque sense discussed above)? In fact, it probably does have a greater share of this requisite than any of Gryphius's other plays. The audience, since it finds its own desires, loves, and passions mirrored in those of the characters, is lured into feeling empathy for them. And while trapped in this relationship of feeling with the characters, the audience is forced to share their metaphorical deaths and resurrections. As the characters are cleansed of sin and rededicated to the eternal orientation of the "lofty spirit," so too is the audience. The sense of joy felt by the audience at the end is not so much relief that Cardenio and Celinde escaped deserved punishment, as vicarious cleansing of the passions. This *memento mori,* no longer subject to the brooding pessimism of its medieval equivalents, leads instead to spiritual victory over death, just as tragic catharsis should always leave, not a sense of depression and defeat, but of exhilaration and triumph.

Daniel Casper von Lohenstein

Gryphius's younger compatriot Daniel Casper von Lohenstein (1635–1683) opened his dramatic career with the martyr tragedy *Ibrahim Bassa* when still a boy in Silesia (1649–50; published in 1653). As he himself admits in the preface to the reader, his *unreiffe Sinn-Frucht* ("unripe fruit of the intellect," 80) owes much to the dramas of Gryphius. In spite of Lohenstein's modesty, however, this drama shows him to possess an original and talented mind, and the play cannot be dismissed as the exercise of a schoolboy. The title figure, Ibrahim, is a mysterious European and former slave who has been made commander of the armies of the Turkish Empire due to his military prowess. The Turkish Sultan Soliman has come to depend upon him to buttress his power at home and abroad. But during Ibrahim's absence on campaigns in Persia, the Sultan has fallen in love with Ibrahim's wife, Isabel. To rescue her from the Sultan's lust, Ibrahim attempts to flee with her to Europe, but the pair is captured and returned to the Sultan. Two *Intriganten,* the courtier Rusthan and the Sultan's wife, Roxelane, convince the Sultan, against his better judgment, that Ibrahim is a traitor who must be executed for his disloyalty. After the execution

Isabel and the chorus of enslaved Christians call upon Divine Retribution to send a crusade to challenge Turkish tyranny.

Lohenstein has borrowed heavily from Gryphius's two early martyr tragedies, *Leo Armenius* and *Catharina von Georgien*, in this play. Like *Catharina, Ibrahim* opens with a prologue spoken by an allegorical figure who delineates the background of the action—in this case "Asia" instead of Eternity. Several of the choruses in each play, too, are similar in that they are commentaries by persons who would be on stage anyway, especially the retinues of the protagonists, while others are allegorical representations of inner psychological processes or forces. Each play opens with the martyr(s) already in the hands of the tyrannical captor and faced with his threats and interrogation. Both Chach Abas and Sultan Soliman waver between good and evil or between keeping and breaking their promises, and both regret their decisions too late to stop the executions. The behavior of Isabel, who believes that she, too, will be killed, is modeled on that of Catharina. As Catharina had maintained the sanctity of her "marriage" to Christ and kingdom against the lust promised in a union with the tyrant, so Isabel is loyal to her real marriage to Ibrahim as she resists the amorous advances of Soliman. In both plays the first chorus is composed of captive Christian women who bemoan the fates of their leaders and plead for Divine Retribution.

Other aspects of the play more closely resemble Gryphius's *Papinian*, written some ten years later, and may indicate a process of reverse influence as well. *Ibrahim Bassa* already demonstrates the tyrant-martyr-*Intrigant* triad of characters which Gryphius also uses in *Papinian*, and which remains an important characteristic of martyr plays in the coming decades (in use earlier in the *Staatsaktionen* of the itinerant stage and in Jesuit plays). And the focus of *Ibrahim Bassa* has shifted more firmly in the direction of history and *Heilsgeschichte* and away from portrayal of Christian steadfastness and religious allegorization, as is apparent in the choice of the allegorical prologue speaker. "Asia" depicts herself as one of several sister continents, each of which held imperial power: "War Ich nicht Asien/ die gröst und ältst und schönste meiner Schwestern?" ("Was I not Asia, the greatest and oldest and most beautiful of my sisters?" line 46). She thus represents Assyria, first monarchy in Daniel's prophetic interpretation of Nebuchadnezzar's dream (Daniel 7, a schema often applied in the seventeenth century to world history), and had been the home of the Garden of Eden (line 48). She had been fertile ground for the spread of Christianity (line 61). But her proud head, once crowned with twelve crowns of the twelve tribes of Israel, now bears the yoke of Gog and Magog, the maverick tribes in the prophecy often equated in Lohenstein's day to the Turks. And her steel legs and stone feet likewise relate to Daniel's prophecy of four great world monarchies. This enslaved Asia, Turkey, is challenged by the fourth and last of the monarchies prophesied by Daniel (as interpreted by Lohenstein's contemporaries): the Roman Empire, now called the Holy Roman Empire, led by Emperor Charles V, in whose armies Ibrahim had fought before being captured and enslaved. And veiled hints reveal to those in the know that Ibrahim himself is none other than the heir of the Palaeologus family, the dynasty which ruled Constantinople until 1453 when the Eastern Roman Empire, the other half of the fourth monarchy, came to an abrupt end in the fall of its capital to the Turks. Ibrahim can thus be seen as Charles's brother-emperor, and his fall becomes more than that of a highly placed army officer—it stands for the slavery and martyrdom of the Eastern Empire and the Eastern Church, a political allegory which is more detailed and lucid than that tentatively discovered above in *Catharina von Georgien*. Lohenstein's choice of subject matter is thus determined, even in this early play so beholden to Gryphius, far more by its ability to express attitudes about the Divine Plan for history (Birken's *Vorsicht*) than about virtue and constancy in a world of transience and vanity, the unifying theme in Gryphius's works. It was probably no accident that the play was first published in 1653, the bicentennial of the fall of Constantinople to the Turks, a date with more significance for this work on the level of political allegory than the actual date of Ibrahim's death during the reign of Charles V in the sixteenth century.

One could see in this play, as in *Catharina von Georgien,* an allegory based on the Song of Songs exegesis which depicted the love of Christ and His Church in terms of human love and marriage. In such an interpretation, the marriage between Ibrahim and Isabel would depict the love and loyalty of Christ for His Church, the Sultan the sinful lusts of this world, and Ibrahim's martyrdom Christ's self-sacrifice for the human soul. But such an interpretation is not hinted at, and it is clear that it was of less interest to Lohenstein than *Heilsgeschichte.*

Ibrahim Bassa undoubtedly belongs to a long train of dramas and other literary works which contain anti-Turkish polemics and even exhortations to launch another crusade against Europe's Muslim challengers. Lohenstein's last drama, *Ibrahim Sultan* (finished and published in 1673), likewise belongs to this tradition and reiterates many of the themes—Turkish immorality and treachery, illicit Turkish rule of Constantinople and Asia, and the Turkish threat to Christianity and the Holy Roman Empire. But this play, named for a tyrant rather than a martyr, belongs to a new direction in German tragedy for which Lohenstein was responsible. This type of drama, historical tragedy, depicts the fall of a tyrant as just punishment by God for his sins. And it is perhaps best to begin discussion of this type of drama with Lohenstein's last work, rather than with the intermediaries, since this tragedy is totally chiaroscuro, like the late Baroque paintings of Magnasco. There can be no doubt that the protagonist is a totaly evil man whose vices find ready servants in his *Intriganten,* but who needs no whispered advice to influence his decisions to do evil. Ibrahim actually rapes his victim, unlike such tyrants as Chach Abas or Sultan Soliman, who may threaten or torture their female captives but do not violate their chastity. And the dramatic interest is not centered on the steadfastness of a Christian martyr, for the briefly depicted Turkish maiden Ambre remains only an exemplary victim and never dominates the scene.

The plot, too, is starkly simplified. Sultan Ibrahim, urged on by a scheming courtier and a female pimp, murders his own son and heir in an attempt to lure Ambre to his bed, and then, that plan having failed, rapes her and sends her home in dishonor. These vile deeds provide the final impetus needed to carry through a palace rebellion and coup. At the play's end Ibrahim is carried down to Hell. The choruses depict the conflict again, this time in dramatized battles between embodiments of the virtues and vices, and judgment in the allegorical figure of Divine Retribution, paralleling the main action, rather than providing narrative commentary. The impression that the play is a morality play is strengthened by the fact that Ibrahim's last words are a lesson directed at the audience, whom he turns to face:

Lernt Sterblichen: wie scharf des Höchsten Pfeile seyn/
Wenn er sie lange Zeit ins Langmuths-Oel weicht ein! (5:813–14)

(Learn, mortals: how sharp are the arrows of the highest Judge,
Even when he has softened them long in the oil of patience.)

But the moral lesson can have had little effect on the audience, for the
play does not attempt to create sympathy for the damned Turkish
Sultan, who was Eastern Europe's most feared enemy at the time the
drama was written (within eight years the Turks will have marched
victoriously to the very walls of Vienna). Instead, the Sultan's depravity
is a depiction *e contrario,* i.e., in contrast to the greatness of the
Christian emperor Leopold, leader of the Holy Roman Empire and
defender of the Faith and the faithful. In the final chorus Leopold is
depicted as being pulled up to Heaven by a chariot of pure white swans;
and the play ends with a presentation honoring his third marriage to a
princess who, it is hoped, will bear him the desired sons and heirs—a
total contrast to Ibrahim Sultan, murderer of his own child for a whim,
who is carried off to Hell in an execution cart pulled by black ravens.

Neither of these "Turkish Tragedies" leads to a purging of the
emotions (although empathy and fear are suitably aroused in *Ibrahim
Bassa,* if not in *Ibrahim Sultan*), but instead to a sense of the necessity to
bring about change through action: a new crusade against the Turks. A
catharsis or purgation of emotions would have freed the audience from
further responsibility, but the intended reaction will, Lohenstein
hopes, lead to a commitment to drive the Turks out of the Balkans and
retake Constantinople for Christianity and the Roman Empire. Tragic
pleasure is aroused through perception of the just punishment given or
promised to each Turkish tyrant, a "prophecy" of events which Lohenstein hopes will overtake the entire Turkish empire.

Another of Lohenstein's historical tragedies, *Epicharis* (published
1665), has usually been termed a martyr tragedy, since the female title
figure is tortured by that arch-tyrant of world history, the Emperor
Nero. However, she is no Christian who maintains her faith or her
chastity in the face of threats and temptations, but an instigator and
participant in a republican revolution against the imperial throne and
its current occupant. Unlike Catharina or Isabel and Ibrahim Bassa, or
even Gryphius's secular political martyr, Papinian, she does not
passively and stoically accept her fate, but curses and taunts her
tormenter and challenges him to try worse tortures, since those he has
applied have failed to gain power over her unconquerable spirit. Her

behavior, however admirable it may seem to us today, would have been considered reprehensible to an audience schooled on Opitz's and Gryphius's stoic male martyrs and suffering but steadfast female martyrs. Her coconspirators, each brought before the tyrant for judgment for his part in the plot, exhibit various unsavory reactions to adversity, from cowardice and treachery to denial of guilt. Only one figure in the play, the imperial adviser and philosopher Seneca, conforms to the traditional ideal of the stoic martyr. And just as Lohenstein's irony dissects the motivations and actions of the conspirators and finds them unworthy of attaining the stature of martyrs for a cause, so it acts even upon Seneca, who must die because he did *not* stand up for a cause, but tried to maintain a distance to both parties. His passivity, now tainted with this negative commentary, extends even to his own body, which refuses to let the blood flow abundantly through the slashes in his wrists he has made in a suicide attempt.

We are faced, then, not with a martyr tragedy, but with a dialectical dissection of the value placed on republicanism, political freedom, and revolution by such "modern" writers as Jean Bodin and Niccolò Machiavelli—both of whose books remained on the Index and were under attack, when not banned outright, by Protestant authorities as well throughout the seventeenth century. In their place Lohenstein elevates the authority of God's Plan for history, *Verhängnüs,* if not Gryphius's outright plea for the Divine Right of kingship, through the medium of the commentary provided in the choruses.

The theme is taken up, in fact, already in the Latin motto from Seneca with which Lohenstein prefaces the play: *Istud tempus, quod alienæ destinas morti, fortasse citra tuam est* ("That time which you determine for the deaths of others may very well be your own," 153). Nemesis, the arm of Divine Providence which carries out retribution, and not one's own intentionality, will ultimately determine fate. The chorus of the first act contains a recitation of strange omens and their interpretations by a seer: tyranny will rule city and empire steeped in blood, and the conspiracy to overthrow the tyrant must fail. Divine Providence (*der Verhängnüs-Schluß*) is named as the cause. The second chorus reinforces this theme. Wisdom, Time (as Fate written in the stars), and Fortune all attempt to claim the honor of being the source of historical events. Yet Divine Providence appears to claim ultimate supremacy. The other forces do not agree, and they decide to cause Nero

to fall at the hands of the conspiracy. But the victory belongs to
Verhängnüs, whose mere handmaidens the other powers are; and her
decision that Nero shall remain in power will be fulfilled. The third
chorus recounts the continual bloodbath of Rome's history, and cannot
account for the horror except as a decision of Divine Providence:

> Der Bluttbrunn muß nach Rom gesätzet
> Durch das Verhängnüs worden sein.   (3:737–38)

> (The bloodbath must have been sent to Rome by Providence itself.)

The geographical allegories themselves are tempted to conspire against
Nero's tyranny, but even Nature is powerless to change the events
foreseen by Providence. More geographical allegorical figures—
Europe, Asia, and Africa—appear in the fourth chorus, where they are
joined by the Cumaean Sibyl. The three continents accuse Rome of
crimes and plead for Divine Retribution. The Sibyl's answer provides
the justification for the evil tyranny which has befallen Rome and the
world:

> Gott strafft mit Fug mit Drangsal und mit Blutte
> Die/ die nicht sind von eigner Bluttschuld leer.
> Ja wißt: Daß euer Meer verdammter Missethat
> Die Tyranney noch nicht halb außgemäßen hat.   (4:653–56)

> (God justly punishes with suffering and blood
> Those who are not free themselves of blood-guilt.
> Indeed, let it be known: that your sea of damned misdeed
> Has not yet been half atoned for by the tyranny you suffer.)

Thus Rome's tyranny is just punishment for its crimes, and relief is still
far off. The rational explanation is coupled with a visual representation:
twelve vicious animals appear which symbolize the first twelve emperors, of whom Nero is only the sixth. The suffering continents are not
satisfied with the first six, but the next six tyrants do fulfill their
demands for retribution. The first three choruses demonstrate that
Divine Providence has caused the tyranny of Nero to flourish; the
fourth indicates that the resultant suffering is just punishment for
Rome's guilt. Lohenstein's audience was aware of the plans of Divine

Providence for Rome beyond the reign of the first twelve emperors—a destiny which demanded purification—to become the Holy Roman Empire and convert the world to Christianity.

The play arouses a rather uncomfortable sense of empathy with Epicharis, with whom the members of the audience continue to identify, even as they see her illusionistically tortured on stage. Coupled with fear of like punishment, this emotional involvement takes them through a process of catharsis which purges similar illicit desires for power and for the overthrow of an absolutist ruler of their own day. At the same time, they become, through Lohenstein's ironic dialectic, aware of the error in her idealism which must separate her from the innocently suffering martyrs of earlier plays, and this awareness restores their critical distance at the end. Above all, they have learned not to resist the destiny posited by the Divine Plan for history—Lohenstein's *Verhängnüs* is Birken's *Vorsicht*.

Lohenstein's other "Roman Tragedy," *Agrippina* (published 1665), likewise takes place during the reign of Nero; and Nero's evil tyranny demands another victim, this time his own mother, the protagonist. It is even clearer in her case than in that of Epicharis that we are not dealing with the wrongful death of an innocent person, but with the just punishment of someone whose guilt consists in resistance to the Divine Plan. Agrippina tries to hold the reins of power for her incompetent son Nero after his accession to the imperial throne, and, upon failing to do so by virtuous and rational means, resorts to a seduction attempt. Fearing that her ploys to gain power will succeed, Nero plots her death, first as an apparent accident (an unsuccessful shipwreck) and then as murder.

Like *Epicharis, Agrippina* focuses on the various manifestations of Divine Providence in world history; but in this play it is the aspect of Divine Retribution which receives, perhaps, the greatest attention. As Lohenstein warns in the introduction to the notes appended to the play, this tragedy depicts *ein Schauplatz grausamster Laster* ("a showcase of the most horrible vices," 113) but is also *ein Gemälde schrecklicher Straffen* ("a painting of fearsome punishments"). This terminology does not refer to the murder of the protagonist or the torture of her servant, but to the various ways by which Divine Retribution is made manifest on earth. For Agrippina retribution takes the form of her fall from a position of power, her mental anguish due to having an ungrateful and unnatural son, and finally a death by treachery which robs her of both life and honor. For Nero retribution is provided by the appearance of his brother's and his mother's ghosts, by his own conscience, and by visions of Hell; in addition, prophecies announce several punitive events which the audience knows later occurred: the great fire and the fall of the first imperial dynasty.

Unlike most seventeenth-century tragedies, in which each chorus conveys a different meaning or analogy, usually bound closely to the preceding act, and like *Epicharis,* all five choruses of *Agrippina* express some aspect of the theme of Divine Justice. For the first chorus the stage opens up, as in Jesuit theater, to reveal Hellfire below and Heaven above the earthly scene, and the text proclaims these as the ultimate punishment and reward for the vices and virtues. The other four choruses demonstrate the various ways by which vice is punished already in this life: through the downfall of an individual and his dynasty, through the instrumentality of the forces of nature, through mortality and transience as conditions of human existence, and through the inner goad of the guilty conscience. *Agrippina* is the showcase of these manifestations of Divine Retribution and Divine Justice.

The two magnificent queens who have the title roles in the "African Tragedies," *Cleopatra* and *Sophonisbe,* fall not in the attempt to usurp Roman power, but in trying to resist conquest by the empire's founders, Augustus and Scipio. Thus while the tyrant/martyr configuration lives on in *Epicharis* and *Agrippina* in a secularized equivalent, tyrant versus usurper/victim, the history play in its purest form makes its appearance in Lohenstein's *Cleopatra* and *Sophonisbe*: a positive ruler/ general who represents Rome pitted against the representative of Rome's illicit challengers, complicated by a subplot which posits a mixed character caught between the two.

The basic plot outline of Lohenstein's *Cleopatra* (first edition, 1660; revised edition, 1680) is well known to English readers through Shakespeare's *Antony and Cleopatra*: Antonius, a member of the triumvirate which ruled Rome after the fall of Julius Caesar, has followed Caesar's footsteps to Egypt, where he, too, has succumbed to the wiles of the beautiful Egyptian queen. At her urging he aids her resistance to Roman expansion, an effort which is thwarted in a great sea battle with Augustus. Thinking her pretended suicide is real, Antonius kills himself in order to join her in union beyond death. When Cleopatra's charms fail to capture Augustus's heart, she too commits suicide. Augustus returns triumphant to Rome, where he will declare the onset of world peace (*pax augusta*).

In Lohenstein's drama Cleopatra is depicted as a woman who holds the reins of power through prostitution of her womanhood—she rules with Roman support due to the sexual favors with which she tempts her protectors. She is often termed "Circe" or "Siren" by the Romans or in the choruses. She is also shown resorting to injustice and tyranny in order to retain her throne. But her vices are merely corroborative evidence of her most damnable deed: resistance to destiny and God's plan for history. Although realizing that destiny has designed her fall, she tries to bend it to her will. At the end, she herself admits her guilt and accepts Divine punishment.

Caught by this siren like the moths drawn to the flame of a candle in the emblem,[15] Antonius subjugates his better nature to his love for Cleopatra. The drama opens with Antonius's despair at defeat. He is depicted as a cowardly and honorless man, ready to put an end to himself and abandon a cause he considers lost. Yet this view of a dispirited and wavering Antonius is contrasted with his earlier victories, honor, courage, and virtue in an account of his life before coming to Egypt (1:228–55). Inextricably trapped by his lust for Cleopatra, Antonius has moved step by step away from his Roman virtue. He conquers lands not allotted to him and gives them to Cleopatra; he becomes tyrannical and martyrs a captive king and ally of Augustus to Cleopatra's whim; and he finally commits suicide due to her trickery, mistakenly thinking to join her in a *Liebestod*. Each of these actions is greeted with abhorrence and shock by Augustus and his fellow Romans. Antonius's catastrophic choice to remain true to Cleopatra rather than to Rome is depicted in the mythological chorus of the second act, where Paris is forced to choose among three goddesses, each of which represents a quality. Juno offers Asia's scepter and is variously termed "majesty" and "pride." Pallas calls herself "virtue" and offers eternal fame. But Paris chooses Venus—"pleasure," "lust," "bewitching Circe"—and his Helena will bring war and fiery destruction to Troy. Juno and Pallas term this fall just punishment:

> Du und dein loderndes Troja wird müssen
> Deine verdammte Verwegenheit büssen.   (763–64)

(You and your blazing Troy will have to
atone for your damned presumption.)

This chorus depicts the meaning of human existence: life is a test in which man has free will to choose wisely or unwisely, good or evil. Antonius, like Paris, has made a disastrous choice which will lead to worldly fall and damnation in the hereafter. As a foretaste of his eternal punishments, he is tormented by the ghosts of those he has murdered who appear as instruments of Divine Retribution (3:300, 412). In spite of the elaborate embalming procedure used to preserve Antonius's body, described minutely in the fifth act, Cleopatra points to the corpse as a supreme *exemplum* of transience (5:1–11).

Augustus, on the other hand, is the ideal ruler whose actions conform, for the most part, with virtue as well as the Divine Plan for history. Augustus is not a military enemy who seeks to expand his power, but a fatherly ruler and friend who wishes to free Antonius from his disastrous and sinful Egyptian fetters and return him to the virtuous Roman fold, even though he would then have to share the empire with him (1:815–16). As in a contemporary depiction of Augustus and Antonius,[16] Augustus here appears as a good ruler because he does not let his passions override his duties, whereas Antonius devotes all his energies to his mistress. Far from being the conditions imposed by a power-hungry man, as Antonius and Cleopatra often claim, Augustus's requests that Antonius give up Cleopatra in order to return to his Roman wife and resume the rule over the previously allotted third of the empire are fair and just. Even when Augustus momentarily gives in to his advisers, resorting to treachery in order to capture Cleopatra alive for exhibit in his triumphal procession, he criticizes it as *Verdammte Staats-Klugheit* ("damned political expediency," 4:238); and when it fails, he quickly returns to his better self: *Jedoch/ was sinnen wir auf Schimpf der edlen Frauen* ("however, why do we plot to heap derision on the noble woman?" 511). He proceeds to grant merciful requests which will endear him to the conquered populace, apparently as much from his own goodness as from motives of expediency and Machiavellism, a representation of the idea that true *Staats-Klugheit* ("political wisdom") coincides with virtue and goodness. Augustus's closing speeches are indications of his magnanimity.

Egypt itself has become the central image of Antonius's sinfulness. Its gods are animals, and their cults are scorned by the Romans for that reason (note, 223). Egypt's queen is often equated to the cow-goddess Isis, and Antonius is named after wild animals by his victims (3:314 ff). Antonius, the virtuous Roman, has been converted into an Egyptian, and he refuses to abandon Egypt, its queen, or even its religion. He insists on being buried *auf Ptolomeisch, auf Römisch nicht* ("after the manner of the Ptolemies," "not Roman style," 3:723, 734). The Romans themselves perceive that Egypt and Cleopatra are synonymous with his fall. Thus the Roman envoy wishes *Daß sein Gemütte nicht zu sehr Egyptisch sei* ("that his character not be too Egyptian," 1:821), and exclaims: *Gantz Rom strafft: daß er hat Cleopatren erwählet* ("All Rome abhores the fact that he has chosen Cleopatra," 1:751).

In sermons of the time the image of Egyptian captivity, out of which the children of God are led by Moses, was frequently used as a metaphor or prefiguration for the sinful state out of which Christ was to lead mankind.[17] In view of this traditional interpretation, Antonius's fall takes on theological implications, as do Roman attempts to rescue him from his erroneous choice. When Antonius's general Caelius tries to reveal Cleopatra's treachery to him, Antonius exclaims, *Wo leitestu mich hin?* ("Where are you leading me?"). Caelius answers, *Zur Warheit und zum Heile* ("To truth and well-being," 1:1047). Attempts to heal (save) Antonius are made in several episodes in the first act, and Augustus is referred to as Antonius's physician:

Wie aber wird der Artzt sie angewehren können/
Indem der Krancke nichts von Kranckheit wissen wil?   (1:696–97)

(But how can the doctor provide a cure
when the patient doesn't wish to know about his illness?)

The equation of illness with unrealized sinfulness extends back to the healing miracles of Christ, and Augustus thus becomes a Christ figure who cares for the salvation of souls: *Wir wolln für aller Heil mehr als für unsers wachen* ("We wish to watch over the salvation of all more than over our own," 4:201).

But the drama is more than a portrayal of Antonius's ethical tragedy, and Augustus, in addition to being a savior figure modeled on Christ, is the very incarnation of the Roman Empire in its teleological function to offer Christ's salvation to the world. As head of the institution given this mission in the Divine Plan, he is charged with attempting to convert others. Since Christ has not yet been born, nor the empire converted to Christianity, his actions can only prefigure the later deeds of such emperors as Constantine and Charlemagne. As the latter were to convert their defeated enemies to Christianity, so Augustus endeavors to transform his into Romans. He does so by attempting to return straying Antonius to Roman virtues and by granting Roman citizenship to the civic leaders of Egypt—important for universal savlation since many patristic and Renaissance historians viewed Roman citizenship, law, language, and virtue as important preconditions for the spread of Christianity throughout the world. As he defeats Egypt in the person of its last queen, Cleopatra, Augustus founds the fourth and final monarchy of Daniel's prophecy, which the Roman Empire, together with its continuation, the Holy Roman Empire, was thought to be. This transferral of supreme power from the third monarchy (exemplified by the tomb which holds its first and last rulers, Alexander and Cleopatra, as well as the many Ptolemies in between) is explicitly depicted in the final chorus, which Lohenstein himself described thusly: *Im Reyen wird unter der Tyber die Hoheit des Römischen Reichs und der neu-angehenden Monarchie beschrieben* ("in the chorus under the guise of the Tiber river the greatness of the Roman Empire and of the newly founded monarchy are described," 212).

If Augustus fails in his role as savior on the level of personal salvation, he succeeds on the level of universal salvation. The references to Christ's imminent birth are frequent and must have been obvious to Lohenstein's audience, which was acquainted with the patristic tradition, even if these references seem oblique today. Augustus will bring universal peace to a world exhausted by war as soon as Egypt's rebellion is subdued, an action symbolized by closing the gates of Janus, the temple of war:

> Euch Göttern sag ich Danck! Nun kan ich unsre Stadt/
> Die Eckel für Verterb und Bürger-Kriegen hat/
> Mit Beut und Fried erfreun; und nach dem Bluttvergüssen
> Zum dritten mal in Rom des Janus Tempel schlüssen.   (5:673–76)

> (To you gods I offer thanks! Now I can please our city,
> which has disgust for destruction and civil war,
> with booty and peace, and after the bloodshed
> close the temple of Janus for the third time).

According to the early Christian historian Orosius, this third closure of the gates of Janus ushering in world peace was the signal for the birth of Christ into history and flesh; Augustus's world peace coincided with Christ's universal peace.[18] A traditional omen associated with Christ's birth which here accompanies Augustus's triumphant entry into Egypt is the fall of pagan idols. Cleopatra and Antonius take their falling gods to be an omen of their own fall (1:509–46), yet the fact that they also signal the imminence of Christ's birth is indicated in Lohenstein's note (162). As Christ's advent coincides with the rise of Rome, so the omens of Egypt's fall—the final step in the founding of the fourth monarchy—could refer to both events. And the meaning of Egypt discussed above—man's sinful nature—takes on significance as an event of universal salvation, when Rome vanquishes Egypt (= sin) as a last stage in preparing for Christ's advent.

A similar historical event provides the plot of *Sophonisbe* (1666; performed 1666? and 1669?; not published until 1680). Sophonisbe, queen of Carthage, is vanquished by an earlier representative of Rome, Scipio, but tenaciously attempts to resist destiny by using her feminine charms to win the African general Masinissa for her cause. When brought to his senses by Scipio's admonitions, however, Masinissa sends her poison and rejoins the Roman effort. The character configuration is exactly parallel to that in *Cleopatra*—a virtuous Roman commander, a North African queen who resists Roman conquest, and a man who is caught between the two, much like Cenodoxus between tempting demon and guardian angel. As in *Cleopatra,* the predestined Roman conquest is triumphant, and the queen commits suicide when her nation falls, rather than be led to Rome in chains. But, unlike Antonius, Masinissa can be rescued from his fatal fascination for a Circe, and thus his subplot can be considered a "conversion drama" not unlike those of Gryphius. In a parallel to the use of the "Judgment of Paris" chorus in *Cleopatra* to illuminate the reasons for Antonius's fall, the intermezzo "Hercules at the Crossroads" in *Sophonisbe* throws light on the intended interpretation of Masinissa's actions: like Hercules making the correct choice between women representing virtue and vice, Masinissa chooses the virtuous path and will be rewarded for it.

The central theme of *Sophonisbe* is human inconstancy—in moral decisions, in marriage, in political alliance—confronted by divine constancy in the form of virtue, Divine Providence, and Divine Retribution. This theme is expressed in two key terms: *spielen* ("to play," with all its derivatives and double meanings) and *Glück,* the blind and inconstant Fortuna. Inconstancy, in the guise of *spielen,* is the subject of the verse dedicatory epistle, in which Lohenstein notes that it is the condition of man and nature to be in a constant state of flux. One theme common in drama from Shakespeare to Schiller and expressed in this epistle is that life is a stage upon which each person plays a part; for Lohenstein and his contemporaries the sum total of the acted roles is history itself, as "performed" at the courts of Europe, a performance which is imitated in this play. Sophonisbe participates in this "playfulness" and "role playing" as she attempts to manipulate both men and events. In fact, the frequent changes of costume and of sex role in this drama are a clear manifestation of the inconstancy inherent in role playing.

This inconstant nature of mankind has its most serious consequences in the moral sphere. Sophonisbe herself is the epitome of fickleness, loving two men at once in bigamous marriages and directing her love according to the accidents of fortune or political expediency. The breaking of oaths of allegiance to Rome by Syphax and Masinissa likewise demonstrates the difficulty of remaining steadfast. And human inconstancy is portrayed graphically in scenes in which Masinissa wavers between two courses of action. Masinissa, who must give up Sophonisbe, is torn by a conflict between passion and reason. In a monologue he changes his mind several times, and each shift is indicated in a terse verbal exclamation:

> Jedoch/ halt! Ich vergeh/ ich zitter/ ich erstarre!
> Geh immer! es ist nicht mehr Zeit zu zweifeln. Harre!
> Verzieh! Ach! Schaue/ wie mir Aug und Hertze bricht!
> Fort! immer fort! der Schluß ist mehr zu ändern nicht.   (4:505–508)

> (On the other hand, stop! I faint, I tremble, I am paralyzed!
> Go on! There is no more time to doubt. Wait!
> Draw away! Oh, look how my heart breaks, my eyes grow dim!
> Away! again away! The decision is *not* to be altered).

The accent rests on the final emphatic *nicht,* a word which indicates the possibility of constancy in human affairs. Human constancy can exist only through the government of the passions by reason and virtue, as in the case of Scipio. The legendary "continence of Scipio," alluded to in Scipio's admonitions (4:299–300), is the supreme *exemplum* of human constancy overcoming the riot of the passions.

In man's limited view, the determining forces outside of him seem to be blind, and he depicts Luck or Fortune as a blind woman. Fortuna is the epitome of inconstancy in human history. The German Baroque poet, Paul Fleming, has offered a view of human vanity in its terms: *Hier ist beständig nichts/ als Unbeständigkeit*[19] ("here nothing is constant but inconstancy"). But in this play even the characters come to admit that the fate they had attributed throughout the drama to Fortune or Luck is somehow related to their guilt. It is their own inconstancy toward Rome which has brought about their fall, not inconstant Fortune. Above human constancy and inconstancy is a force of divine constancy which has two aspects, Divine Providence (destiny) and Divine Justice (nemesis). In this drama, as in *Cleopatra,* the former is represented by the victorious Romans, while the latter appears in the image of flames. Like Paris's Troy, Carthage goes up in the flames of its queen's funeral pyre.

In the final chorus, *Verhängnüs* appears in order to put the historical events portrayed in the drama into the framework of *Heilsgeschichte.* She sits in judgment over Daniel's four monarchies and asserts that these empires had been set up by her and that their power derives from her Divine Plan. Then each empire presents its claims for the highest honor, but Rome's case is judged the best. Rome's claims will be realized in part by the victories of Scipio, whom Lohenstein considers in a note to be an important founder of the Roman "Monarchy": *Diese in gegenwertigen Trauerspiele berührten Siege des Scipio haben den wahren Grund zu der Römischen Monarchie gelegt* ("the victories of Scipio dealt with in this play laid the basis for the Roman monarchy," 410). Thus while in *Cleopatra* Augustus's defeat of Egypt is stressed in order to provide for the birth of Christ into history, this chorus shows that Lohenstein's intentions in *Sophonisbe* were to concentrate on a historical event as part of the Divine Plan as revealed in the prophecy of the book of Daniel. But for both dramas, the purpose is to illuminate the destiny of Rome to be a primary ingredient in Birken's *Vorsicht.*

In these two dramas, Lohenstein has provided very clear examples of the dual function of Baroque tragedy in its effect on the audience. The latter responds rationally to the representatives of virtue, Augustus and

Scipio, able to admire and emulate these figures for their virtues and greatness in the *exemplum* tradition. But the spectators are also involved emotionally with the play as they notice the passions aroused in Antonius and Masinissa reflected in their own feelings, whether in life or in the fascination felt for the two queens. And these passions are purged in a kind of catharsis, in the perception that Antonius is punished for his passions, while Masinissa is converted from his.

These two "African Tragedies," like the "Turkish Tragedies" *Ibrahim Bassa* and *Ibrahim Sultan,* are designed to affect the audience in another way, as well, namely as anti-Turkish, pro-Habsburg polemics. One purpose they share is to instill in the audience the desire to crusade against the Turks in a new Christian union. All four plays do so emotionally, by showing the horrors of Turkish tyranny (Cleopatra and Sophonisbe, as queens of North Africa, under Muslim control in Lohenstein's time, represent Turks in a symbolic manner, while Sultan Soliman and Ibrahim Sultan do so directly). They also constitute a rationally perceived call to a crusade in that they demonstrate the historical necessity of such an action. The use of historical drama depicting events of the distant or recent past for polemical purposes is based on contemporary attitudes toward history. The stories from ancient Rome are viewed as examples from which modern man can learn virtue and wisdom and which he can emulate. But they are also seen as parallels to present or future events, and thus have a typological relationship with them. Just as Augustus defeated Egypt and prepared the world for Christianity, so Holy Roman Emperor Leopold should defeat the modern inhabitants of North Africa and Asia, the Turks:

> . . . Leopold/ der dem August es gleiche thut.
> . . . .
> Wir sehen schon sein siegend Schwerdt/
> Den Adler für dem Mond am Nil und Bospher gläntzen.
> (*Cleopatra*, 5:838–48)

> (Leopold, who does just what Augustus did . . .
> We see his victorious sword already,
> And the eagle shining above the moon on Nile and Bosporus.)

Leopold himself is thus exhorted to call a crusade, and by implication the audience is called upon to follow him in this venture. In *Sophonisbe* such typological layers of historical events become threefold: Scipio, who conquered Carthage, is the prefiguration for the deeds of Charles V and his sons, who battled Turks near the site of ancient Carthage and in the Mediterranean Sea nearby. And the current emperor, Leopold, receives Dido's "prophetic destiny," figured on those of Scipio and his own Habsburg dynasty, which calls upon him, as in *Cleopatra,* to retake North Africa. The fourth chorus ("Hercules at the Crossroads") also refers to Leopold, who, it is stated, will conquer Istanbul and has already won a great victory over the Turks (Battle of St. Gotthard on the Raab in 1664). And he will eventually conquer the entire Turkish domain, as the Romans had conquered Carthage.

By setting modern deeds or possible future deeds in a typological parallelism with famous actions and pivotal events from the past, Lohenstein confers the aura of truth and historical necessity upon them. And an audience, which has just been convinced that certain actions they are called upon to perform conform to the Divine Plan, is much more likely to perform them than if preached to in a sermon or oration. Lohenstein, himself convinced of the necessity of uniting behind the Holy Roman Emperor to save European Christianity from the Turks, has used the most powerful weapon at his disposal: *Trauerspiel,* an imitation of pathetic events which arouse fear and empathy and which teach virtue through providing an *exemplum* for emulation.

Johann Christian Hallmann

Johann Christian Hallmann (ca. 1640–1704) followed his Silesian models Gryphius and Lohenstein in creating a series of martyr dramas and historical tragedies in the high style of the *Kunsttragödie,* and although he has been labeled an epigonal writer, the best of these dramas are effective and fascinating. The martyr play is represented in his *oeuvre* by the standard early Christian story culled from the martyrologies, *Die Himmlische Liebe/ Oder Die Beständige Märterin Sophia* [Heavenly Love, or the Steadfast Martyr Sophia, published 1684] and by a political "martyrdom," *Die sterbende Unschuld/ Oder Die Durchlauchtigste Catharina Königin in Engelland* [Dying Innocence, or Her Excellency Catherine, Queen of England; written 1669–73, published 1684]. *Sophia* is too close to *Felicitas* to warrant its own treatment; *Catharina,* however, is an interesting play for a number of reasons.

Hallmann, who was a convert to Catholicism, expresses in this play the Catholic outrage at the actions of King Henry VIII of England which culminated in the introduction of Protestantism there. As the play opens he has divorced Catharina and banned their daughter Mary in order to wed a second time. Catharina makes an unsuccessful attempt to kill the new wife, Anne Boleyn, and finds herself in prison as a result. Neither a parade of persons pleading for Catharina's freedom and reinstatement on the English throne nor supernatural warnings of the consequences dissuade Henry, who renews his attacks on the Catholic Church. Catharina dies in prison of shock and sorrow, but the fifth act is reserved for Divine Retribution which manifests itself in Henry's belatedly troubled conscience and in a series of tableaux, representing visions, which prophesy Henry's heresy and five marriages and the horrors perpetrated by his heirs. Instead of the heavy tragic alexandrine verse of Silesian tragedy, Hallmann uses the irregular madrigal verse of opera, for he has designed this short play as a "musical" tragedy. The resultant irregularity, brevity, and simplicity are refreshing. Allegorical dualism seems absent, and Hallmann's purpose is clearly to polemicize in favor of the Holy Roman Empire and the Catholic Church. His attack on the English Reformation can perhaps be applied to German Protestantism, thus making this play one of the few strictly sectarian *Kunstdramen* of the period.

Hallmann's historical tragedies, *Die Göttliche Rache/ Oder Der Verführte Theodoricus Veronensis* [Divine Retribution, or the Emperor Led Astray, written and performed 1666; published 1684] and *Die Beleidigte Liebe Oder Die Großmütige Mariamne* [Mistreated Love, or Magnanimous Mariamne, 1670], on the other hand, remind one of Lohenstein and of the historical tragedy of Jesuit theater (where both subjects are likewise treated). And his double titles may give us insight into the sort of interpretative *explicatio* Lohenstein would have used for his dramas had he, too, used double titles. In his *Theodoricus* Hallmann depicts the corruption of a ruler who changes from an ideal prince to a tyrant due to use of *Staatsraison* ("political expediency"). This Roman Emperor, under the influence of *Intriganten,* persecutes both Christians and wise counselors. When Theodorich's closest adviser, Cassiodorus, abandons him and political affairs for monastic robes in a dramatic scene in which he changes costume on stage, Hallmann is making a statement in favor of monastic self-denial and distance from the corrupting influence of the political arena. But the play as a whole functions as a mirror for princes, an anti-Machiavellian textbook. The play also functions, like those of Lohenstein, to present Divine Providence as it manifests itself in Roman history. The spirit of the first emperor, Augustus, appears (3:2) in order to view the deeds of Theodorich from this perspective. He laments the sorry state of Rome and predicts that the future translation of the imperial power to Charlemagne and his German descendants will occur due to Rome's current corruption, thus justifying the contemporary idea that the Holy Roman Empire was a divinely ordained continuation of the ancient empire. His "prophecy" extends to the present Holy Roman emperor, Leopold, who, he predicts, will restore the empire to its former glory. Augustus addresses Leopold and calls upon the latter to emulate himself by victories which restore lost Roman provinces, particularly in Asia:

Sey/ tapffrer Leopold/ sey ferner ein August!
So fühlt mein längst verfaulter Leib auch in dem Grabe Lust.
Schau/ wie der Hund vor deinem Adler kni't/
Wie der blasse Mondenschein deiner hellen Sonne weich't/
Wie der Boßphor vor der Donau die gesänckten Segel streich't.   (3:151–55)

(Become, bold Leopold, henceforth a second Augustus!
Then my decayed body could feel pleasure even in the grave.
Look, how the [Turkish] dog kneels to your [Austrian] Eagle,
How the pale [Turkish] moon gives way to your bright sunlight,
How the Bosporus lowers its sails before the Danube [ship of state].)

Thus Hallmann, like Lohenstein, uses historical tragedy dealing with ancient Roman deeds to praise and exhort the present emperor. Both aim to influence Leopold's political decisions and to urge him to attack the Turks.

Theodoricus, Hallmann's first dramatic attempt, is a ponderous and heavy-handed drama which deadens interest by its overly long monologues and passages of Stichomythia and by its abnormally elevated level of emotional exclamation throughout. But true Baroque pathos is successfully achieved in his most famous play, *Mariamne.* Herod, appointed king of Judea by the Roman overlords, marries the heiress of the previous ruling dynasty, Mariamne, but fears that his crown will be taken from him again by her deposed relatives. He has her brother and grandfather, a Jewish priest, killed, and her mother imprisoned, but Mariamne too is a threat to his safety on the throne in his paranoid mind. Yet his love for her is a consuming passion and his need of her to sustain his tenuous claim to the throne is very great. Wavering between love and fear, he seeks to test her love for him, but is rebuffed by the insulted Mariamne, whom, during a recent absence, he had placed under the guard of his brother-in-law with orders to kill her if he himself did not return from the journey. After he has killed her relatives, he again seeks her love, but she denies him her bed and calls him a murderer. Meanwhile, the intrigues of his sister Salome have made the king believe his wife has deceived him with his brother-in-law and also tried to poison him. She is tried and convicted of treason and beheaded. At the end Herod is haunted by the ghosts of those he has killed, including Mariamne herself.

Herod is one of the most fascinating Baroque characters, for the passions which rule him, jealousy and paranoia, are demonstrated vividly in all of his actions. These passions are derivatives of Lohenstein's *Libe* ("love") and *Ehrsucht* ("lust for power and honor"), but are more extreme in their domination of Herod's personality and more severe in their results. His jealousy leads to inhumane expressions of his "love": the threat of death for Mariamne if he should die and the execution of his brother-in-law when this man is accused of adultery with her. His paranoia about his throne will lead to the execution of his wife's relatives and ultimately herself. These passions combine to becloud his mind to such an extent that he becomes putty in the hands of Salome, whose goal is the death of Mariamne. And when the latter is dead, Herod realizes the full horror of his raging passions, for they have slaughtered the woman he loved. He, perhaps more than any other Baroque protagonist, attains the level of a tragic hero.

But victimization by the passions is no valid excuse in the seventeenth century. However befuddled Herod's reason may become, he cannot escape the full fury of Divine Retribution for his inhuman deeds. Eternal damnation will be his just punishment in the hereafter.

Even the worst of tyrants have a place in the Divine Plan, and Herod's position is an important one. As he obliterates all traces of the last ruling dynasty of Israel (he will even have his two children by Mariamne killed), he prepares for the figurative reinstatement of a previous dynasty, the House of David, in the impending birth of Christ. And just as he saw in Mariamne's family a threat to his precarious hold on the throne, so he will fear a political takeover from the descendant of David. His efforts to destroy his feared opponents in the drama succeed, but when he orders all male infants killed (according to the biblical account) in the attempt to destroy the infant Christ, he will fail, as the audience knows. In that case Herod's paranoia will be even more ridiculous than in the play, for Christ's kingdom is not of this world and poses little threat to Herod's kingship, even if He was to be termed "King of the Jews" by another Herod at His crucifixion.

Herod's victim, Mariamne, is also a kind of prefiguration of the later sacrifice of the Savior, for many elements of her passion and execution mirror those of Christ.[20] She is falsely accused of treason and is tried by a Jewish court which subjects her to the same injustices as Christ; she is betrayed by false testimony; she accepts death and the burden of another's guilt with equanimity; she forgives her enemies and echoes Christ's words *Es ist vollbracht*! ("It is finished," 5:573; John 19:30). Her martyrdom, modeled like that of most Baroque martyrs on Christ, takes on additional importance since it immediately precedes and prefigures his. Herod's later victims—the infant boys of Jerusalem—are likewise prefigured in her innocence and in the failure of the results to quell Herod's paranoia.

Herod's other function is that of Lohenstein's Nero: to punish the guilt of his state by his outrageous and cruel deeds. In the final chorus, a lamenting Palestine is told by the spirit of Solomon that Herod is only the first of many horrors in store for her, for the Jews will be guilty of disbelief when they reject Christ as the Messiah only sixty years later. Herod's tyranny will be followed by Roman tyranny, culminating in the destruction of Jerusalem and scattering of the Jews by the emperors Titus and Vespasian, then by the tyranny of the Muslim conquerors, the Saracens and Turks. Victories of Christian crusaders like Godfrey of Bouillon will be transient until an ultimate Christian victory under Leopold.

Thus this play, like Lohenstein's dramas, demonstrates Birken's *Vorsicht,* the Divine Plan for history. Like Lohenstein in his *Cleopatra,* Hallmann chooses historical subject matter from the turning point in world history in the Christian perspective, Christ's birth, in order to express effectively the divine origin of all events of human history in the wisdom of Divine Providence. And like Lohenstein, Hallmann provides a pseudoprophecy of victory over the Turks in the context of "prophecies" which have already proved true in order to urge the current emperor to call a new crusade against the Islamic foe.

Other Dramatists

A third dramatist of the High Baroque whose treatment of history in the *Trauerspiel* resembles that of Lohenstein and Hallmann was Nicolaus Avancini, a Jesuit from South Tyrol, who wrote and designed theatrical performances for the imperial court in Vienna. Twenty-seven of his dramas, all written in Latin verse, were collected and published in the five-part *Poesis dramatica* between 1674 and 1686, but were performed much earlier, between 1633 and 1673. They cover the entire range of favorite themes for Jesuit theater: saints and martyrs (Francis Xavier, St. Idda), biblical subjects (Judith, David, and Susanna), ancient history (e.g., Semiramis, Cyrus, Marius, Eugenia), European history (Genoveva, Charlemagne, conversions of kings of Norway and Denmark), early Christian history (Theodosius, Constantine). As in Lohenstein's works, many concern the defeat of an evil tyrant by a good prince or hero. But Avancini's victorious figures receive more stress than do the falls of those they conquer, and thus tend to glorify the rulers whom the plays are designed to honor, the emperors Ferdinand II and III and Leopold, rather than dissuade the audience from evil actions or encourage them to good actions through evil and good *exempla*. Most have the double titles which reveal both topic and moral lesson to be learned.

For purposes of this study, it will be sufficient to examine one of Avancini's dramas, *Pietas Victrix, sive Flavius Constantinus Magnus, de Maxentio Tyranno Victor* [Piety Victorious, or Constantine Victorious over the Tyrant Maxentius], written and performed in 1658–59 for the coronation of Leopold in Vienna. It is an account of the battle between Constantine and Maxentius which Constantine wins with God's help after converting to Christianity. The outcome is predicted in Constantine's vision in which he sees the sign of the cross and an inscription with the words *In hoc signo vinces* ("With this sign you will conquer"), and the thematic half of the title of the play confirms the centrality of the idea that God will aid the faithful in their battles. Maxentius dreams of his fall in terms of an Old Testament story, the people of Israel led out of Egyptian captivity by Moses and through the Red Sea, while their pursuer, the Pharaoh, drowns. Thus Constantine, a second Moses, will lead the Romans away from their stone idols and sinfulness and to worship of the living God. Roman piety will guard the world, Roman law will insure justice everywhere, and Christianity will become the state religion of Rome, uniting the whole world in worship of Christ (198–99). The choruses contain commentary by personifications of virtues and vices, predominantly *pietas* and *impietas*. At the end of the play, a "prophecy" connects the events of Constantine's victories to the history of the Habsburg dynasty and to hopes for similar triumphs by the new emperor Leopold over the current "impious" enemies of the empire, the Turkish residents of the Bosporus.

A fourth Silesian dramatist, August Adolf von Haugwitz (1647–1706), is often discussed in the context of a "Silesian School," but some have claimed that his serious dramatic efforts, *Schuldige Unschuld oder Maria Stuarda* [Guilty Innocence, or Mary Stuart] and *Obsiegende Tugend/ Oder Der Bethörte doch wieder Bekehrte Soliman* [Conquering Virtue, or the Corruption and Conversion of Soliman], are a bridge to the shorter and less excessively ebullient drama of the Enlightenment or the first in a chain of German *Seelendramen,* which show character development or depth.[21] The unfortunate habit of earlier scholars to see value in Baroque literature only insofar as it resembles and thus supposedly leads to the more favored works of the *Goethezeit* does little justice to these plays and does not constitute valid judgment of their quality. Indeed, it is clear that they are instead a colorless and rather inept imitation of a genre of historical drama which their author does not understand, an imitation which fails due to the lack of those qualities which elevate the dramas of Gryphius and Lohenstein: stylistic virtuosity, encyclopedic knowledge, and depth of metaphysical/ religious insight. Yet since these two dramas attempt to embody patterns and meanings similar to those found in certain plays of Haugwitz's great Silesian predecessors, a brief analysis will help to fill out the picture of serious drama of the German Baroque.

While Haugwitz claims influence from Gryphius, his plays more closely resemble contemporary Jesuit plays in terms of their subject matter, treatment, and even religious orientation. *Maria Stuarda* relates the events surrounding the execution of the Catholic Mary, Queen of Scots, by her Protestant cousin and fellow monarch, Queen Elizabeth I of England, from the perspective of Catholic apologists. Thus the descriptive title, *Schuldige Unschuld* [Guilty Innocence], is a misnomer, for Mary never confesses any guilt whatsoever, and, as Robert Heitner has shown, it was an afterthought added when Haugwitz became aware of the version of those historians who were of Protestant persuasion.[22] Mary's very existence threatens Elizabeth's throne since her followers continually plan coups in order to free her or even to place her on the English throne, thus restoring Roman Catholicism to the island. Elizabeth, persuaded by her advisers to draw up the order of execution, seemingly wavers in her intention to carry it out—behavior which is later revealed as a clever ploy to avoid any blame for the deed herself. Her henchmen, ignoring her delaying tactics, carry out the execution. Attempts to convert Mary to Protestantism fail, and she dies as a martyr for her Roman faith, knowing that her execution will become a cause célèbre for the Counter-Reformation.

The meaning of the play is less clear than it would be in Gryphius or Lohenstein, but Mary seems to stand for the wrongfully deposed Catholic dynasty of English rulers while the personification of Religion in the chorus of the fourth act decries the miserable state of religion in England—both an apparent call for restoration of true religiosity, if not Roman Catholicism itself. Heitner has pointed out the rampant borrowings from Gryphius, from the title (derived from *Carolus Stuardus*) to the prologue-speaker (Eternity, from *Catharina von Georgien*) and the chorus of captive maidens (ibid.). The long monologues and extensive stichomythia likewise remind one of *Carolus Stuardus,* but both characteristics lack the significance underlying their usage by Gryphius—commentary and polemic. Adages abound, and are even set off by quotation marks to indicate they should be noticed; but they are generalizations which do not carry a central theme. And when one compares Haugwitz's notes to those of Gryphius and Lohenstein, his shallowness as a man of learning clearly emerges.

On the other hand, two characteristics of this play are new to German audiences and literature. Haugwitz is the first major dramatist to make extensive use of the tragic monologue. And he endeavors, more than most authors of historical drama, to avoid putting unhistorical words in his characters' mouths or motives of his own devising in their hearts. But this very historicity is his doom, for it also deprives the story of the interest which it will attain in Schiller's less historically accurate treatment.

If we are to believe the prologue speaker, Eternity, the purpose of the play is to cleanse the members of the courtly audience of *Ehrsucht* (desire for power and honor):

> Dieses Spiel das soll euch rauben
> Den so hoch getrotzten Geist.   (97–98)
>
> (This play is supposed to rob you/
> Of the overbearing ambitious spirit.)

It will do so by creating the dual tragic effects: rational instruction through presenting an *exemplum* of earthly transience, and cleansing through the emotions aroused by Mary's tragic fall:

> Kommt und schaut Mariam an/
> Die euch eures Grabes Länge
> Nach dem ihren messen kan/
> Die euch wird gar sanffte kühlen
> Durch ihr jetzt bald fliessend Blut.   (90–94)
>
> (Come and look at Mary,
> Who can measure your grave
> According to the proportions of her own,
> And who will cool you gently
> With her own blood, soon to flow.)

Haugwitz's other serious play, *Bekehrter Soliman,* is termed a *Misch-Spiel* ("mixed play" or tragicomedy) rather than a tragedy by its author, and it conforms to the format of the conversion drama. This play has the same story as Lohenstein's *Ibrahim Bassa*—the persecution of Ibrahim and Isabella by the Turkish Sultan Soliman—but it follows Madeleine de Scudéry's nontragic version in her novel *Ibrahim ou l'Illustre Bassa* (translated into German by Philipp von Zesen in 1645) rather than looking, like Lohenstein, to the historical sources which indicate the tragic ending. In Haugwitz's play, Ibrahim and Isabella are released and forgiven their flight by a Soliman whose wavering ended not in the decision to execute Ibrahim, but in the choice of virtue over vice. Unlike Lohenstein, whose anti-Turkish polemic precluded such treatment of Turks as individuals with potential for moral action, Haugwitz sees Soliman as a human being whose faults can be cured as easily as those of any Christian, and without becoming a Christian. Unlike

Lohenstein's Soliman, who sleeps through Ibrahim's execution in accordance with the priest Muffti's sophism enabling him to break his oath to protect him, Haugwitz's Sultan awakens in time—both literally and figuratively. He is thus the *exemplum* of *selbst regieren*—ruling oneself. Identification of the audience with him will presumably produce a similar conversion to virtue in its members.

Yet the anti-Turkish polemic abounds in this play as well, against all rhyme and reason. Ibrahim is explicitly identified as Justinian, heir of the Byzantine dynasty and thus rightful ruler of Constantinople/ Istanbul; Ibrahim and Isabella are Christian slaves; Ibrahim refuses to fight against the emperor Charles V and his Christian armies; and visions of Charles's armies at the gates of Constantinople haunt Soliman. This aspect of the material Haugwitz may have taken over from Lohenstein, without, however, understanding that his treatment of the plot nullified the polemical intent. Another indication that Lohenstein's tragedy may have influenced Haugwitz's version is the use of a chorus of virtues and vices who battle over Soliman's soul in the second act.

A non-Silesian dramatist, the Thuringian Caspar Stieler (1632– 1707), better known for his earlier comedies, wrote one tragedy, a version of Kyd's *Spanish Tragedy* he titled *Bellemperie* after his heroine (1680; written and published in Weimar just prior to Stieler's stint as theater director there). While the use of prose and the choice of a plot with the revenge theme ally it to the itinerant stage, several characteristics of this play demand treatment here.

The princess of Castille, Bellemperie, loves the son of a high-ranking courtier. In order to clear the way for her marriage to his friend and ally, the prince of Portugal, her brother and the latter ambush and murder her beloved. She and her beloved's father plot revenge which will end in *ein gerechtes Bluthad* ("a justified bloodbath") (120)—the killing of the two murderers during a performance of a play at court in which they are actors. The prose acts are followed by verse choruses spoken by Roman deities who comment on the action; the final one, the epilogue, is spoken by *Nemesis/ Die Göttliche Rachel/ von dem Schluß des Himmels auf die Erde gesant* ("Nemesis, Divine Retribution, sent down to earth by the decision of Heaven"), and indicates the usual Baroque figurative (if not literal) backdrop of Heaven and Hell. The servant Scaramutza provides comic relief. The play ends in a *Totentanz* ("dance of death").

Some insight into courtly theatrical productions can probably be gleaned from the performance of a play within the play, here (unlike *Hamlet*) part of a plan for revenge rather than for detection preparatory to revenge. And, unlike *Hamlet,* this play is performed not by a professional acting troupe but by the members of the royal household itself. Certainly such a practice may have some basis in fact, for both Louis XIV of France and the emperor Leopold are known to have participated in performances (albeit not strictly theatrical) at their courts; and the younger generation, the royal heirs, participated in performances arranged by their tutors, just as middle-class schoolboys did. Stieler's thoughts on the purpose of tragedy emerge in the discussion among the royal amateur actors: tragic theater is of great importance since it is a mirror of human existence, a school for manners, a purification of excessive passions, and a time-honored method of soothing the spirits of kings and princes (64–65).

Unusual for German *Kunsttragödie* ("high tragedy") is the intrusion of comic interludes and a comic character, Scaramutza, inherited from Stieler's earlier plays, six comedies often termed the *Rudolstädter Festspiele,* to be treated below. Scaramutza's comic interjections and activities interrupt even the tragedy-within-the-tragedy and constitute a kind of comic relief which is perhaps needed for such a heavyhanded and grisly play, but which also reflects the *Hanswursterei* attacked so viciously by Gottsched in the early eighteenth century. Scaramutza, however, is no slapstick comedian of the alimentary-tract variety. He is a witty and clever character whose ironic comments destroy pretensions, break theatrical illusion in order to show that life itself acts out roles, and offer political satire. After the bloodbath ending the tragedy within the tragedy, Scaramutza steps to the front of the stage to claim the vacated thrones of the two kingdoms, Castille and Portugal. A buffoon would rule them better than rulers who put themselves above justice and the law.

The tragedy performed by the protagonists is in itself of considerable interest. It is a typical Turkish play: the story of a Christian slave woman (played by the princess) wooed by her Turkish captor (played by her unwanted suitor). Since a stabbing is called for by the plot of the playlet, the audience must be informed that the two men are really dead and not just acting out their roles. This is done by members of the courtly audience within the play, the fathers of the victims, who are in turn stabbed by Bellemperie and her ally, who then commit suicide. Presumably the actors playing the dead protagonists who had previously played dead men rise at the end and begin a dance of death, a chain dance of late medieval origins which could eventually include members of the audience. The play within the play has merged at the catastrophe with the main play, blurring the distinctions. The audience, which had experienced tragic pleasure, according to Aristotle, upon viewing tragic deeds it knew to be imitations which did not affect its own safety, thus likewise loses its sense of being distinct from what it has viewed, being drawn into the procession proclaiming man's mortality. The effect could be a devastating emotional experience of one's own transience, not merely a conscious recognition of it through the means of *exemplum*.

Thus the tragedy of the High Baroque (1640–1680) can be seen to exhibit a variety of types of serious drama and of tragic effects, rather than a unified drama of which each individual tragedy could stand as a representative. The *Trauerspiele* of Gryphius tend to express the transience and vanity of earthly life and the glorification of martyrs for religious or ethical ideals; those of Lohenstein and Hallmann are more concerned with figural relationships between secular and sacred history, past and present. Hallmann's protagonists, like those of Gryphius, are martyrs, while those of Lohenstein include virtuous rulers pitted against tyrants, as do many by Avancini. Conversion dramas, whether tragic or not, also belong in the serious *Trauerspiel* category: Gryphius's *Leo Armenius* and *Cardenio und Celinde*, Haugwitz's *Bekehrter Soliman*, and the subplots in Lohenstein's *Cleopatra* and *Sophonisbe*.

Chapter Five

Comedies of the High Baroque (1640–1680)

Comic Theory

The other dramatic type mentioned and briefly described in Opitz's *Poeterey* is the *Comedie*. Opitz defines it by the social class of its characters and by its subject matter:

> Die Comedie bestehet in schlechtem wesen unnd personen: redet von hochzeiten/ gastgeboten/ spielen/ betrug and schalckheit der knechte/ ruhmrätigen Landtsknechten/ buhlersachen/ leichtfertigkeit der jugend/ geitze des alters/ kupplerey und solchen sachen/ die täglich unter gemeinen Leuten vorlauffen. (20)

> (The comedy consists of low-class concerns and persons; it deals with marriages, parties, games, the deception and roguery of servants, self-glorification of mercenary soldiers, affairs of the heart, frivolity of youth, miserliness of old age, match-making, and such things as happen daily among ordinary people.)

Although Opitz does not provide an example of this genre, as he does for tragedy through his translations of ancient dramas, he evidently has seen or read some, probably from among those performed on the stage of the itinerant theater. He mentions a type of comedy popular throughout seventeenth-century Europe, that which concerns the love stories of persons of noble or even royal blood; and he criticizes such usage as a violation of the classical genre distinctions:

> Haben derowegen die/ welche heutiges tages Comedien geschrieben/ weit geirret/ die Keyser und Potentaten eingeführet; weil solches den regeln der Comedien schnurstracks zuewieder laufft. (20)

(Thus those have strayed far from the path who, in this day and age, write comedies which introduce emperors and potentates as characters, since such an action runs against the rules of comedy.)

Later theorists, whose poetics are more descriptive and less pre- and proscriptive, tend to differentiate among various types of comedies, each with its own set of characteristics. Both practice and theory tend to break seventeenth-century comedy down into four types which can be termed "satirical," "italianate" (romantic), "pastoral," and "allegorical."

Harsdörffer defines two main types of comedy, *Freudenspiel* (Joyful play) and *Hirtenspiel* (shepherd play).[1] The *Freudenspiel* takes place among the city people, the bourgeoisie, and must be happy and humorous in content and ending. The structure of the plot is based on *Veränderung* ("peripety"), and at the end complications are solved by *Erkenntnis* ("recognition"). The *Hirtenspiel* deals with peasant life, but in the ancient sense of a Golden Age when shepherds spoke and felt the lofty thoughts attributed in the present only to kings. It is thus a more serious dramatic genre, and beneath its surface lies a hidden meaning (*ein Verborgner Verstand,* 101) with religious import. The pagan gods should not be named; the disruptive satyr becomes the Devil; the result is Christian insight:

Die Betrachtungen der Geschöpfe Gottes/ der Eitelkeit der Welt/ Todesgedanken und deß höllischen Satyri Betrug/ rc. ist der beste Inhalt der wider erneurten Hirtengedichte. (103)

(Contemplation of God's creatures, of the vanity of the world, of thoughts of death and of the deception of the Hellish satyr and so on, are the best contents of the reborn pastoral poetry.)

The names of the characters may point to this meaning, whether Latin (e.g., *Urania* means the contemplation of heavenly things) or German (e.g., *Seelewig* means eternal soul). Harsdörffer mentions the ancient satyr play, *Schimpfspiel* ("derision play"), which satirizes vice, as originally related to the pastoral play, but disdains it as not properly poetic (99).[2] A fourth type, a mixture of *Freudenspiel* and *Hirtenspiel* which he defines but does not name, does receive detailed treatment. In such a play (later termed by Stieler *Allegorie*) the characters are allegorical figures, and their conflicts are those of the virtues and vices or other forces they represent. A key (*Schlüssel*) is necessary in order to understand the meaning of such plays—often, although Harsdörffer himself does not say so, in the form of significant names such as those he suggests for the *Hirtenspiel* (97–98).

August Buchner defines three types of nontragic drama: *Satyra* ("satyr plays"), *Comödien,* and *Schäfereyen* ("pastorals"). The satyr or satirical plays treat the vices and errors of human beings and improve the audience through laughter; comedies deal with the everyday life of common people; and the pastoral plays, which depict the life of shepherds, serve to honor princes.[3]

Perhaps more than any theoretician before him, Sigmund von Birken describes comic genres practiced in contemporary literature. His pastoral genre (*Schaeferspiel*) corresponds to that of Harsdörffer and Buchner, and his *Lustspiel* is, like their *Comoedie,* a portrayal of the life of city people, particularly those in the household: parents, children, and servants. But he adds two tragicomic genres to the list, the *Tugendspiel* ("virtue play"), which depicts the victory of virtue among the lower classes, and the *Heldenspiel* (hero play), which depicts heroic, positive deeds of the nobility and royalty.[4] The latter type he defines in great detail and with examples. The plot should involve serious complications which are resolved at the end:

Die Zier von Heldenspielen ist/ wann alles ineinander verwirrt/ und nicht nach der Ordnung/ wie in Historien/ erzehlet/ die Unschuld gekränkt/ die Bosheit beglückt vorgestellt/ endlich aber alles wieder entwickelt und auf einen richtigen Ablauf hinausgeführet wird. (329–30)

(The beautiful thing about heroic comedies is when everything is jumbled up together, and not according to chronology, when the innocent are depicted suffering and the evil happy, but in the end everything is untangled and led to a proper conclusion.)

Among his examples Birken includes dramas (*Androfilo* and *Psyche*) which correspond to Stieler's *Allegorie* (see below) and Harsdörffer's unnamed middle type between pastoral play and comedy.

Daniel Georg Morhof defines two types of comedies which seem to correspond to the satirical and pastoral plays, *Possenspiele* ("farces") and Hirtencomödien ("pastoral comedies").[5] He also notes the existence of

Satyrae, which he also calls *Schimpf-Gedichte* ("diatribes," 191), but does not know of any German examples (he considers Gryphius's *Horribili-cribrifax* a *Possenpiel*). He differentiates sharply between verse and prose drama, claiming that the latter is not poetry but oratory, and names Rist and Filidor as writers of prose comedy.

Caspar Stieler, who under the pseudonym Filidor wrote primarily prose comedies, composed his *Dichtkunst* in alexandrine verse (all others are prose). His treatise, not published in the seventeenth century but dated 1685 in the manuscript,[6] is the last important poetical treatise of the High Baroque. It clearly distinguishes four types of nontragic drama: *Lustspiel,* which is a satirical mirror of the vices and vanities of mankind as depicted in the lives of members of the lower classes; *Heldenspiel,* which depicts the loves and deeds of persons of high class rather than their vices or downfalls; *Schäferspiel*; and *Allegorien.* His depiction of the latter will establish it as a genre in its own right. He begins by describing the freedom of the poet working in this genre to create story, setting, and characters out of his own imagination, then insists that these must still be plausible. Allegories must aim both at *delectare* and *docere,* giving pleasure and teaching. And, above all, they must contain a hidden meaning:

Zumal, wann drunter ist was heimlichs zuverstehn,
so Allegorisch heißt. Die Wahrheit will verbildet
und ümgekleidet seyn, verzuckert und vergüldet.   (111; lines 1712–14)

([Plays fit this category] when underneath [the plot] there is something secret to be understood, which is called allegorical. Truth likes to be reshaped, disguised, sugar-coated and gold-plated.)

The names of characters in such plays should aid the interpretation, and thus they should be derived from German words (e.g., *Gottlieb,* "love of God"; *Reinhart,* "honorableness").

In his *Frauenzimmergesprächspiele* [Conversation Games for Women—a multi-volume work derived from Castiglione's *The Courtier*] Harsdörffer provides a further distinction among comedies, this one based on characteristics of the performance. The *Freudenspiel* is a comedy performed by professional actors for monetary gain, while the *Lustspiel* is performed by noble amateurs for their own enjoyment.[7] The

Lustspiel is additionally defined as following the Italian fashion of being presented musically, and thus conforms further to the "italianate" type of romantic comedy which Stieler terms the heroic comedy.

But from this jumble of terminology for the varieties of comedy some unity can be perceived. The *Freudenspiel* (or *Comedie* or *Satyra* or *Possenspiel*) deals with vice and error through presentation of the common people; when it becomes particularly scurrilous it may qualify as a *Schimpf-spiel*. It will here be termed the satirical comedy. The *Heldenspiel* (Stieler) or *Lustspiel* (Harsdörffer's *Gesprächspiele*) is an italianate or romantic comedy which deals with the loves and intrigues of the nobility and has a happy ending based on virtue. The *Allegorie* (Stieler; Harsdörffer defines but does not name it; Birken calls it *Heldenspiel* or at least includes it under this designation) contains a hidden meaning, which, rather than history or anecdote, is the source of the plot: the interplay of abstractions or figural events. The Pastoral play (*Schäferspiel, Hirtenspiel*) is usually a romantic comedy in pastoral guise, but may carry a hidden allegorical meaning.

All the theorists after mid-century mention Horace's *delectare et docere* as the dual purpose of comedy. Buchner and Harsdörffer see the latter purpose accomplished by means of laughter, which frees the audience of the very vices at which it laughs. But Birken, following the Jesuit theorist Jacob Masen, sees two comic emotions aroused in the audience, *Hoffnung und Freude* (335; Masen's *spes et gaudium,* "hope and joy"). Birken defines these concepts in Christian terms as hope for salvation and joy due to God's Grace. While such emotions may not be aroused by the satirical comedy, which Birken disregards or condemns anyway, they certainly are appropriate for the other types. Baroque comedy, then, insofar as it is not merely satirical, has the potential to fulfill the same function as Dante's *Divine Comedy*: to reveal ultimate truths in the Christian view of man and his world.

Another (perhaps related) serious side to Baroque comedy is the metaphysical one defined by Richard Alewyn,[8] who discerns that the essence of comedy, from Shakespeare and Italian Renaissance comedy to the German Baroque, is the contradiction between appearance and reality, mask and underlying truth, role and actor. He points to the tendency to rely on disguises, misunderstandings, mistaken identity, deception, fraud, and play-acting for the plot complications as well as for humor. Similar elements in tragic drama lead to disaster and fall, but in comedy they are triumphantly overcome by the reinstatement of Truth and Order at the end and by the resultant arousal of Birken's "comic" emotions, i.e., hope for similar Divine Aid for oneself and rejoicing with the characters who have received it.

Satirical Comedy

Satirical comedy, which seeks to arouse laughter in members of the audience at vices they may share with the characters, is the only comic genre which has roots in German literature: the later Protestant *Fastnachtspiel,* especially that of Hans Sachs. Heinrich Julius von Braunschweig's *Vincentius Ladislaus* (treated in Chapter 2), although derived from the Latin and romanic *Capitano* tradition, deserves consideration as the first Baroque comedy of this genre, since its verbal felicity and verbal humor distinguish it from the coarser *Schwank*-oriented quality of its German predecessors. Among later satirical comedies of literary quality, two by Gryphius stand nearly alone as representatives of the only type of Baroque comedy respected by most scholars: *Absurda Comica/ Oder Herr Peter Squentz* [Comic Absurdities, or Peter Squenz] and *Horribilicribrifax.*

Gryphius himself terms his *Peter Squentz* (written ca. 1648–50; published 1657) a *Schimpf-Spiel,* and the basis of its plot is a practical joke played by members of a royal court on a group of well-meaning but unsophisticated and silly subjects who have offered their services as a theater troupe for the entertainment of the court. The plot, and many of the names, derive indirectly (via the itinerant theater) from the subplot of Shakespeare's *Midsummer Night's Dream.* Under the leadership of the pretentious schoolmaster Peter Squentz, the amateur actors, all of whom are uneducated craftsmen, blithely carry through their attempt at a serious dramatization of the story of Pyramus and Thisbe—with unwittingly ridiculous and hilarious results. The members of the courtly audience are indeed richly entertained, but by the ineptness rather than success, and the prince pays by the mistake when it is time to reward the players. While the play within the play is in *Knittelvers,* the verse form of the amateur theater of the preceding century (e.g., *Fastnachtspiel,* Hans Sachs), the *dramatis personae* of the Peter Squentz action speak in prose which is matched in elegance or coarseness to the social class of the speaker. One member of the court, the king's fool, Pickelhering, joins the amateur actors and plays Pyramus; his language remains that of the court, as befits his function: gently to ridicule his fellow players and intellectual inferiors from his loftier perspective— even the court fool is less foolish than these pretentious craftsmen. Peter Squentz himself speaks the ludicrous modish language of someone who has received sufficient education to acquire affectations but not enough for self-knowledge, and his malapropisms and factual errors (e.g., Ovid and Aesop were Church Fathers) provide a good deal of the verbal humor in the play. Additional humor is provided by the deadly seriousness with which the "actors" take their play, their falling in and out of their roles, slapstick, verbal misunderstandings, scatological language, and sexual *double entendre.*

A central theme in the play is role-playing itself. The real audience watches actors—probably amateurs from a court or school—play the parts of an audience on stage and amateur actors who perform a play for that "audience." At the end of the play within the play, the amateurs assure an "audience" they assume to be worried about the deaths of Pyramus and Thisbe that they are only playing dead and will rise up from the "dead" to walk off stage. At other points, they express concern that the "lion" might frighten the ladies, and so ought to growl quietly; or that Klotz-George's beard might give away the fact that a man was playing the role of Thisbe. Their fears are hilariously unfounded, for their performance is anything but illusionistic. Characters fall in and out of roles to criticize, comment, or scuffle; forget their lines; and act and speak their lines as woodenly as puppets. One of them even forgets the rhyme words in his speech, substituting nonrhyming synonyms.

From inadequacies of their role-playing in the playlet, one progresses to inadequacies in the character of Peter Squentz himself, who has "assigned" himself a role in society considerably above his station and talents. The mistakes he makes as he "plays" a well-educated and creative man—Latin malapropisms, inability to multiply simple numbers, misuse of the titles of royalty—reveal that his claims to greatness are a sham and that beneath his self-assigned role he is a silly fool. His "audience" perceives the vanity of his pretentiousness, but the real audience of the play can see both his and theirs; the theme of the world as a stage extends Gryphius's irony beyond Squentz and his comrades to the smug members of royalty themselves, whose roles may befit their stations, only to disappear at death, leaving nothing but naked human souls marked by pride and lack of self-knowledge.

The play contains criticism directed at the amateur theater of the previous century as exemplified in the *Meistersänger* syndrome of the shoemaker Hans Sachs, and at the early seventeenth-century drama which derived from it (a number of serious Pyramus and Thisbe plays were written and performed in Germany between 1600 and 1650).[9] The play within the play is a parody of such drama. It is designed and performed by *Handwerker,* members of craftsmen's guilds. It is written in *Knittelvers,* with all the failings of that verse form taken to extremes: forced and overused rhyme, uneven line length. It ends with a Hans Sachs–style formula, when Peter Squentz finishes his epilogue by wishing the audience a good night and naming himself as the author. Prologue and epilogue explain the story and comment upon it, and the author sits on one side of the stage as prompter and commentator.

Such a parody of pre-Opitzian drama and theater can serve as a dramatized negative *Poeterey* in which Gryphius seeks to put as much distance as possible between the unsophisticated amateurish product of the middle class of the previous period and the sophisticated drama produced by himself and his fellow authors, members of a new kind of higher middle class which considers itself closer to the nobility than to the lower-middle-class tradesmen. The new Baroque authors write drama as a kind of pleasurable scholarly pastime, not for monetary gain (Squentz's *Trinkgeld* = "tip"). Their pride in their status and their desire to disassociate their literary production from that of earlier "poets" thus would find expression in this play.

It has been suggested that *Peter Squentz* was designed and performed as a satyr play in the ancient manner to follow upon Gryphius's tragedy *Cardenio und Celinde,*[10] conforming to Birken's suggestion that a short comedy following a tragedy or interspersed with it would cheer the audience after its exposure to the terrible and the tragic (*Rede-Bind,* 327–28). The shortness of the play, only around 1,200 lines, would even allow it to be performed right after the tragedy, as in ancient Greek practice. Thematic connections make the supposition well worth considering. Both *Cardenio und Celinde* and the *Pyramus und Thisbe* inner play deal with a tragic love which rashly subsumes all else to passion.

Both plays tend to dethrone love, rather than glorify it romantically—*Cardenio und Celinde* through the realization of its vanity and the rejection of its power, *Peter Squentz,* in spite of the sentimental *Liebestod,* through the words of the epilogue:

> Lernet hierauß wie gut es sey
> Daß man von Liebe bleibe frey.   (37, lines 12–13)
>
> (Learn from this how good it may be
> That one from love remain free.)

Thus Cardenio and Celinde overcome the power of earthly love in an earnest encounter with the supernatural and their own mortality, while *Peter Squentz* provides the comic pendant in a travesty of a play which glorifies love through a romantic *Liebestod.*

A further indication of the interweaving of the two plays is the quibbling—serious in *Cardenio und Celinde* and humorous in *Peter Squentz*—about genre designation. Nowhere else does Gryphius seem at a loss to know to what genre, tragedy or comedy, a particular play belongs. He terms *Cardenio und Celinde* a *Trauerspiel* in spite of the fact that the catastrophe is averted through the conversion of the protagonists to a sense of higher values, but he feels the need to defend this designation in the preface: *Die Personen so eingeführet sind fast zu niedrig vor ein Traur-Spiel* ("The characters introduced are almost too lowly for a tragedy," 5:99). Similarly, Peter Squentz cannot decide whether to term his play tragedy or comedy. The king, he tells his comrades, is a patron *von allerley lustigen Tragoedien und prächtigen Comoedien* ("of all sorts of funny tragedies and magnificent comedies," 6). His proposed play, too, mixes the terms in an apparent malapropism: *als bin ich willens / durch zu Thuung euer Geschickligkeit eine jämmerlich schöne Comoedi zu tragiren* ("So I intend, with the help of your skill, to tragedize [as in "to perform a tragedy"] a lamentably pretty comedy," 6). Later he decides, *Wir sollen es heissen eine Comoedi oder Tragoedie* ("we should call it a comedy or tragedy," 11). The Meistersänger in the group, Lollinger, replies with Hans Sachs's definition: a sad ending, such as this play has, makes it a tragedy. Pickelhering argues that by the same definition it is a comedy: *Contra! Das Spiel wird lustig außgehen / denn die Todten werden wieder lebendig / setzen sich zusammen / und trinken einen guten Rausch / so ist es denn eine Comoedi* ("On the contrary! The play will end happily, for the dead will become alive again, sit down together, and drink themselves into a drunken stupor; thus it is a comedy," 11). Squentz prefers to equivocate, since a happy ending, for him, involves a handsome reward—something he does not yet feel sure of getting: *Darumb ist es am besten/ ich folge meinem Kopff und gebe ihm den Titul ein schön Spiel lustig und traurig/ zu tragiren und zu sehen* ("For that reason it will be best if I follow my head and give it the title: a beautiful drama, happy and sad to perform and to see," 11), although in the prologue he terms it *die fröliche Tragoedie* ("the happy tragedy," 18).

In *Cardenio und Celinde,* too, the characters "rise from the dead," that is, the protagonists literally climb out of the tomb and thus figuratively out of their *memento mori* experiences alive, if not unchanged—an ending seemingly calling for the comic designation more than does the "happy ending" involved in realizing that the tragic deaths on stage in *Pyramus und Thisbe* were merely playacting. Gryphius's irony seems to be at work here. At the end of *Peter Squentz* the genre discussion surfaces again. The epilogue speaker still equivocates:

> Hiermit endt sich die schöne Comoedie,
> Oder wie mans heist die Tragoedie.   (37)

> (Here comes to an end the beautiful comedy,
> Or, as one could say, the tragedy.)

For just as *Cardenio und Celinde* is a tragedy diverted from its usual course, so *Pyramus und Thisbe* is a travesty of a tragedy which induces tears of laughter in the audience, not tears of pity or fear. It cures the audience of excessive interest in worldly love through laughter at the follies of those who take it seriously—the purging effect of laughter—while its companion piece does so through the tragic emotions, fear and empathy, and the catharsis they bring about in spite of the nontragic ending. Not content with the power to affect and change his audience developed in the twin thrusts of tragedy, catharsis and *exemplum,* Gryphius turns to a third in composing a pair of theoretically related dramas: comic purification through laughter.

Gryphius's other satirical comedy, *Wehlende Liebhaber/ Oder Horribilicribrifax* [Pairing Off, or Horribilicribrifax; written ca. 1648, published 1663], probably was not meant as a pendant to a tragedy, as its approximately 2,400 lines and lack of thematic ties to any tragedy would tend to indicate. Horribilicribrifax and his friend Daradiri-datumtarides, both military officers of the bragging and preen-ing variety already seen in *Vincentio Ladislaus,* are in the mood for wooing, as are the noble maidens and gentlemen of the court and their servants. After much scrambling and mismatched wooing, seven ap-propriate marriages are arranged at the end of the play which reward virtue and punish vice.

The two captains may derive from a tradition of *capitano* satirical dramas which date back to Plautus, but they had special relevance at the time this particular play was written. The Thirty Years War, which had disrupted Germany's political, economic, and social life for three decades, had just come to an end, leaving thousands of its creatures—military officers who had scrambled their way up through the ranks with the help of the fortunes of war—out of a job and in a social vacuum. They who had been powerful, important, useful, and oc-cupied during a war which started before some had even been born, and which had dominated their entire adult life, were now reduced to being classless vagabonds. The feudal class system of prewar Germany was restored, and there was no place in it for these sorry figures whose expectations had been raised by their military status. The two captains in this play are making the attempt, not entirely unsuccessfully, to merge the military hierarchy with the social hierarchy; as officers they expect to be treated as equals by the nobility. They show their presump-tion not only by gate crashing and bragging about their glorious deeds, but also by wooing ladies of the court.

They are rebuffed, for their expectations are too high. Their claims to greatness are undermined by a number of incidents. For instance, in one scene these supposedly brave men are terrified by a housecat, envision-ing in its glowing eyes some sort of dangerous monster. Their pompous speeches are full of malapropisms; their bombastic quasi-noble names, *Windbrecher von Tausend Mord, Erbherr in und zu Windloch* ("Wind-breaker of thousand killings, hereditary lord in and at Windhole") and *Horribilicribrifax von Donnerkeil auf Wüsthausen* ("Terrifying sieve-maker of the lightning bolt upon destroyed village"), do not impress the other characters. They are social climbers and upstarts; their pride must go before a fall. Daradiridatumtirades manages to marry a noblewoman, Selene, who is his equal both in false ambition and empty pockets. Horribilicribrifax worships the exquisite Coelestina, whose beautiful and virtuous charms will be deservedly granted to another. At the end he is matched to an ugly castle employee. Yet they have been accepted into the hierarchy, if at a lower level than they had expected, and have not been chased from court—and the stage—by a barrage of rotten eggs, like the protagonist in *Vincentius Ladislaus*. Nor have the members of the court played a trick on them, as in that play, for their own sadistic enjoyment. The hierarchy has become more flexible than it was before the war.

Another character in the play also comes to court with delusions of grandeur: Sempronius, a village schoolmaster, thinks he is a scholarly and brilliant man whose attainments also deserve the hand of a courtly lady. His pseudo-learned bombast, more obnoxious and less charming that that of Peter Squentz, earns him the hand of an ugly old procuress ("Cyrilla, eine alte Kuplerin"). He, too, represents a classless group rising in postwar Germany, a group which likewise seeks a niche at the upper end of the old feudal hierarchy: the educated elite whose wealthy city families bought for them an education no worse than that of a king's son. Gryphius himself belonged to this group, and an element of self-irony enters his work. Although he himself did not make use of his acquired title, most of his peers did: Daniel Casper von Lohenstein, Christian Hofmann von Hoffmanswaldau, even Christoffel von Grimmelshausen and Caspar von Stieler. As the educated elite began to infiltrate the hereditary noble class of feudal tradition, a new concept of nobility based on knowledge, skill, and diplomatic service to the ruling houses began to arise, a sort of natural nobility or elite class of superior individuals.

Another kind of upward mobility, however, is depicted and idealized in this play. The young noblewoman Sophia, whose family, once powerful and wealthy, had lost everything in the war, has no pretensions of grandeur at all. She disdains the usual vanities of her sex and age group, preferring virtue, chastity, and self-respect to primping or catching a rich husband. To support herself and her mother, she finally cuts off and offers for sale her beautiful golden hair—which the local ruler no sooner sees than he falls in love with its unknown owner. When her virtue proves as admirable as her self-sacrificing action, he offers to share his throne with her, thus elevating her to a kind of hierarchy of virtue. It is this natural nobility based on virtue and wisdom, rather than that based on learning, which Gryphius espouses in this play.

Thus the comedy is an examination of the old feudal hierarchy threatened by the new conditions present in postwar Germany. It satirizes the affectations of two groups of people, discharged military officers whom skill and the fortunes of war had elevated to high rank, and the educated elite whose learning raised them above their middle-class peers. While the play recognizes the dilemma of these classless groups, it does not propose a solution but instead satirizes their pretensions to high status. In revealing their follies and self-deceptions, Gryphius forces the members of the audience to laugh at these qualities not only in the characters but in themselves as well, insofar as they may exist there. And the play also proposes a new hierarchy based neither on inheritance nor on status, but on the natural nobility of virtue and natural vulgarity of vice. The apotheosis of Sophia to the highest nobility due to her virtue, and the relegation of others to particular social ranks through marriage appropriate to their moral status, constitute the creation of the only hierarchy important on Judgment Day, that based on the good and evil accrued by each soul. Gryphius's proposal is probably not a suggestion for social change, but rather a way of demonstrating the ultimate irony constituted by the confrontation of man's imperfect view of relative status with that of the absolute, God.

Italianate Comedy

The romantic or italianate comedy, Stieler's *Heldenspiel,* contains intermittent rather than constant humor, and its primary effect on the audience is not accomplished by laughter, but by the eventual disentangling of complications and the unmasking of deception by means of virtue and truth. The finale is the announcement of multiple marriages (an element which Gryphius took over in *Horribilicribrifax*). The emotions aroused in the audience are *spes et gaudium* ("hope and joy"), the opposites of tragic fear and pity (*metus et misericordia*): hope that one's own problems can be quickly solved by an equally benevolent world order and vicarious joy over the successful solution of problems of those deserving characters with whom one identifies.

Gryphius tried his hand at this type of comedy in a translation probably written during or immediately after his travels, the *Seugammel/ Oder Untreues Hausgesinde,* discussed in Chapter 3. His only original contribution to the genre, however, is his double comedy *Verlibtes Gespenste/ Die Gelibte Dornrose* ([Love-sick Ghost/ The beloved Dornrose]; 1660; published 1661) composed of two short self-contained but parallel four-act comedies. The *Gespenste* plot deals with the problem of a parent falling in love with her child's suitor.[11] Chloris's mother, Cornelia, steps between her daughter and Sulpicius, who love each other to the point of love sickness, in order to pursue Sulpicius herself. Sulpicius's friend Levin, who loves Cornelia, suggests a scheme which will solve all the problems: Sulpicius is to sham death after eating candy containing a love potion given him by Cornelia. During his "death," Levin will have time to win a repentant Cornelia, leaving Sulpicius free to wed Chloris when he "miraculously" rises from the dead. All the characters hail from the upper middle class, and, since this play is a *Singspiel,* the speeches are all in verse. In the dialect prose *Zwischenspiel,* Gregor Kornblume and Lise Dornrose, children of feuding peasant families, share a love which is seemingly ill-fated, in spite of their attempts to overcome the animosities. Gregor's uncle and Lise's father hurl accusations about dirty tricks—a prize chicken gets a leg cut off and a dog is scalded—perpetrated during the most recent outbreak of violence. Gregor manages to stop the violence, and the case is taken to court at the end of the play. Lise's unwelcome suitor Aschewedel tries to win her love by force, but she is rescued by Gregor and her father, who take Aschewedel to court. In the court scene at the end, these two cases are tried and all problems are eliminated by the genius of the judge's solutions: Gregor and Lise united in marriage, the family feud halted, Aschewedel condemned to marry an ugly procuress/sorceress who gave him evil advice.

The two plots reflect and parallel one another in a particular relationship which illuminates both rather than one plot providing commentary for the other. Although the Dornrose play is termed a *Zwischenspiel,* it is not merely an interlude which restates the same themes on a mythical or pastoral plane, even though it does seem to be a localization of the imported pastoral fashion. Instead, as a play of equal length, it restates the central theme—the miracle-working power of love—and illuminates it from several new points of view. While each play is self-contained, the whole is greater than its parts, for the double comedy provides a dual perspective and thus a deeper insight than either one alone could do. This use of a semi-independent drama as a

Zwischenspiel is also practiced contemporaneously by Sigmund von Birken,[12] but without the freshness and vitality of Gryphius's peasant play. Gryphius's class-conscious effort proves the universality of love and offers to the royal wedded couple for whom it was written a sort of congratulatory greeting card signed by all of the prince's subjects, high and low.

Human love in these two comedies of the italianate variety is an allegory for divine love,[13] and thus the use of the term *Wundertaten* ("miracles") to describe love's triumph in both plays is more than a figure of speech. Each play demonstrates one aspect of Christ's love for the human race: Sulpicius's "death" and "resurrection" signify both Christ's act of Divine Love—his sacrifice on the cross, descent into Hell, and resurrection—and the results for mankind, resurrection to eternal life in Heaven; the trial in *Dornrose* stands for both Divine Aid and divine approval offered the human soul in its *Feuerprobe* ("ordeal by fire"), its earthly testing, and for Christ's function as judge at the Last Judgment. The fact that Wilhelm von den Hohen Sinnen, the local judge, is at first a pretentious buffoon, not unlike Kleist's Dorfrichter Adam in the nineteenth-century drama *Der zerbrochene Krug* [The Broken Jug], but then becomes endowed with the wisdom of a Solomon, is an indication of divine intervention in this case (and of the divine model for human justice in general).

In *Gespenste,* the loving sacrifice of Christ, as figured in Sulpicius's resurrection, unifies the true lovers in a sort of *unio mystica,* while it offers opportunity for repentance and conversion of the straying soul, Cornelia. *Dornrose* likewise ends in the marital union of the virtuous lovers; Gregor, as rescuer of his Dornrose from rape and dishonor, can be seen as savior of his bride, the soul, and Aschewedel thus plays the role of the devil who seeks her ruin. But another marriage punishes Aschewedel for his attempt to force Dornrose to his will—he must marry his evil female counterpart, Salome. Marriage can thus be an allegory for eternal reward *or* punishment, and each is sentenced by the divine judge to his just deserts.

The double comedy also contains a political allegory, which, oddly enough, is carried by the peasant play alone, rather than by the more politically powerful middle class or by a hypothetical appearance of royalty (who do appear in other italianate comedies). The marriage of Kornblume and Dornrose brings about harmony between two feuding families who threatened the peace of the society, just as dynastic marriages of royal families help to end political hostilities and unify nations into a single political entity. Thus marriages arranged by God (as indicated by true love and the court's judgment) conform to political wisdom as well as to divine will. Such usage agrees with Birken's prescriptions for the pastoral play, which is designed to reflect the affairs of kings, and is one indication that Gryphius's *Dornrose* is a Germanized pastoral.

This double comedy was written to celebrate the marriage of Gryphius's prince, the Silesian Duke Georg of Brieg and Liegnitz, to the Palantine Countess Elizabeth Maria Charlotte. In this capacity, it was expected not only to laud and flatter the new pair and entertain the wedding guests, but also to comment on the meaning of marriage. Thus it is appropriate that the play demonstrates the sanctity of marriage through the use of the analogy to Christ's "marriage" to the soul, as Birken advised;[14] that it points out the political wisdom of dynastic marriages arranged, as it were, in Heaven, as a way to achieve peace, harmony, and unity; and that it alludes to the ultimate purpose of dynastic marriages, the production of an heir, as indicated in the song of the god of marriage and the happy couples at the end of the play:

> Und kröne die Verlibten Sorgen/
> Mit viel Charlotten und Georgen.
> (*Tanz der Geister und der Liben,* lines 78–79)

> (And may Heaven crown the cares of the lovers
> With many little Charlottes and Georges.)

Although we term these plays comedies (Gryphius called them *Singspiel* and *Scherzspiel,* respectively), arousal of laughter is not their primary goal. In fact, the double drama contains little slapstick (only in the scene with the two feuding peasants), few verbal puns, and no alimentary-tract humor. While the audience might chuckle at Sulpicius's lovesickness or at Kornblume's stuttering when he tries to ask for Dornrose's hand in marriage, such comic effects are purposely avoided. The usual sources of humor, the servants and peasants, have a dignity which elevates them above it: the servants in *Gespenste* woo in a serious, if flippant manner; the peasants in *Dornrose,* although they speak dialect, are not the stupid bumpkins they are in almost any other play of the time. Instead, Masen's and Birken's "comic emotions" are the goal: hope and joy are Gryphius's appropriate wishes for the newly wedded couple.

The main contributor of italianate comedy to German Baroque literature was Caspar Stieler, whose translation of an Italian comedy, *Ernelinde/ Oder die Viermahl Braut,* was discussed in Chapter 3. His three original italianate comedies use romance-language novellas as their source in much the same way that Shakespeare made fruitful use of this treasure trove of romantic plots. All of his six early plays—the so-called *Rudolstädter Festspiele* published under the pseudonym Filidor—were written during his tenure as secretary to the Count of Schwarzburg-Rudolstadt, Albrecht Anthon, from 1665 to 1667, and all celebrate various important events at court: princely marriage, birthdays, the birth of an heir. This occasional function does not prevent them from having the effects and functions characteristic of comedy, however, but instead adds a further dimension to them.

The first comedy of the series is *Der Vermeinte Printz* (1665), performed on the occasion of Albrecht Anthon's marriage to Aemilia Juliana of Barby. A king, whose wife loses the ability to produce further children as a result of childbirth, raises the infant daughter as a son in order to allow her to inherit the throne. As the play opens, the assumed prince, now eighteen years old, learns her true identity, and she agrees to continue her father's deception. Yet Nature thwarts the best-laid plans, and she falls in love with an exiled prince who arrives at court. The resulting complications and intrigues wind their way to the usual happy resolution and multiple marriages. The rule of male inheritance is set aside, so that the princess inherits her father's kingdom after all, and her union with the prince turns out to be an important dynastic marriage.

Mistaken identity, disguises, and deceptions form a network of intrigue and complication based on the disparity between appearance and reality, between the artificial and the natural. Close brushes with "crimes against Nature" such as transvestitism, transsexualism, and homosexuality are the result of insistence upon an "unnatural" law (the Salic Law of male-only succession) and upon deception as the solution to the problems it causes. But the princess's "natural" feminine feelings intervene in the network of artificiality and sham, albeit by using its own weapons—more disguises and lies. With the aid of her cleverness, the natural and the godly win out; the artificial laws of men are set aside in the face of the Law of Nature and the Divine Will. The potentially tragic disparity between appearance and reality is turned into a weapon for the cause of Nature and inclination, and then finally vanquished altogether by the unifying magic of love.

The victory of Nature and love over human laws is graphically portrayed in the mythological *Zwischenspiele,* which include choruses, a prologue, and an epilogue. In these scenes, the ancient gods, as personifications of certain qualities, guide the events on the human plane. Jupiter, as personification of political wisdom, sets the god of shapeshifting, Vertumnus, to work to solve the political problems caused by the birth of an heir of the wrong sex. But these politically oriented actions based on *Staatsraison* ("political expediency") ignore the demands of Nature, and it is the love-god Amor who eventually overturns the trickery of Vertumnus, revealing the ultimate divine approval of natural feelings, love, and marriage.

This theme is appropriate for a comedy whose function it was to honor a royal marriage. As in the case of Gryphius's double comedy, love assumes great importance as a sign of divine approval and of dynastic continuity—the ultimate in values for the Christian ruler. It is a cipher for divine love, the love of Christ for the human soul. And in this play it is also seen as the ultimate in *Staatsraison,* for the marriage unites two kingdoms as well as two dynasties into a single and therefore stronger entity. The marriage of Albrecht Anthon to the Countess of Barby will, it is hoped, likewise unite two principalities and two dynasties, and provide a single heir to rule both.

But the play has an additional function not seen in the usual marriage play; to convey a political polemic which lays claim to a particular territory for a patron. For Aemilia Juliana had lost her claim to her patrimony due to the same Salic Law which causes the complication in the play. Her father had died in 1641 and his only son, Aemilia's brother, followed him to the grave in 1659, six years before her marriage. She and her three sisters were deprived of any claim to Barby when it was split among its neighboring states, all of which had some sort of traditional feudal status as overlord over parts of it. The comedy, in ruling the Salic Law of male-only succession unnatural, thus lays claim to the inheritance of the bride for her bridegroom and constitutes an attack on the seizure of it by its neighbors.

Thus the hope and joy aroused in the audience at the end of this comedy can be defined not only as metaphysical but also as political. The joy at the satisfactory solution of the protagonist's problems carries with it a hope that those of the princely bride and bridegroom in the audience might have a similar conclusion. Italianate comedy or *Heldenspiel*, which treats the affairs of the heart of highly placed persons, can thus have a function as potentially political and serious in nature as that of tragedy: to carry matters of policy polemically to the public and to bring a subtle sort of diplomacy to bear on weighty affairs of state. It is perhaps for this reason that its main purveyor in Germany, Stieler, ignored Opitz's objections to the appearance of royalty in comedy, and followed the romantic traditions of "heroic comedy."

Die erfreuete Unschuld (1666), which Stieler terms (like *Ernelinde*) a *Misch-Spiel* ("tragicomedy"), also belongs to the italianate comedy group. It honors the count's sister, Sophia Juliana, on her birthday, through the presentation of the story of a virtuous woman wrongly accused but eventually vindicated. Queen Eleonora, left in the care of the king's marshal Pancalier during the absence of her husband, is subjected to the deputy's attempt to seduce her. When she furiously rejects his advances, his passion for her turns to hatred and the desire for revenge. He accuses her of adultery and has her sentenced to die at the stake, but agrees, if she can find a hero to fight for her honor, that he will fight him for her life. Eleonora applies to the prince Mendoza, whom she secretly loves but had renounced in favor of chastity within marriage. He declines, saying that his own land is under siege, but comes in disguise to ascertain whether she is guilty. Posing as a monk, he hears her confession, and, convinced of her innocence, he duels and defeats Pancalier, who must now himself die at the stake. Word is then received of the convenient death of Eleonora's absent husband, and she and her hero marry and live happily ever after. The comic figure Scaramutza, Pancalier's servant, seems silly and stupid, but his speeches not only criticize the illicit behavior of his master but also provide social criticism directed at the audience, as when he parodies the parasites or turns to the audience, saying that he sees adulterers everywhere.

The *Zwischenspiele* provide the clues for a theological interpretation of the play which conforms to fourfold biblical exegesis. The four distinct levels of interpretation, literal, tropological or moral, allegorical, and anagogical, ally this play to pastoral and allegorical comedy without weakening the entertainment value constituted by the unraveling of the intrigue or the verbal humor. In the interludes a dragon appears, accompanied by Gog and Magog and the Babylonian Whore, to persecute the personification of the Christian Church (also called Zion and Jerusalem). At last, in answer to her prayers, the archangel Michael, her spouse, appears with gleaming sword to drive off her persecutors. Two standard Christian hymns, which plead for divine aid and express thankfulness for it, also appear in these choruses.

The events depicted in the choruses are parallel to those in the plot of the comedy: Pancalier is the dragon, Eleonora the persecuted Church, Mendoza her guardian angel and eventual bridegroom. Thus Eleonora's Christian virtue, on the moral level, is depicted under siege by the Devil and defended by divine aid. The Babylonian Whore, the Devil's ally, represents the lust which Pancalier tries to arouse in her, or perhaps her earlier transgression; the maverick tribes Gog and Magog, associated with Babylon according to Ezekiel (38:39), attack Israel (Eleonora) by God's command as a punishment for past sins (her love for Mendoza), but Israel's (Eleonora's) eventual victory over them is a sign of divine forgiveness and favor (39:25–27).

Examination of the passages in Revelations dealing with the Whore of Babylon, however, leads to another level of interpretation; that conveying anagogical or final things. The Whore appears at the end of the world as representative not only of lust but of the Antichrist, for her horns represent the kings who make war upon the Lamb (Christ). The beast on which she rides is the apocalyptic dragon, also an image of the Antichrist, which will likewise make war on Christ. After the capture of the Antichrist at the hands of the hero/savior whose sword is the word of God, the celebration of the marriage of the Lamb with his bride, the New Jerusalem, will take place. And "blessed are those who are invited to the marriage supper of the Lamb" (19:9). The parallel of the interludes and, by extension, of the comedy itself, to this set of passages then yields the following interpretation: Eleonora, the Church or congregation of Christ's followers, is attacked by the Antichrist at the Last Judgment, but is rescued by the appearance of her divine and merciful bridegroom, Christ, with whom she then contracts the spiritual marriage which represents the union of God and mankind for eternity. It is the story of erring mankind, forgiven and defended by divine grace, and welcomed to its heavenly home after sin and travail on earth.

Yet one name chosen for the bride—*die Verfolgte Kirche* ("the perse-cuted Church")—when taken together with the appearance of Gog and Magog in Turkish costume, may indicate yet another meaning, this one dealing with the story of the Christian institutions and their attempts to provide for the salvation of mankind. Eleonora's story would thus stand for the Christian Church under attack by the Turks in the Balkans and in the Mediterranean. The identity of the "savior" is probably, as in Lohenstein, the emperor Leopold (although his name is nowhere men-tioned), since only two years earlier he had won a decisive victory against the Turks in Hungary. Gog and Magog were frequently linked in anti-Turkish polemic to the Turks, who were likewise considered a scourge of God and a sort of Antichrist. Such imagery from Revelations and the Old Testament prophecies dealing with the end of the world, when equated to the present conflict with the Turkish Empire, took on added importance; reiteration of the ultimate happy ending, the aboli-tion of mortality and of the gulf between man and God, is an appro-priate subject for the sort of comedy as defined by Birken and Masen, that which arouses *spes et gaudium,* hope for eternal life and joy at its attainment.

A third romantic comedy, *Der betrogene Betrug* [Deceived Deception, 1667], seems less susceptible to interpretation as anything more than slightly risqué entertainment. Don Ferdinand, already wed to Victoria in Toledo, abandons her and travels to Madrid, where he is to wed Elvira. Victoria discovers his intentions and sets out to deceive this bigamous deceiver. She thwarts his marriage plans but deceives him into reconsummating their own marriage by making him believe he has a rendezvous with Elvira. Ferdinand returns to Victoria, Elvira marries the man she really loves (Don Alexandro), and even the servants Scaramutza and Lisille are planning a wedding at the end of the play. Surrounding the three acts of this romantic comedy is the four-act mythological masque of Jupiter's seduction of Danae in a rain of gold and the promise of the birth of their heroic son, Perseus.

As the title indicates, the play revolves upon the theme of deception and its overthrow. Ferdinand thinks to deceive his wife and his new betrothed, but is instead deceived; Danae's father Atrisius thinks to deceive Fate, which had decreed that his daughter's son would kill him, by confining her in a cruel prison where she will have no chance to fall in love, wed, and bear a child, but instead Jupiter's deceptive disguise penetrates the prison and the divine lover impregnates her with the fateful son. The deceptions—Ferdinand's bigamy and Atrisius's attempt to cheat destiny—are defeated by counterdeceptions which rely on disguise. Victoria changes her name and her social class, and her new garments and position as a servant in Elvira's household make her real identity impenetrable to others; even though she faces Ferdinand himself, he cannot recognize her. Venus, to help carry out the destiny the fates have decreed, disguises herself so cleverly that Atrisius is blind to her real identity, and her father, Jupiter himself, cannot see through her rags and wrinkles. Jupiter, who appears at first as a shower of gold to Danae, is also not recognized: her *Hilf Jupiter* ("help, Jupiter!" 27) is ironic, and not until he reveals himself to her in her dream does she realize she has been ravished by a divinity: *Ach Jupiter* ("Ah, Jupiter," 27). Deceivers and innocents alike are deceived in the eternal tragicomedy of the dichotomy between appearance and reality, between facade and essence. But in the end the veils are lifted to reveal Divine Providence as the ultimate helpmate of virtue and right.

This play, although superficially a romantic comedy, is, like Gryphius's *Verlibtes Gespenste,* a conversion drama. Ferdinand's hidden evil is discovered by the abandoned Victoria, who curses him as *du vermumter Vertumnus, der sich in einen Engel verstellet/ und das gantze Hellenheer in seinem Hertzen beherbergen darf* ("you disguised Vertumnus, who dresses up as an angel, but who may be host to the entire army of Hell in his heart," 2). His lowest moment comes when he coarsely derides Victoria's widowhood, desiring a virgin for his wife instead: *Sie mag hinfahren. Ich habe mir nie vorgenommen eine Witthe zu heyrathen. Jungfer Fleisch ist niedlich. Die Pfütze/ worinn ein ander gebadet/ mag ich nicht aussauffen* ("She can go to Hell. I never intended to marry a widow. Virgin flesh is a dainty morsel. To lap up the bilge water in which another has bathed doesn't appeal to me," 54). Victoria's actions, seen by a thankful Elvira and her father to derive from Divine Providence (40), culminate in the conversion scene. Victoria accuses Ferdinand of perfidy; he is admonished to repent; he confesses his guilt and repents of it; he pleads for forgiveness and is ultimately forgiven by the woman he had most wronged, his wife.

In this play, marriage is not the *unio mystica* of Christ as bridegroom with his spouse, the human soul, but the earthly manifestation of divine grace and forgiveness. As Victoria redeems her wayward husband and returns him to their marital union, she has provided for his spiritual redemption as well in rescuing him from sin and in offering him forgiveness. Just as Christ lowered himself by being born a lowly human being in order to redeem the human race, so Victoria has lowered her social class and received the derision of her servant and the duress of serving another with equanimity in order to redeem Ferdinand.

The interlude also seemingly deals with adultery: Jupiter must quickly woo and win his human paramours in order to escape the wrath of his wife, Juno, queen of the gods. Yet this motif is a blind one in the *Zwischenspiel,* for Jupiter's roving eye has positive results. Instead, the meaning of this masque must be viewed from the perspective of traditional allegorizations of this tale from Ovid's *Metamorphoses,* most of which view the shower of gold as Divine Love miraculously achieving union with the soul. Divine Providence, in the guise of the chief Roman god, fulfills the oracle of Fate by breaching the prison walls to provide for the birth of a culture hero who will battle tyranny, evil, and vice and punish the blasphemous man (Atrisius) who has tried to resist destiny.

The prologue and epilogue of the play provide commentary on the function of this theatrical performance and, by extension, all such occasional literature. The *Vorredner* (prologue speaker) is the poet Horace, who brings the ancient gods with him out of Hades, like Orpheus leading Euridice, to entertain the courtly patron. The following relationship of poet and patron emerges: Stieler's patron's fame will live on eternally in the poet's praises, just as Horace's patron (Augustus) is famed partly due to his poetic expression. The play should attack vice by ridiculing it and should demonstrate the virtuous way (2); but it should also entertain, celebrate the joyous occasion of the birth of the heir, and arouse pleasure and joy (*Lust und Freud,* 3). The mythological representatives of poetic inspiration, Apollo and the Muses, appear as the epilogue, and they provide best wishes from the author and his actors for the health and future of the newborn heir. The appropriateness of the *Zwischenspiel* for this occasional function is clear, since it is the story of the origins of the hero Perseus, whose birth metamorphoses into that of the Schwarzburg infant in the epilogue.

Pastoral Drama

Pastoral drama closely resembles italianate comedy, for its plot consists of the same series of intrigues and complications resolved at the end in multiple marriage. But its setting is Arcadia; its characters are garbed in shepherd's robes. Beneath this playful guise allegory can have full rein, as was the case in Hofmannswaldau's translation of Guarini's *Il Pastor fido*.[15] Original pastoral comedies in German were popular in the 1660s and 1670s, including one by Caspar Stieler (*Basilene*, 1667) and several by Johann Christian Hallmann (*Die triumphierende Keuschheit/ Oder Die Getreue Urania* [Triumphant Chastity, or Loyal Urania], 1667; and *Die Sinn-reiche Liebe/ Oder der Glückseelige Adonis und Die Vergnügt Rosibella* [Sensible Love, or Blessed Adonis and Delighted Rosibella], 1673.

Stieler's *Basilene*, as Höfer has shown (97–101), is a reworking of Antoine de Montchrétien's *Bergerie* which returns to Montchrétien's source, Guarini's famous *Il Pastor fido*, for some of the important changes. Others are Stieler's original contribution. As in his two sources, Stieler's Arcadia has been cursed by the goddess Diana and must sacrifice a human being each year on her altar in an attempt to stay her anger. The oracle has provided a loophole: should a faithful shepherd appear to die for his beloved on the altar, Diana will be appeased. As the priest in each play prepares to sacrifice the maiden, the faithful lover steps forward to take her place. The curse is lifted and multiple marriages are announced.

Just as *Der getreue Schäfer* of Hofmannswaldau has been shown to have an allegorical significance based on its figural relationship to the story of Christ dying on the cross in order to redeem the human soul, so *Basilene* recreates the primary events in universal salvation: Christ, referred to in the Bible as the good shepherd as well as the sacrificial lamb who died for mankind's sins, is the model for the self-sacrificing shepherd, while Basilene, who is to die as a scapegoat for the unnamed sins of her people which had angered Diana eleven years before, is the human soul who must suffer under the effects of the Fall in spite of the lack of individual guilt. The original sin which condemns her can be overthrown only by the ultimate act of divine grace: self-sacrifice of the son of God, who loves her in spite of her resistance. The marriage at the end will signify the union of God and the human soul in divine love.

Stieler's *Basilene* was written to honor the Schwarzburg count, his patron, on his birthday. This function is fulfilled in part by specific laudatory references in the prologue and epilogue. But the laudatory passages and their message are united to the thematics of the play. The prologue-speaker Mars, god of war, claims he appears because March, the prince's birthday month, is named for him, but also because of the current conflict in Eastern Europe (wars against the Turks); Irene, goddess of peace, takes his place as epilogue speaker. The two can parallel the progression of the ages of mankind delineated in the play, blood and violence replaced by peace, harmony, and love. But they also refer to the political actuality: a healthy, vigorous prince who has hopes to continue his dynasty through royal marriage (love) provides for a land graced by peace and harmony. Albrecht Anthon's birthday is not a private celebration, but a public observance of an occasion which is for the public benefit.

The other pastoral of 1667, Hallmann's *Urania,* uses the pastoral disguise for another purpose, to demonstrate allegorically that man's focus should be on heavenly things rather than on earthly delights. Urania, whose name means contemplation of Heaven, is wooed by a crazed lover, in spite of the fact that she is a married woman. Here, as in *Cardenio und Celinde* and *Die Gelibte Dornrose,* the rejected lover tries to win love through the application of magic. But Urania remains true to the virtue of marital chastity, while in the choruses famous adulteresses of history are consigned to Hellfire. In the end, those crazed with love are cured and the virtuous are rewarded in a paean to the victory of *caritas* over *amor* (heavenly over earthly love). In the final chorus, the two mythological heroes symbolizing virtuous resistance to lust, Hercules at the crossroads and Ulysses tied to the mast as he listens to the Sirens, reiterate the triumph of chastity.

More successful is Hallmann's famous pastoral of 1673, *Adonis und Rosibella,* which he wrote for the marriage of the emperor Leopold to Claudia Felicitas. The love-lorn shepherdess pursues her beloved Adonis, but in vain, for this shepherd has joined in a cult worshiping Diana, the virgin goddess, and swears to emulate her life without love. But Venus, goddess of love, also has her adherents, and Rosibella joins in a plot to bring the enemies of love to their senses. Rosibella, like Sulpicius in Gryphius's *Verlibtes Gespenste,* feins death in order to capture her beloved's heart, then revives to enjoy the newly awakened love.

This play only seemingly contradicts the paean to chastity sung in *Urania,* for both plays are in favor of virtuous love and marriage. While the crazed wooers who love illicitly must be cured and converted to virtue, those who love virtuously will overcome all obstacles to union with the beloved. Like Sulpicius, whose "resurrection" from the dead cures illicit love and paves the way for virtuous marriage as an allegorical representation of Christ's divine love for the soul, Rosibella woos and wins love in return by her "death" and "resurrection."

This thematic treatment of love is appropriate for this play since it, too, celebrates a dynastic marriage. And certain facts concerning the particular background of this marriage find expression here. In the dedicatory poem, Hallmann claims that princes are shepherds of a sort, thus equating the marital deeds of his shepherds with those of the prince honored by the play and indicating that the events on the stage will be relevant to his situation. The prologue (*Vorspiel*) is an honorific musical/ballet which lauds Leopold and his bride. It uses word plays on the bride's name, Felicitas ("felicity," "blessedness," "happiness"), to indicate that she will bring these qualities to Leopold and that she is the heaven-sent reward for his patient virtue. It also makes reference to Leopold's European importance as a bastion against Turkish encroachment into Europe, as does the epilogue (*Nachspiel*), which terms him hope and shield of Christendom and which wishes for the defeat of Istanbul at his hands. The epilogue continues the *Felicitas*-thematics by means of an apotheosis of the imperial couple in a chariot drawn up to Heaven. And it connects this theme of the blessedness of marriage in the conflict between the personification of death (*Tod*) and the love god Cupid. Cupid, standing for both *amor* and *caritas* at once, defeats death. Death was, indeed, on the minds of the audience, for Leopold had recently buried his first wife. Thus the continuation of the dynasty in the form of a new marriage to a young and vigorous princess is celebrated by the victory of the partnership of divine and earthly love, marriage, over death. Even the conspiracy in the play to give chaste Diana the primacy may be a reference to fears that Leopold, a man of monkish training and tendencies, might refuse to embark on a second attempt at marriage. The victory of Venus and marriage is thus once again a statement to the effect that dynastic marriage is the basis of earthly harmony and political wisdom.

Allegorical Drama

While religious and/or political allegory can be shown to underlie most dramas of the period, whether tragedies, romantic comedies, or pastorals, several authors furnished examples of a type of drama which makes the allegories completely transparent. This allegorical drama uses significant names and invented plots which usually parallel the chief events of *Heilsgeschichte* to make its figural meanings clear. The translation of Jakob Masen's *Androfilo* in 1656 by Sigmund von Birken (discussed in Chapter 3) opens the chain of allegorical dramas in German, although Birken claims to have written his original one, *Psyche,* before he read Masen's.[16] But Harsdörffer's opera libretto *Das Geistliche Waldgedicht, oder Freudenspiel, genannt Seelewig* [The Spiritual Silvan Poem, or Comedy, Called Seelewig, 1644] belongs to this genre and thus actually precedes *Androfilo* and *Psyche.*

Seelewig seems to be a pastoral, but the author has stripped away most of the details designed to veil hidden meanings in pastoral drama, leaving only the allegorical kernel, plus a series of beautiful nature poems. Its simple plot depicts the attempts of the satyr Trügewalt ("deceptive power") to seize the nymph Seelewig ("eternal soul") through deception. His servant Sinnegunda ("the senses") and three shepherds with equally significant names conspire to lure her with pleasure, honor, and love, but her companions Gwissulda ("praise of conscience") and Herzigilda ("golden heart") rescue her. At the end she prays to God as a repentant sinner, and a chorus of angels promises salvation. The names are formed of old German roots, as Harsdörffer and Stieler advise, which give the clue to interpretation: the eternal soul is nearly perverted by the devil, but is rescued by her conscience and her loyalty to God, which convince her to turn her back on the glories and pleasures of this life and to seek God's forgiveness for her sins.

The presentation of the salvation of the soul here seems to be a criticism of Guarini's *Il Pastor fido,* for *Seelewig* attacks the values of that play by using the pastoral elements, but inverting their effect on the audience. The shepherds are not noble lovers who deservedly win the love of the noble shepherdesses through self-sacrifice, but henchmen of the devil-figure, the satyr. The echo dialogue does not constitute some kind of divine consolation to the shepherdess, but is a means the satyr uses to deceive her; he, not her noble lover or God, provides the echoes to her queries, and his answers are designed to lead her astray. The blind-man's-bluff game, during which a blindfolded Seelewig embraces the satyr, is a commentary on Guarini's blindfolded kissing game which playfully unites his two virtuous lovers. Love is here not an allegorical presentation of divine love, but of earthly love; to love earthly values threatens the salvation of the soul. Thus Harsdörffer makes a statement that he disapproves of the erotic pastoral play;

whether he understood its more veiled allegorical presentation is unclear. His *Seelewig,* which inaugurated the allegorical play in German literature, is his answer to the danger he perceived in pastoral drama.

Birken's *Psyche* (in Latin in 1652; translated and published in his *Rede-bind* of 1679) is a much more elaborate allegorization of *Heilsgeschichte* and is remarkably similar to Masen's *Androfilo.* Psyche ("the soul") and her brother Sarcander ("the body") are placed by Anarchus ("without beginning," God) in his farmyard, a veritable Garden of Eden. But the treacherous Alastor ("Lucifer"), who has been ejected from Heaven, seeks to subvert Psyche's virtue. Using deception and trickery, he manages to lure his victims into the forbidden grove, whereupon the garden is laid waste and a dragon, Death, is loosed on the world. But the Son of God, Theagenes, lowers himself to Psyche's human level by becoming a shepherd in order to rescue her, for he has long been enamored of her. He kills the dragon and drives off Alastor. He then leaves her while he makes preparations for the heavenly marriage, but promises to return soon. At the end, he does so, taking her from Cosmopel ("earthly city") to Uranopel ("heavenly city"). Once again the significant names give the clue to the allegorical deeds which although veiled are quite obviously parallels to the biblical events. The prologue speakers, Cupid ("earthly love") and Philanthropia ("divine love"), set the stage, for Cupid is accused of being a shameful pagan poem (that is, figment of the imagination) and is chased from the stage by an irate angel, Philanthropia, who then tells the members of the audience to seek Psyche's identity in their own breasts.

Caspar Stieler's comedy *Willmut* (1680) likewise belongs in the category of dramatic allegory. Willmut, a rash and headstrong young prince, chafes at the restraints his parents have put upon him, refuses to marry the princess they have chosen as his wife, and sets out instead to woo Scheingude. Eventually brought to his senses by his advisers, he comes to agree freely with his parents' wishes. In his *Vorsprache an den Leser* Stieler states that the meaning of his tale will be clear to all those who have sense for *Sittenkunst* (the art of proper behavior, "etiquette"), and that the prologue and epilogue speakers will help the reader/ audience to understand the play. But he here analyzes the meanings of the names of the characters to be certain that their significance will not escape the reader. The names of the king and queen, Adelheld and Redewinne, stand for understanding and reason, Willmut's name for the will (*voluntas*), his bride, Allguda von Seelewig, for the supreme good (*summum bonum*), the seductive Scheingude for the apparent good (*bonum apparens*) whose servant is Wunne, lust (*voluptas*). Willmut's three servants, who influence his original choice of vice and lust, represent his senses and sexual appetite, while the loyal advisers who come to his rescue are Kührmann, the free will, and Wahlbrecht, correct choice. The prologue speaker, Hercules, calls on the audience to discover the hidden truth in the play: *Greift nach dem Kern/ dem Absehn vom Gedicht!* ("Grasp for the kernel, the intention of the piece!" 12). At the end of the play, the epilogue speaker, Mercury, offers an analysis and allegorization which is completely superfluous by this time, even to a modern reader: Willmut as mankind has freedom of the will to choose wisely (heavenly orientation) or ill (earthly orientation); after first plunging into error he listens to reason and ultimately makes the choice which will be rewarded with salvation. Somewhat alienating in this allegory is the appearance of Stieler's omnipresent dramatic homunculus, Scaramutza, whose slapstick humor performs with its usual congenial coarseness and whose illusion-breaking techniques continually remind the audience that they are watching a play. But even Scaramutza receives an allegorical identity—*Wahn* ("delusion")—an ironically appropriate significance for the fool who creates and breaks illusions and at the same time demonstrates mankind's foibles.

Like tragedy, comic drama in the German seventeenth century thus exhibits a multitude of forms, but here the various manifestations receive distinguishing names—*Lust-* or *Schimpf-Spiel, Heldenspiel, Schäferspiel, Allegorie.* While Gryphius devotes his comic muse to satirical and romantic comedy, Stieler provides examples of romantic, pastoral, and allegorical comedies, and Hallmann confines himself to the pastoral play. Laughter is the emotional mechanism by which the satirical comedy affects its audience, while hope and joy for the attainment of religious or social/political goals are the results of the other types, in which humor may be relegated to the position of "comic relief."

Chapter Six
Festive and Musical Theater

Outside the strictures of the poetical treatises and literary tradition based on ancient theory and usage, a wealth of dramatic or semidramatic forms flourished in the court theaters and informal gatherings in the homes of the *literati—Festspiel,* ballet, fireworks, *Singspiel,* opera, and oratorio. Free of prescriptions and proscriptions, these genres could, and did, use and abuse the set dramatic forms, tragedy and comedy, with impunity; they could combine dramatic with other genres (narrative, oration, lyric, song); they could add music, often to the detriment of the verbal arts, but to the delight of the ear. Those performances designed for the courts could count on lavish expenditures to enhance the pleasure aroused by a total assault on the senses; the operas and the more operatic of the *Singspiele* and *Festspiele* constituted the first veritable *Gesamtkunstwerke,* art works which appealed to all the senses—visual, aural, tactile, olfactory—through the creation of a myriad of stimuli. Illusionistic stage design, elaborate costumes, titanic gestures, and dramatic lighting effects teased the eye. A variety of musical forms, instrumental, vocal, and choral, delighted the ear. Appropriate odors permeated the audience: incense, sulphurous fumes, perfume. Wonder at the miraculous stage effects, a sense of freedom derived from the suspension of the strictures of real time and space, loss of self in vicarious experiences of a romantic or heroic nature, pride in the self-image promoted by the prince—these are the results of the escapist intentions of this group of performing arts, seemingly so alien to the purposes of comedy as well as tragedy as depicted in this study. Yet even such apparently pure entertainment has a social and political function, if not always a religious or metaphysical one. As the courtly audience shares the pleasurable sensations aroused by the performance, it coheres into a single group united behind the purveyor of pleasure, the princely patron of the arts. His patronage demonstrates his magnanimity, his sensitivity, his affection for the group of people with whom he has surrounded himself; the production may augment this image by glorifying the prince or his ancestors directly.[1]

Festspiel

Important occasions at the great courts (Vienna, Munich, Dresden) traditionally required theatrical entertainment as a part of the festivities, and many of the lesser courts (notably Wolfenbüttel, Weimar, and Rudolstadt) followed suit. As has been shown, many tragedies and comedies were designed to be performed at such occasions, but the unofficial dramatic genres predominated. Preeminent among them from the point of view of polemical value is the *Festspiel,* which can be divided into two main types, mythological masque and genealogical play. The mythological masque was already popular in the early sixteenth century when it was brought to German courts by the Humanists, who had seen such performances in Italy, and it was revived after the turmoil of the Reformation and its prejudice against pagan gods receded late in the century. But the revived masque shows a different usage of mythology. Whereas the Humanist plays sought to flatter the prince through equating him with a mythological hero and to espouse certain princely virtues in the *exemplum* tradition, the Counter-Reformation and seventeenth-century Protestant usages tend to be allegorical. The Roman Gods stand for the abstract qualities most often associated with them (e.g., Mars is War, Pallas is Wisdom, Apollo is Art and Music, Jupiter is political wisdom or divine judgment, Venus is Lust, Cupid is Blind Love), and their interactions constitute a concretized conflict of abstractions. Examples of this genre in choruses or interludes of plays by Lohenstein (the Judgment of Paris, Hercules at the Crossroads) and Stieler (the *Zwischenspiel* for *Der Vermeinte Printz*) were already described above, but masques could also be isolated from "realistic" action and become plays in their own right. The many *Festspiele* celebrating the Peace of Westphalia and earlier attempts to end the Thirty Years War; Gryphius's *Majuma,* celebrating the coronation of Ferdinand III; and *La Contesa dell'Aria, e dell'Acqua,* designed for Leopold's first marriage, are the famous examples to be discussed here. In addition, the festival play designed by Lohenstein for the ancient Rome of his *Arminius* novel exemplifies the courtly mythological masque, and since it is depicted in a courtly setting, it demonstrates actual audience reaction and the use of the *Festspiel* in social situations.

The *Irenaromachia* of Ernest Stapel and Johann Rist (performed and published in Hamburg in 1630) is the first of a series of *Festspiele* celebrating apparent or real hopes for peace during the Thirty Years War. Rist himself provided two more of these masques, one in 1647 and another in 1652. The *Irenaromachia* typically posits a conflict between Irene, the goddess of peace sent down to the war-torn world by a benevolent Jupiter, and Mars, the god of war. Their battle is eventually fought in a courtroom scene presided over by Justitia, and a triumphant Irene leads Mars away in chains at the end. In the scene on Olympus at the beginning, however, the prevalent view of the war emerges: the devastation has been sent to earth by Nemesis as the deserved punishment for human sinfulness. Only the repentant humility of Germany can sway Jupiter to rescind the sentence imposed. And, in fact, this *Festspiel*, like the others of Rist, leaves the Olympian plane to descend to the earthly showplace where mankind's sinfulness is amply demonstrated in genre scenes depicting the inhumanity and vices of the lower spectrum of society, peasants and soldiers. The use of dialect for these scenes in the *Irenaromachia*, attributed to Rist, becomes a device used for village interludes in comedies from Gryphius's double comedy to Weise's *Niederländischer Machiavellus*, while the use of pagan gods as personifications of abstractions is to define the mythological masque for the remainder of the century. The peasants reject Irene, refusing her lodgings, thus making her eventual conquest of Mars a clear case of divine forgiveness.

While the *Irenaromachia* is written entirely in prose, writers of masques turned increasingly to verse due primarily to the addition of music. Gryphius's *Majuma*, written in 1653 to be performed *gesangsweise* in celebration of the coronation of Ferdinand IV as Roman king, uses a variety of verse forms, including alexandrines, alternating alexandrines and pentameter lines, four-beat and three-beat lines, but without resorting to the Italian madrigal form so well suited to the musical presentation of drama. The heartbroken nymph Chloris nearly abandons hope for the return of her lover Zephir (the West Wind), but he finally reappears to pledge his eternal love and report that he had been held captive in ice by the North Wind, Boreas. As an allegory for the return of spring after winter, this masque carries an appropriate theme for a celebration in the month of May; as a dual allegory for the return of peace and renewed confidence in the continuity of the Holy Roman Empire under German control, it carries an appropriate significance for a celebration of the election and coronation of the emperor's son to the position of assured heir to the empire. Political harmony is established, and the continuity of peace is assured. Mercury's praise of the coronation as *einen neuen May* ("a new Maytime") for the exceedingly joyful world ties these two allegorical meanings together in a paean of hope for an improved political situation in Germany.[2] As in the *Irenaromachia,* Mars has brought destruction to the earth (he has destroyed the heroine's garden)—an allusion to the Thirty Years War, which ended only five years earlier. With the help of Pan, god of idyllic pastoral life, Chloris, Maja, and Zephir capture Mars and set him to work guarding the revitalized garden in which they themselves become flowers—the threefold *Kaiser-Kronen* ("imperial crown flowers") representing the Holy Roman Empire—while Mars metamorphoses into the Habsburg eagle which guards the empire. The final chorus honors the newly crowned Ferdinand directly and calls upon him to preserve peace among Christians, retake Constantinople from the Turks, and follow the virtuous and heroic traditions of his ancestors through deeds and dynastic continuity.

Among the many *Festspiele* created for important occasions at the imperial court in Vienna, the one which stands out as the most spectacular was that performed to celebrate Leopold's marriage to the heiress of Spain, Margareta Theresia, in 1667 (designed in 1666). In this multi-media event, as described by Francesco Sbarra, Gottlieb Rinck,[3] and others, one section involves personifications of air, water, fire, and earth vying in a ballet on horseback amid extravagant floats, temporary architecture and earth sculpture, and fireworks. Sbarra provided the libretto, partly in Italian and partly in German, for operatic sections. Court composers wrote instrumental music for both the Spanish riding school "ballet" and the ballets danced by members of the court, including Leopold himself. Even Scaramuccia *der Kurtzweiller* ("the time shortener"), borrowed from the *commedia dell'arte,* French comedy, or even Stieler's Rudolstadt plays, entertained the audience with his satirical commentary. To commemorate the event and to glorify the emperor, who sought to outshine his French rival, Louis

XIV, Sbarra published descriptions, accompanied by lavish engravings, of the various phases of the entertainment.

Yet even that extravaganza was not produced only to give pleasure and evoke admiration, for political polemic abounds in various segments of the *Festspiel*. For example, in connection with the presentation of water in the battle of the elements, the myth of Jason and the Golden Fleece is performed. Jason and his Argonauts sail over the sea to the land where a monster guards the Golden Fleece. The king's daughter, Medea, helps Jason win the treasured fleece due to her love for him, and returns with him to his home, abandoning her own family. The golden fleece was a symbol firmly connected with the Habsburg dynasty by the mid-seventeenth century, and it has multiple layers of meaning in the context of the wedding to Margareta. Leopold's forebear, Maximilian I, had married Mary, heiress of Burgundy, and thereby brought control of the prestigious Order of the Golden Fleece to the Empire, as well as the wealthy state of Burgundy. In a polemical genealogy of the House of Habsburg (*Ostländischer Lorbeerhäyn*, Austrian Laurel Grove, 1657), Sigmund von Birken draws a parallel between this acquisition of a twofold "golden fleece" and another Habsburg dynastic marriage, that of Maximilian's son Philip to the heiress of Spain, Joanna the Mad, thus bringing a Spain made wealthy by the gold of the New World under Habsburg control. The marriage *Festspiel* celebrating Leopold's union with another heiress of Spain thus reuses this symbolism to indicate both the value of the marriage in material terms (it will keep the Spanish throne under Habsburg control by marrying the last of the Spanish line to the head of the German line) and the greatness of Leopold emulating the marital deeds of his illustrious ancestors whose dynastic marriages had led to the popular motto *Bella gerant alii, tu felix Austria nube* ("Let others wage war; you, blessed Austria, marry!"). The Golden Fleece may also symbolize the sanctity of dynastic marriage, for in an emblem of the period the fleece is interpreted as the salvation offered by Christ, the pascal lamb.[4] And the polemic of the Order of the Golden Fleece, which turns to two biblical accounts, those of Gideon's (Judges 6:36–40) and Jacob's fleece (Genesis 27:16), both signs of God's special grace and favor, provides further support for such a religious interpretation complementary to the political/dynastic significance of the marriage.[5]

A detailed account of the performance of a fictional mythological masque honoring the Roman Emperor Augustus on the occasion of the peace treaty between Germany and Rome appears in Lohenstein's monumental novel about German prehistory, *Großmütiger Feldherr Arminius oder Hermann* (written in the years before Lohenstein's death in 1683; published in 1689–90). This *Festspiel* takes the form of a triumphal procession, a frequent *topos* in both German Humanist and Italian 'Renaissance masques of the sixteenth century. The personifications of all the Roman provinces, bound with golden chains, are paraded past the viewers, Germania in last position and holding up the symbol of her pact with Rome. The personification of Rome claims supremacy over the previous world empires and demands obeisance from them. She avers that Roman conquest does not degrade the conquered peoples, but offers superior law, justice, and government, lowers taxes, and raises the level of responsibility and wisdom of the citizenry. Then the personifications *Glück* ("fortune") and *Tugend* ("virtue"), contest for supremacy. Fortune claims that when she allied herself with Rome after leaving the earlier three world monarchies in turn, she abandoned her inconstant Wheel of Fortune and acquired the anchor (= constancy) as an attribute. Victory (*Der Sieg*), too, allies itself with Rome, listing the other monarchies as mere stage stops on her way to Rome, who conquers due to her twin attributes, Fortune and Virtue. A golden age of peace, when the wolf (= Rome), lamb (= Christianity), lion (= Judaism), and rooster (= France?) will live in harmony, is prophesied; and this age will begin when Augustus closes the gates of the temple of Janus (= signal for the birth of Christ; see the interpretation of Lohenstein's *Cleopatra* in Chapter 4). As in contemporary *Festspiele,* the princely spectator, a fictionalized Tiberius, is urged to emulate his predecessor Augustus, who has laid the foundation for the fourth world monarchy and prepared the world for the advent of Christ through the establishment of universal peace and the extension of Roman law and citizenship to the entire world. Tiberius is exhorted to deserve divine support through adherence to virtue; his generals, also in the audience, are addressed by *der Sieg* ("Victory") and told that their future fame depends on the recognition that it is divinely ordained that the emperor be set over them; the provinces (German princes are in the audience as representatives of Germania) are exhorted to support Tiberius by being shown the futility of resistance in the face of the support of Divine Providence for his predecessor, Augustus, and Rome.

The German princes in the audience are chagrined to find the image of Germania in the group of Roman provinces honoring the emperor, for they had hoped to be treated as equals and friends after the treaty, not as a conquered province to be engulfed by the expansion of the Roman Empire. But the Romans have made their position clear in such a diplomatic and courteous fashion—Germania, depicted heroically as Hercules, wears a myrtle garland signifying freedom rather than golden chains—that the German princes swallow their objections, thus giving tacit approval to Germany's new status as a Roman province. The rules for courtly courtesy and the behavior of guests toward their host are thus used in the very *Festspiel* performed in their honor in order to entrap them. Theatrical performance thus accomplishes for the Romans what battles and peace conferences alone could not.

Two *Festspiele* which have survived the ravages of time represent another strain, the dramatized legend of a famous ancestor and presentation of the genealogy of the house of the prince honored by the play. Genealogical poems, works of art, and even processions had served to honor princes since the emperor Maximilian I (d. 1519) devoted most of his artistic patronage to genealogical commissions; but their dramatization awaited the theater-conscious milieu of the mid-seventeenth century. Lohenstein's choruses and "prophecies" honoring the House of Habsburg illuminate pseudogenealogical connections between the current imperial dynasty and the founders of the Roman Empire in the format of Baroque tragedy, but such genealogical polemic forms the very core of the two ancestor plays by Andreas Gryphius and Caspar Stieler. Gryphius's *Piastus* converts the story of a legendary ancestor into a Christian parable, while Stieler's *Die Wittekinden* depicts the foundation of the Schwarzburg dynasty in the form of a heroic comedy.

As in the case of his double comedy *Verlibtes Gespenste/ Die Gelibte Dornrose,* Gryphius seems to have written *Piastus* in 1660 for performance at the court of one of the Silesian dukes, this time Christian von Wohlau, on the occasion of the pregnancy of his wife, Louise—one of the last chances to provide for the continuation of the Piast dynasty and thus for the independence of this Protestant region from Catholic control. Jöns speculates[6] that the title refers not only to the name of the dynasty and its founder, but also to the name chosen for the unborn child, and that upon refusal of the Church to agree to the heathen name, the *Festspiel* was returned to a drawer, not to be published until 1698 in the *Nachlaß*.

To tenth-century Poland, persecuted by the proud and inhuman tyrant Popiel, God has sent two angels who are to attempt to convert him, and, failing that, to find a man worthy of being made king. When the angels, dressed as poor pilgrims, are chased from the castle as worthless vagabonds, they conclude that the servants who deride them must reflect the opinions of their master. Popiel fails the second test as well: as the invisible angels listen to his behavior in a decision-making session, during which he displays cruelty, heartlessness, and finally blasphemy, they consign him to his deserved punishment at the hands of Divine Retribution. They then set out, like Diogenes in mythology and in the *Irenaromachia,* to find one good human being. The determination will be made on the basis of decency and generosity to strangers. After being rejected by the powerful and the rich, the disguised angels are offered hospitality by the poor man Piastus. Much to his surprise, the meager food and drink he can offer multiplies as in the legendary accounts of magical tables and saddlebags or in Christ's miracle of the loaves and fishes. The manhood rites for his son on the following day become a city-wide festivity attended by the powerful and wealthy, including the twelve princes who will soon elect him king. The angels leave Piastus with a prophecy about the family tree of which he is to be the root, naming the famous rulers and heroes among his descendants, culminating in the three ducal brothers of the present and allusions to the unborn heir hoped for from Louisa's womb.

The short play (six acts in only 625 lines) honors the future heir and his parents by placing his birth in a continuity dating back some seven hundred years to the election of his legendary ancestor Piastus to kingship. The future heir thus joins an unbroken chain of rulers and heroes whose greatness will presumably influence his own character; and he, it is hoped, will be a link to future generations of Piast dukes, just as his illustrious ancestors were to him. He will join not only a dynasty of long secular tradition, but, as Gryphius's treatment of the legend demonstrates, a divinely sanctioned ruling family whose founder was selected by God's own emissaries. Surely such divine sanction in the past will protect the present representatives from the feared and threatened break in continuity due to lack of a surviving male heir, or so Gryphius hopes as he celebrates the expected birth in this play.

But, as one might expect from Gryphius, this play has other, more general functions as well. It is a *Fürstenspiegel* ("mirror of princes") which demonstrates through *exemplum* and precept the proper behavior of the ruler, and as such it is directed at the ducal audience and high-ranking guests. The tyrant Popiel is the epitome of the evil ruler: bloodthirsty, lacking in mercy, uninterested in the well-being of his subjects, and so proud of his own power that he is blind to the ultimate power over kingdoms and kings, God. Popiel's behavior prompts the angels to comment on the qualities of a good ruler in several precepts: he is accessible to the complaints of his subjects and hospitable to strangers. When Popiel persists in his evil ways, and ultimately challenges God himself to reveal His power *wofern er kan* ("insofar as He is able"), the angels call on Divine Retribution, who then appears, personified, in a barrage of fireworks to damn Popiel for his pride and guilt and to predict a gruesome end: he will be devoured by mice. The angels later tell the moral of Popiel's story to Piastus, the future ruler:

Liebe denn vor allem Tugend; spiegel dich an Popels Ende/
Schütze die man unterdrucket/ habe rein und milde Hände.   (6:21–22)

(So love virtue above all; learn from Popiel's end:
Protect those who are oppressed, have innocent and mild hands.)

Gryphius's parable portrays life as a test in which man does not recognize his divine examiners until he has already revealed his virtue or vice and thus already passed or failed the test. The lesson to be learned is twice explicitly stated: *Jeder schau auf Gott und sich* ("Each should perceive God and himself," 1:120; also 1:14–15). Recognition that God is omniscient and that He has established life as a test of virtue, coupled with recognition of one's own limits and mortality, will lead mankind to salvation.

Contrary to the prevailing opinion that *Piastus* was suppressed, the appearance of a similar genealogical play some six years later seems to imply performance, or at least circulation in manuscript, of the unpublished Gryphius *Festspiel* shortly after its creation. Caspar Stieler's *Die Wittekinden* (1666) is a full-length play and has comic elements, but otherwise conforms to the form and purpose of *Piastus*. The elder Wittekind, leader of the heathen Saxons defeated and converted by Charlemagne, is now general of Charlemagne's armies fighting the Saracens in Spain. In his absence from court, several of Charlemagne's French nobles, jealous of the emperor's preference for Wittekind and of Countess Brechta's love for him, plot to discredit and overthrow the Saxon hero. They spread rumors of his defeat and death, and report the apparent treason of his young and confused sons. Wittekind returns in glory, the French nobles are unmasked but forgiven, and the hero's sons, the younger Wittekind and Walprecht, convert to Christianity after a miraculous vision. The elder Wittekind receives Anjou as hereditary duchy to be passed down to his children by his new wife, Brechta, while his sons Wittekind and Walprecht receive the duchies of Schwarzburg and Gleichen. A series of tableaux introduces the famous rulers and heroes who followed Wittekind, culminating in a sort of dramatized ancestor cabinet (small room in many princely houses of the time containing busts or statues of ancestors).

Like *Piastus, Die Wittekinden* serves to honor the princely patron on a festive occasion, in this case the twenty-fifth birthday of Albrecht Anthon. The depiction of the count's heroic ancestor and the miraculous events surrounding the founding of the Schwarzburg principality—the receipt of the feudal lien directly from Charlemagne as a reward for service for the Christian faith on the part of the newly converted Saxon warrior and the divine vision which effected the conversion to Christianity of the younger Wittekind—portray the divine sanction the dynasty had from its very outset. Coupled with the series of illustrious ancestors presented in tableau "visions" at the end of the play, this depiction of a dynasty in its entirety functions to express the basis for political stability in the principality: divine sanction and dynastic continuity in the person of the ruler, whose health, and thus the health of the state, is celebrated on his birthday.

Rather than merely presenting the glory and conversion of the illustrious ancestors, Stieler adds elements which place the ancestor play in the fabric of a typical Italianate comedy—an intrigue which threatens the honor and happiness of the hero and a subplot concerning the wooing of the ubiquitous Scaramutza. The elder Wittekind, apparently a widower, has been given the hand of Brechta, countess of Blois, as a reward for his services to Charlemagne, and she loves him with a tender and chaste passion. The jealous Burckhardt, who tries to woo her

in his absence and is rejected, attempts to convince her that he is dead
by providing a poem full of such lies to the itinerant *Flugschrift* poet
Michael (singer of crude broadsheet songs on newsworthy themes and
events). Brechta believes the tragic "news" and falls into a seemingly
mortal decline rather than, as Burckhardt had hoped, into his waiting
embrace. Burckhardt's henchman Robert goads the hero's sons into
hatching treasonous plots against the emperor which he reports, causing them to be thrown into prison. Even Scaramutza, who has the
misfortune to be attacked by Burckhardt as he attempts to enter his
beloved Blonje's chamber for a midnight rendezvous, languishes in
prison. But Wittekind returns unannounced from his battles against
the Saracens in Spain to effect the "cure" of the joyous Brechta, the
release of the prisoners, and the forgiveness of the repentant *Intriganten.*
The apparently tragic ending is unmasked as a network of deception,
and hope and joy are the results.

Opera

By far the most successful theatrical genre of all time, if one is to
judge by the number of performances and published texts, is the opera.
K. G. Just claims that some 30,000 libretti have been published since
the first one in 1600.[7] Opera was so popular that within fifty years, in
spite of the ravages of war, Vienna had five opera houses, in addition to
the court and public theaters and the Jesuit stage. In Munich by 1650
opera had replaced the local Jesuits in the court theater; an opera house
opened in Hamburg in 1678. Adding to the quick spread of opera after
1650 in Germany, Emperor Ferdinand III brought along an entire opera
production when he journeyed to the *Reichstag* (imperial parliament) in
Regensburg in 1653 and had it performed before the admiring princes
and nobles gathered there. Braunschweig and Hamburg in the North
were centers for librettists and composers in the fourth quarter of the
seventeenth century, while Vienna and Munich tirelessly patronized
the new form of theatrical entertainment.

The first opera was designed in Florence in 1594 by a group of *literati*
who theorized that the Greek tragedies had originally been sung in
their entirety, and who wished to found a modern dramatic form based
on that theory. The result was *Dafne,* with a text by Ottavio Rinuccini
set to music by Giulio Caccini and Jacopo Peri. The earliest operas used

recitatives, but within a few years the aria began to intrude and the recitative sections to recede (e.g., Monteverdi's *Orfeo,* 1607). *Dafne* was translated into German by Martin Opitz as his second contribution to the making of models for German dramatic forms and performed in 1627 to music by Heinrich Schütz (score now lost). The first original German libretto was apparently that for the allegorical opera *Seelewig* by Harsdörffer (1644, discussed in Chapter 5). Not only is the score by Siegmund Staden appended; the subtitle states that it was presented *Gesangweis auf Italienisch Art gesetzet* ("set to vocal music in the Italian style") and the list of characters gives both an identifying tag and the voice type of the singer who plays each part. The musical instruments needed for particular scenes are also specified.

The scope of this study will not allow treatment of opera or other mixed forms as *Gesamtkunstwerke,* and thus only the texts of *Seelewig* and other operas and oratorios will be discussed here. Subject matter, plot, verse form, language, textual interpretation, and theatrical elements will be the chief concerns. The verse forms of *Seelewig* betray two basic structures, recitative (in alexandrine, five-beat, or four-beat lines) and song or aria (shorter lines, often grouped into strophes). There is no narrator, and the actions and reactions are carried totally in the monologues (in song form), dialogues (recitative or song), and ensembles. The prologue and epilogue, sung, respectively, by *Singkunst* ("Art of Singing") and *Mahlkunst* ("Art of Painting"), present Harsdörffer's theories about opera as a *Gesamtkunstwerk* to which the musical, verbal, and visual arts all contribute equally.

Opitz's *Dafne* is the first German *opera pastorella,* Harsdörffer's *Seelewig* the first of many allegorical operas. Other types also roughly correspond to dramatic genres discussed in this study: *opera seria* ("tragedy"), *opera buffa* ("satirical comedy"), and *opera comica* ("italianate comedy"). One of the most famous operas of the period, *Il Pomo d'oro,* was designed as a *Festspiel* to be performed for the marriage of Emperor Leopold in 1667. No effort was spared in its creation: the chief court librettist, Francesco Sbarra, wrote the Italian verses, the court composer Marc Antonio Cesti provided the music, and some 100,000 *Reichstaler* ("imperial dollars") were spent on the creation of the set for the performance in 1668. The plot, derived from Greek mythology, originally explained the causes of the Trojan War: Priam's son Paris is doomed by the gods to award the golden apple of discord to the most beautiful of three quarreling goddesses, Juno, Athena, and Venus. When Venus promises him the most beautiful woman in the world, Helen, Paris offers her the apple. But in the opera Jupiter ends the discord and war caused by Paris's choice by taking the apple from the goddesses and offering it to the new empress. The opera was apparently reused for Leopold's third marriage—to Eleonora in 1676—with but slight adjustments. The court historian Priorato wrote an account of the marriage celebration to send to personages who could not attend,[8] including engravings of the decorations, one of which depicts the hand of God emerging from the sky to hand a globe to the three goddesses. Priorato points out that Eleonora, the new empress, is Leopold's third wife, and that the three goddesses thus now represent all three spouses, each of whom was handed the *Reichsapfel* ("imperial apple" or sphere signifying world empire) by the emperor, whose own possession of it was divinely ordained. Thus the libretto now honors the beauty of Eleonora, alludes to her position as third wife, and transforms the apple of discord into the imperial symbol of divinely ordained power, thereby contrasting Paris's disastrously foolish choice to Leopold's dynastic marriage(s) based on Christian virtue and political wisdom. The fame of the opera was so great that it earned mention in Birken's poetic treatise (325), and the libretto was translated into German by Caspar Stieler at the request of Duke Johann Ernst of Weimar.[9] Some fourteen years later, the anonymous pamphlet celebrating the joint coronation of Eleonora and the heir she produced (Joseph)[10] reused the imagery from the imperial marriage in a continuation of this allegory: Eleonora is all three goddesses in one and, in her position as third wife, is *dreyfach Erbenreich gekrönt* ("crowned thrice with heirs," her three children). Leopold was fortunate and wise enough to be able to offer his golden apple to the best qualities of all three goddessess (= government, wisdom, and love) at once, as embodied in Eleonora. His third attempt at dynastic marriage has succeeded in bringing an end to speculations about the succession; the "apple of discord" has truly metamorphosed into the *Reichsapfel* of imperial power—political stability. Thus opera and *Festspiel* merge in an apotheosis of the Holy Roman Empire.

   One of the centers of opera in Northern Germany, the courts of the dukes of Braunschweig/Wolfenbüttel, could boast of a ducal librettist, Anton Ulrich, a literary talent whose efforts as novelist and poet place him among the most important Baroque poets. Between 1656 and

1667 he wrote at least ten libretti, most of which were set to music by the court musician Johann Jacob Löwe. The text of his *Daniel* (1663),[11] performed for the eighty-fifth birthday of his father, closely resembles Harsdörffer's *Seelewig,* except that the recitative sections of dialogue carry more of the action than do the arias. Wolfenbüttel/Braunschweig was also a center for the *Singeballet* or *Balletoper,* a mixture of two genres. One example, F. C. Bressand's *Doppelte Freude der Musen* [Twofold Joy of the Muses, 1695],[12] was performed to honor Anton Ulrich on his sixty-second birthday. The other North German center of opera was Hamburg, and there, under the leadership of Christian Heinrich Postel, the German libretto (set to music by Reinhard Keyser) finally freed itself from the alexandrine verse inherited from Baroque tragedy and used a shorter and more flexible verse for the recitative sections.

From around 1600 on, many German dramatists used music in their verse comedies, although not to the exclusion of spoken dialogue. The first German to do so, Jakob Ayrer, who claims to have been influenced by the English Comedians, terms such musical comedies *Singspiele,* and this term can be used for many musical comedies of the seventeenth century (e.g., Stieler's *Die Wittekinden,* Gryphius's *Verlibtes Gespenste* and *Majuma*). The music, usually in the form of songs, is thought to have used tunes already known to the audience in other contexts, which accounts for the lack of musical notation. While there is no unanimity about the definition of the *Singspiel,* a term whose meaning is further confused by its use in the significance of *operetta* or light opera in the eighteenth century, in the seventeenth century it most often was applied to dramatic works with songs and music interspersed, in which the spoken text received the most emphasis—unlike the opera, which tended within several decades after its first appearance to stress the musical presentation at the expense of the text.

Oratorio

The least specifically courtly and most serious of the unofficial dramatic genres is the oratorio, which likewise uses musical presentation. Its origins lie in the public "performances" of biblical texts offered by the Counter-Reformation lay brotherhoods sponsored by the Jesuits in Italy. The title of the genre derives from the name of the building designed for these brotherhoods, the *oratorium* (e.g., the oratorio of San

Felippo Neri in Rome). But the popular opera increasingly influenced both music and format. The early Catholic performances of predominantly Old Testament texts involved musical presentation, but not the visual effects of a true dramatic performance. The protagonists were the reader/singer of the text and the chorus—narrator and commentator, respectively—both aspects of narrative or epic presentation, not dramatic representation. At the imperial court in Vienna, performances of oratorios sung in Italian were extremely popular throughout the seventeenth century and until the death of Charles VI in 1740; the musical emperor, Leopold I, even contributed several of his own design.

When Protestants finally turned to the oratorio, they altered its format and its function in a substantial way. Instead of narrating Old Testament stories, they used the oratorio to present the Easter and Christmas events from the Gospels as a replacement for the Passion Plays and liturgical dramas which once accompanied the appropriate masses of the liturgical year. Since the oratorio needed no stage or special effects, it could move the performance of the deeds of Christ back into the church or meeting room of pious groups. But the narrative character of the Italian tradition was rejected in favor of a more dramatic and operatic representation: to the narrator and commentator the Protestant composers added the monologue and dialogue, the aria and the duet. The personages of the New Testament—Mary, the disciples, Herod, Pilate, and Jesus himself—now are portrayed musically, although still not theatrically, by individual singers.

The early Protestant oratorios had little room for a poet or librettist, for they were expected to use the exact words of the *Evangelium,* Luther's New Testament, for which the music provided a setting. Heinrich Schütz, who introduced this genre in 1623, framed the biblical text, spoken to a simple instrumental arrangement, with a-capella choruses sung by a boys' choir. At appropriate moments, well-known church hymns were introduced, and the audience was expected to join in. This participatory form of the oratorio was thus closely allied to the format of the Protestant church service and accordingly was even further from dramatic performance than its Italian models. The decisive change in favor of the poetic and the dramatic came about due to a new musical form, the cantata, a song for a soloist to which biblical passages, reformed into verse, could be set.[13] This principle, applied to the texts used in the oratorio, resulted in a potential for dramatization and an interest on the part of poets in writing libretti. Poets like Neumeister, Hunold, Reuter, and Brockes provided appropriate verses or even entire libretti for the new oratorio in the opening years of the eighteenth century.

Christian Reuter's *Passions-Gedanken* [Passion Meditation, 1708; music originally by Johann Theil] represents perhaps the purest form of the new oratorio libretto. It consists of solo paraphrases of the biblical narration by the Evangelist, comments by two choruses, and monologues by the protagonists—Jesus, Judas, Petrus, Caiphas, Pilatus, etc.—closely modeled on direct discourse from the text. True dramatic dialogues, however, are not allowed to take place, for the Evangelist intrudes with his narration between the solos of the protagonists.

Dramatic interchanges do occur in B. H. Brockes's *Der Für die Sünde der Welt/ Gemarterte und Sterbende Jesus* [Martyred Jesus, Dying for the Sins of the World, 1712], although the Evangelist/narrator still is responsible for the movement of the action. A typical dramatic scene begins with the Evangelist's account of Jesus' walk to the Mount of Olives and ends with the requisite narrative introduction of direct discourse: *Woselbst Er dann zu Seinen Jüngern sprach* ("Whereupon he spoke to his disciples"). Jesus states that one of the disciples will betray him, the chorus of disciples replies with an avowal of loyalty, and Jesus recites the appropriate Old Testament prophecy which will be fulfilled by the betrayal. Peter then professes his intention to remain faithful, and Jesus answers that Peter himself will betray him three times before the cock crows twice. Peter swears that he will not, and Jesus leaves them to talk with his Heavenly Father. This little dramatic scene is followed by the soliloquy/aria of Jesus praying. And indeed, even in the soliloquies, the presentation is predominantly dramatic rather than narrative in nature, as is especially clear in the case of the role of Petrus. Intermingled with the Evangelist's narration of his betrayal, feelings of guilt, and grief, the arias of the future founder of the Church directly demonstrate an inner process rather than merely narration or commentary as in earlier oratorios. The way has been paved for the great musical theater of the disembodied voice exemplified in Bach's *St. Matthew's Passion* and Händel's *Messiah*. The commentators—the choruses of the Christian churches and of the Believing Souls, the Daughter of Zion, and *Die gläubige Seele,* the leader of the group of the Believing Souls—

fulfill in this oratorio the same function as the chorus of captive
Christians in Gryphius's *Catharina von Georgien*; but the nontheatrical
elements—lack of visual representation and the intrusions of the narrating Evangelist—separate the mature oratorio libretto from its dramatic
cousins.

Before the middle of the seventeenth century, one author, Johann
Klaj, created a variant of the oratorio which remains anomalous among
Baroque poetic forms: the *Redeoratorio* ("spoken oratorio"). Between
1644 and 1650, apparently at the instigation of his mentor Harsdörffer,
Klaj wrote six semidramatic performances of the great New Testament
events, the birth, passion, and resurrection of Christ, and the apocalyptic battle of angels and dragons from Revelations. Like the musical
oratorio, Klaj's *Redeoratorien* offer a mixture of narration, commentary,
and action. Brief passages from the biblical text are followed by longer
poeticized and versified narrations of events interspersed with commentary (in alexandrine verse); the protagonists recite versified monologues
and dialogues (in songlike or madrigal versification); and the sung
choruses—sometimes the words of protagonists also furthering the
action—provide a running commentary or reaction to the events. Like
the early Protestant oratorios of Schütz and others, Klaj's *Redeoratorien*
depict New Testament events; unlike the others, however, Klaj follows
Catholic practice in creating an original libretto which transforms the
prose Bible text into poetry. And although the four acts are surrounded
by musical choruses which utilize voice and instruments, the main text
is designed for declamation, not song or even musical recitation.
Flemming claims that the original performances did not underline the
dramatic tendencies, but rather bordered on epic narration, for Klaj
apparently recited all the nonmusical roles himself rather than assign-
ing parts to several speakers.[14] As one might expect, the stress in the
Redeoratorien is on verbal rather than musical presentation and felicity;
the resulting poetry is one of the most attractive groups of literary
works of the period.

Herodes, der Kindermörder [Herod the Infanticide, 1645] stands out
among these works perhaps because, as Klaj claims in the subtitle, it is
written *nach Art eines Trauerspiels* ("in the manner of tragedy"). For a
Christmas oratorio Klaj here chooses to focus attention on one of the
peripheral events which had also fascinated the makers of Passion Plays
in the late Middle Ages, the "slaughter of the innocents" at the hands of

a crazed King Herod in the vain attempt to eliminate the newborn
Christ child. The paranoid king of Judea, hearing from the three wise
men who have followed the star in search of the Christ child that He is
to be a king of kings, fears a threat to his earthly crown. The full horror
of Herod's order to kill all the male babies in Judea is portrayed through
the anguished speeches of their mothers as well as in rather graphic
narrative passages. Herod is the typical arch-tyrant of Baroque tragedy,
motivated only by pride, paranoia, and political expediency and lacking
in human kindness, ethics, and common sense. Like most Baroque
tyrants, he is haunted by ghosts of his victims (the ghost of his wife,
Mariamne, promises Hellfire) and by his own conscience, as a foretaste
of the Divine Retribution to come. And the ultimate justice of Divine
Providence already makes itself known in that the Christ child has
escaped slaughter and has arrived safely out of his reach in Egypt. The
oratorio ends with a personified Germany pleading, like the Jewish
mother Rahel, for an end to the "slaughter of the innocents" being
perpetrated currently in the form of the Thirty Years War, thus allying
this work to the early Irenistic *Festspiele*. Here even the liturgical
calendar and the Protestant progeny of the medieval Passion play are
made to participate in a polemical appeal for peace.

The other *Redeoratorio* which demands individual treatment here is
Freudengedichte Der seligmachenden Geburt Jesu Christi [Happiness Poem
of the Salvation-Bringing Birth of Jesus Christ, ca. 1650], for it
likewise strains the form of the religious oratorio to provide political
commentary. Along with the traditional events associated with the
birth of the Savior—the Annunciation, the journey of Mary and Joseph
to Bethlehem, the worship of the angels and shepherds, and the arrival
of the three wise men—Klaj has mingled events from secular history.
The Roman Emperor Augustus recounts recent world events involving
bloodshed and war, then announces a change in policy: he intends to
shut the gates of the Temple of Janus for the third time, a signal of
world-wide peace, and lay aside weapons and conquest to concentrate
on self-conquest and self-improvement in the form of reason, wisdom,
humility, justice, and law. As a first step in unifying the world under
Roman control, he proclaims a universal census and taxation for which
every citizen must proceed to the city of his birth. The narrator then ties
these "secular" events to the birth of Christ by showing that it is for this
reason that Mary and Joseph find themselves on their way to Bethlehem

where the Holy Child will be born. A chorus of Romans recites the list of omens associated with Christ's birth: fountains of oil, cracking temples, falling idols, and a vision of the holy mother and child on a heavenly altar. Thus Klaj, like Lohenstein, sets biblical events into their secular framework, and the result is *Heilsgeschichte,* the progress of universal salvation in human history.

While Klaj does not explicitly link the Rome of Augustus to that of the Holy Roman Empire, the connection between the two is ubiquitous in the traditional historical accounts on which his material is based. But his purpose in using this framework may be different from that of Lohenstein, for at the time this oratorio was written the celebrations of the end of the Thirty Years War were still underway, and the dual story of Christ and Augustus as princes of peace, authors of the coincidental *pax christiana* and *pax augusta,* would be entirely appropriate. Just as pacification of the world under Rome and Augustus prepared the way for the birth of Christ, so the celebration of the anniversary of His birth is augmented by the end of hostilities among Christians in Europe; only in such a peaceful climate, in fact, can the full joy be experienced anew in emulation of that first Christmas; conversely, the celebration of Christmas, the onset of a new spiritual *pax christiana,* is the liturgical event best suited to express Germany's joyful relief after three decades of war.

Thus, in a sense, all the unofficial dramatic forms, with the exception, perhaps, of the musical oratorio, can participate in a political polemic which does not distinguish between religious and secular events or between *delectare et docere,* and few can be disregarded as mere flattery or pure entertainment. Like the officially sanctioned forms of dramatic performance, tragedy and comedy, the major forms appearing on the festive stages of Germany's courts fulfill crucial social, political, and religious/metaphysical functions. And they continue to provide pleasure at festive courtly occasions throughout the eighteenth century (cf. Goethe's *Paläophron und Neoterpe,* performed for the birthday of the Duchess Amalia of Saxony-Weimar in 1800).

Chapter Seven

The Rhetorical Theater: Prose Tragedy and School Drama

Throughout the seventeenth century there existed in Germany a type of drama which resembled that of the itinerant theater in its use of prose and of coarsely comic scenes, but which shared the moralizing and educational purposes of the *Kunsttragödie* and *Komödie*. The rhetorical tragedy aspires neither to verse nor to elevated speech, but imitates actual usage, and in so doing it disregards the many admonitions of Opitz and other theorists of the literary Baroque to use verse and elevated language, avoid foreign words, treat the German language in a creative and innovative manner, use rhetorical devices and imagery for embellishment, or provide a hidden meaning. It intersperses comic scenes in dialect which, as in the itinerant theater, tend to overpower the serious scenes, although they may now carry complementary or parallel "morals of the story." The comedies are usually of the satirical sort, as befits their didactic function, and are thus not as different from the *Kunstkomödie* as are the prose tragedies, except that they tend to diffuse the focus from a single person or couple to the scattered representatives of the entire spectrum of society in a plot which is necessarily episodic rather than Aristotelian or linear. The biblical dramas provide a link to sixteenth-century school drama, thus indicating some kind of continuity into the late seventeenth century, albeit limited to this peripheral dramatic genre.

Older scholarship tended to view the most famous and prolific of the creators of didactic prose drama, Christian Weise (1642–1708), as one of the opponents of the "second Silesian School" (seen to include Lohenstein, Hoffmannswaldau, Hallmann, and Haugwitz). Some recent studies demonstrate that his dramas participate instead in a tradition dating back to the middle of the Thirty Years War, if not to Heinrich Julius von Braunschweig on the very threshold of the seventeenth century. The dramas of this tradition, heavily influenced by the plays of the English Comedians, do not constitute a literary movement based on disagreement with Opitz's vision of an elevated literary product, but rather a continual theatrical activity designed with primarily practical rather than aesthetic purposes in mind—to teach rhetoric, or the art of public speaking, to amateur actors (primarily schoolboys). One theorist, Daniel Georg Morhof, whose poetical treatise appeared only a few years after Christian Weise began his dramatic production, recognizes that the distinctiveness of this dramatic genre from *Kunstdrama* derives from its pedagogical purpose. He names Johann Rist and Filidor (Caspar Stieler) as two prominent authors of the genre.[1] Unless he was acquainted with works of Filidor presently unknown, his relegation of Stieler's prose comedies to this category is based on misapprehension, for, as this study has tried to demonstrate, the latter's Rudolstadt plays had polemical and even allegorical functions, not didactic or rhetorical. Use of prose alone cannot have been his criterion, for Morhof refers to Gryphius's prose comedies as good examples of the *Kunstkomödie*. But Johann Rist's dramatic production—the irenistic *Festspiele* and his tragedy, *Perseus*—do indeed constitute the models for later prose dramas of the rhetorical type.

Johann Rist

While most of the later representatives of the didactic prose tragedy genre were associated with the standard educational method of teaching schoolboys polite speech and manners, political wisdom, and moral behavior through participation in theatrical performances designed and directed by school rectors, the play which provided the model emulated throughout the century, Johann Rist's *Perseus* (1634), was not a school drama. It seems to have been designed for courtly or civic performance, perhaps using schoolboys as actors; but its primary function was apparently to acquire for its author patronage and/or a secure position—possibly as a school rector.[2] Rist comments in his foreword on the function of drama, and while he repeats Opitz's theories from the *Poetery* and foreword to *Die Trojanerinnen* practically verbatim, even though he does not follow them, his discussion of the *delectare et docere* principle does not conform with Opitzian theory.[3] Not only does he stress the entertainment function in a most anti-Opitzian manner—perhaps due to his attendance at performances by English Comedians—but he also evolves a theory of the usefulness of dramatic performance which is decidedly didactic. Rist lists five pedagogical benefits to be gained by the actors (obviously not itinerant professionals): their judgment and understanding will be enhanced by acquaintance with so many excellent histories and stories; they will learn to be enemies of the vices depicted by the comic and evil characters and to emulate the virtues of the heroic and noble characters they portray; their memories will be improved by the memorization of lines; they will improve their ability at public speaking and diction; and they will acquire admirable manners, overcome shyness, and be prepared to state their opinions boldly in any company. The spectators, who in Opitzian theory are the persons primarily to be affected by the play, however, are of secondary interest to Rist, who only notes, following Opitz, that a picture is worth a thousand words.

The play, based on an anecdote told by Livy, recounts the bloodbath surrounding the accession of Perseus to the throne of Macedonia. The deaths, which involve the execution of a prince, two murders, and five suicides, include the worst of capital crimes: responsibility for the deaths of a brother and a father. Perseus, the elder son of Philip of Macedonia, is jealous of his brother Demetrius because of his success in wooing and in battle games, and he plots to bring his younger brother into disfavor. When Demetrius is removed from the scene (Perseus contrives to have him sent to Rome as a hostage guaranteeing peace), Perseus woos his fiancée, Eudocia. Her rejection of his suit leads to persecution which culminates in the suicide of herself, her brother, and her father. Upon Demetrius's return, Perseus convinces their father that Demetrius had plotted the king's death, and thus brings about his execution; but Philip soon repents, turning against Perseus, who murders him and the uncle to whom Philip now wished to give the crown. Perseus's Machiavellian politics have finally won him the coveted crown, but he does not live long to enjoy it before his guilty conscience, ghosts, and demons torment him to the point of taking his own life. His ally, the fellow conspirator Dido, like the biblical traitor Judas, has already hanged himself in despair. The background of this depiction of the illicit rise to power and precipitous fall of a tyrant is the same that is to be found in the later tragedies of Lohenstein—attempted rebellion against Rome.

Like the northern itinerant theater and unlike the Silesian *Kunsttragödie, Perseus* is written in a contemporary prose reflecting the fashions of courtly bureaucracy: stilted and stiff, filled with socially proper forms of address, euphemisms, and French expressions, demonstrating that sort of rhetoric which demands complicated circumlocutions and avoidance of direct confrontation, pretentious without achieving the stylistic elevation demanded by Opitz. Like the English Comedians, Rist adds a wealth of comic scenes involving, in this case, the army recruiter Hans Knapkäse, his simpleminded recruits, and the clever village maiden, but he enhances their effectiveness by the use of low German dialect and he links them thematically to the main action, as well as to contemporary events. Hans Knapkäse, whose name connects him with Hans Wurst and the comic figures of the *Wanderbühne,* exhibits a coarseness which vies with the vilest of English clowns in terms of profanity of speech, scatological and vulgar sexual references, and black comedy (e.g., he wants to shoot the poor fiancée and her brother and father, who lie in a pool of blood already, having just pathetically taken their own lives in a tear-jerking scene). The tragic love story, the use of character types, and the gruesome deaths portrayed on stage rather than relegated to reports all link Rist's *Perseus* to the English Comedians, as do his borrowings from the collections of *Wanderbühne* plays of 1620 and 1630[4] and his use of moralizing direct address to the audience. Yet unlike these, *Perseus* lacks real dramatic dialogue and conflict in the serious segments, where each speech is a lengthy exposition of a point of view—a miniature oration or, at most, a response in an organized pedagogical debate—rather than a constituent part of a conversational dialogue. And certain speeches, rather than deriving from those of the typical tyrant of the *Haupt- und Staatsaktion,* seem to be modeled on Heinrich Julius's *Vincentius Ladislaus,* the braggart and exaggerator, or on the corresponding tradition in the *commedia dell'arte* or Humanist drama. Likewise, the introduction of Lurco the parasite, a comic type alien to the English Comedians, indicates influence from the *commedia dell'arte,* Humanist drama, ancient comedy, or Jesuit theater.

Rist's opposition to the ongoing Thirty Years War is clear in this work, just as in the various peace plays, and it emerges in both the main action and in the comic interludes. Perseus's desire to rebel against the Roman Empire must be seen as a criticism of those who presently fight the Holy Roman Empire (in spite of Rist's position as a North German Protestant). The warnings of a wise adviser about the dangers and evils involved in raising an army surely also echo Rist's own sentiments. On the other hand, the lies and ploys by which Hans Knapkäse deceives a naive peasant boy into enlisting and the inadequacy of the other specimens Hans manage to recruit (one has a game leg, the other only one eye) constitute a commentary upon current practices, while their unquestioning support of the tyrant Perseus provides further condemnation of the political absolutism which must rely on a mercenary and therefore patently amoral army.

Johann Sebastian Mitternacht

The next dramatist to produce prose didactic dramas meritorious or fortunate enough to arouse the attention of scholars was Johann Sebastian Mitternacht, rector of a *Gymnasium* in Gera. While only two of his dramas were published, he mentions in a preface that he has authored several dozen, some in Latin but most in German, for performance by the boys in his school. His two published plays probably represent the norm of the didactic prose school drama as practiced throughout the century.[5]

Mitternacht's *Trauer-Spiel/ Der Unglückselige Soldat Und Vorwitzige Barbirer/ genant* [Tragedy Called the Unfortunate Soldier and the Inquisitive Surgeon, 1662] is the tale of a prodigal son who rejects his father's plans for him to become a scholar and instead joins the army as a mercenary, only to desert after becoming disillusioned. On his way home, however, he is kidnapped by a vivisectionist who dissects him alive in order to discover the mechanism of the circulation of the blood. The moral of the story is clear: schoolboys who do not obey their parents and teachers come to a bad end, for God is not always so merciful to the thankless and rash as he was in the biblical parable. Mitternacht also exploits the grisly end of his prodigal in order to damn the godlessness and *superbia* of the New Science which relied on experimentation and observation rather than on revealed truth. Commentary on the action is provided by a philosopher who appears after each act as a kind of sermonizing chorus. Comic interludes have few set speeches, but apparently end each act with the semiextemporaneous slapstick of the itinerant stage—a frivolity which Mitternacht chooses not to preserve in his published versions.

The play has captured the interest of recent scholars who are delighted to find there the seeds of the *Bürgerliches Trauerspiel* ("bourgeois tragedy") due to flower a century later. The source is a newspaper story; the main characters are from the educated professional class—a merchant's son and a barber/surgeon—rather than the kings or potentates demanded by Opitz and apparent in all *Kunsttragödien* except for the problematical *Cardenio und Celinde.* But in his defense of his usage in the preface, Mitternacht unwittingly reveals his lack of sophistication and understanding when he excuses the lower-class characters by claiming that the demand for high characters is fulfilled by the introduction of peripheral figures—the judges and the pagan gods.[6]

Mitternacht's second play, *Politica Dramatica/ Das ist/ Die Edle Regiments-Kunst In der Form oder Gestalt einer Comoedien* [Dramatized Politics, or, The Noble Art of Governing, in the Form of a Comedy, 1667], depicts the tyrannous persecution of three social classes (peasants, city folk, and gentry) by their superiors (the local officialdom, the city councilors, and the king), leading to a general revolution in which the oppressors are slaughtered. A new king, who is well advised by Christian Politics, is elected, and a more just society is founded to replace the old order. The choruses constitute a classroom demonstration of the Socratic method, for a philosopher and a young prince, his student, discuss the preceding act in a Socratic dialogue. The philosopher becomes the commentator/guide, while the young prince represents and thus provides a model for the real adolescent prince in the audience. Both in this commentary and in the preface and prologue Mitternacht makes it clear that he does not condone revolution. The purpose of the play is not to criticize absolutist government, but rather to provide the Christian precepts which will guide it on a good and safe course. The election of the new king receives Divine sanction, since the gods contribute to his instruction by sending the adviser, Politica Cristiana. The comic scenes are, as in *Soldat/Barbier,* primarily extemporaneous activity of schoolboys too young to have speaking roles. There are no central characters, nor is there much in the way of dramatic action. Instead, reports of events and of decisions alternate with long monologues, and the characters rarely interact.

The prose style of Mitternacht's plays, like that of Rist, is the stilted and unnatural rhetoric of the chancellory bureaucracy, and although clear and relatively free of metaphors and mystifications, it retains a bombastic heaviness due to circumlocution and stiff attention to proper forms of address. Mitternacht's dialogues are even less dramatic than those of Rist, and they lack color and concreteness. Long monologues, many delivered by personified abstractions directly to the audience, further detract from theatricality and add to the sense that one is listening to an oration or debate instead.

Mitternacht's plays, even viewed within the strictures of the didactic drama genre, are particularly irritating in their tone of smugness, moral complacency, and pretension to a high level of wisdom. His obsequious yet naively immodest prefaces aimed at noble patrons conjure up Gryphius's ridiculous schoolmaster Herr Peter Squentz. Yet to the extent that his plays often reflect personal and social realities, Mitternacht emerges as one of the most revealing dramatists of the seventeenth century in terms of the concerns of the common man. Of peasant background himself, he depicts the miseries of the peasants—burdened with ruinous taxation and vexed by the unrelenting tyranny and corruption of petty officialdom—with the concreteness of firsthand knowledge, while the injustices of the town hall and the flagrant disrespect of his fictional king for the nobility likewise have the ring of truth about them. The critique of the behavior of soldiers and the horrors of war seems to reflect the author's own experiences in 1640, when he lost his wife and possessions during a Swedish raid. His dealings with dissatisfied schoolboys and their overly demanding parents, too, are mirrored in the *Soldat/Barbier* tragedy. Mitternacht's plays are interesting as *Zeitgeschichte* ("contemporary history") and as pedagogy, if not as contributions to Opitz's literary revolution.

Christian Weise

Only in Christian Weise does the didactic prose drama achieve distinction as good theater and quality literature. Weise's creative phantasy achieved, in some forty extant plays dating from 1678 to 1708, in spite of the limitations placed upon him by the exigencies of school performance, a success which ignores rather than challenges

Opitz and the Silesian *Kunstdrama.* Except for a period from 1688 to 1702, when he wrote plays only for small in-home performances, he generally wrote and produced three plays a year—an historical drama, a comedy, and a biblical drama—in which the entire school took part. In 1682, for example, his students presented the biblical drama *Jacobs doppelte Heyrath* [Jacob's Double Marriage], the tragedy *Von dem Neapolitanischen Rebellen Masaniello* [The Neapolitan Rebel Masaniello], and a *Parodie eines neuen Peter Squenzes* [Parody of a New Peter Squenz]. While the biblical plays do not deviate sufficiently from sixteenth-century school drama to warrant intensive treatment here,[7] one tragedy and one comedy which are much discussed in scholarship will serve to characterize Weise's vast oeuvre.

Like Mitternacht's *Politica Dramatica,* and perhaps written under its influence, Weise's *Masaniello* deals with a revolution of the weak against the taxation and tyranny of the powerful, and the title figure, as in Mitternacht's *Soldat/Barbier,* is no high personage, but a representative of one of the lowest socioeconomic classes, a fisherman. Masaniello emerges as the leader of the spontaneous revolution against the Vice Roy and nobles of Naples. When he reluctantly accepts the role of ruler, however, he is afflicted with a madness which produces paranoia, tyrannical behavior, and finally his fall from power and murder at the hands of his comrades, all in a matter of ten days. The Spanish Vice Roy regains his throne, the society returns to its materialistic activities, and the privileges won by the revolutionaries have little chance of survival.

Conforming to its nature as a school drama, *Masaniello* utilizes a cast of some seventy-eight speaking roles plus numerous silent mime roles for the smaller children. While Masaniello has the title role, his speaking part is no greater than that of some dozen other main characters—perhaps a condescension to the need to let all of the older boys of high social status obtain a major speaking role. Indeed, in order to satisfy all the boys and their doting parents, Weise seems to have invented an episodic structure which utilizes countless short, lively scenes involving representatives of all social classes with only minimal repetition of personnel, thus allowing a maximum number of boys to take part while holding the attention of the audience members when their own sons are not on stage. Rather than relating to one another in the classical structure of logical and chronological order, the scenes are independent. The total impression gleaned from the sum of all such scenes forms the unifying thread for the thematics of the play. Against this background, the minimally developed but decidedly classical tragedy of Masaniello unfolds. While recent scholars have pointed out similarities to the "modern" episodic structure of Lenz and Georg Büchner, it should be noted that these authors retained a central character.

Although Weise chose to use prose rather than verse, his style is in many ways closer to that of *Kunstdrama* than to that of his fellow pedagogues. Less encumbered by the elaborate courtly terms of address and the circumlocutions characteristic of *Kanzleisprache,* the speeches in *Masaniello* have a vigorous concreteness to them, enhanced by their affinity to real conversational exchange instead of rhetorical speeches and by a richness in the use of imagery derived from the Silesians. The result is not so much the elevated style demanded by Opitz as it is a genial aesthetic equal to it on another plane. And Weise, having freed his style from the primarily rhetorical function, works to integrate, as no school drama had done before, literariness and theatricality. But even as Weise overcomes some of the barriers imposed by the function of this dramatic genre in the creation of a new structure and style, the contradictions in his attempts surface in a destructive fashion to confound the reader with blind motifs (e.g., imagery connecting Masaniello to another fisherman, St. Peter) and an equivocal statement on revolution. Weise's attitude toward revolution and absolutist monarchy appears, if one confines oneself to the body of the play, to be progressive. Many scenes from the proletarian perspective are sympathetic to their sufferings and paint the injustices and persecutions of their social superiors frankly and critically; the scenes set among the nobility reveal their hypocrisy and cruelty. But Masaniello himself, as his deterioration indicates, is unfit to rule, and his female relatives exhibit a vanity and pretentiousness which further comment on the inappropriateness of rule by the masses. The finale (5:25) unabashedly celebrates the overthrow of the illicit revolutionary government, restoration of monarchy, and political wisdom and virtue of the Vice Roy; the *Nachredner* ("epilogue") likewise reveals Weise's abhorrence for the inversion of the social class structure and satisfaction that Divine Providence did not allow such an unnatural state of affairs to have much duration. He terms the end a happy one, in spite of the tragedy of Masaniello:

So werden wir auch alle mahl rühmen/ daß der MASANIELLO in seinem
Lebens-Lauffe zwar einen unglückseligen Ausgang/ gleichwohl aber dieses
Schau-Spiel ein glückseliges Ende gewonnen habe. (373)

(Thus we will all laud, too, the fact that even though Masaniello's life had an
unhappy end, this play itself has achieved a happy ending.)

If one views the play from the perspective of its finale and epilogue,
Weise's opinions are not revolutionary: monarchy, in the sense of the
limited and diffused structure of imperial privileges as ruled by principles of a benevolent Christian Politics, is the divinely ordained form of
government. Oligarchy leads to abuses of power, whereas mob rule
leads to anarchy and social chaos. While revolution is not condoned, it
is inevitable when politicians and rulers involve themselves in
Machiavellian expediency. The present class structure is natural and
foreordained, and rebellion against it is an illicit challenge to society
and God. In his pragmatic and rather pessimistic view of man, however, Weise's role as teacher of practical politics emerges, as he demonstrates in this play the wisdom of backing away from confrontation
(e.g., Roderigo promises what the rebels demand, as do the church-
men) while surviving to restore their earlier privileges as soon as their
patience is rewarded by the fall of the revolutionary government.

The central theme of the play, that of inappropriate role-playing,
supports the contention that Masaniello and his revolution are considered illicit.[8] Masaniello's fortunes are linked to his changes of clothing.
While in his first appearances he continues to insist that he is merely a
fisherman wearing the clothes appropriate to his station (2:2), he is
forced to don the rich garb of a ruler when his political power elevates
him above the hereditary rulers (4:12). In a frenzy of insanity, he tries to
tear the silver robe from his body in order to return to his fisherman's
clothing, and thus to his real identity. While Weise motivates this
madness with a drug administered by his enemies, this touch merely
weakens a sequence of developments in Masaniello portrayed con-
cretely in his attitude toward clothing: first humble in the appropriate
fisherman's pants, then forced to don the ruler's clothing which conforms to his present social role, he finds the silver robe first a temporary
and somewhat embarrassing encumbrance, but then progressively a
trap which reduces him to terror and even physical pain, like Hercules
in his scalding cloak. Just as the robe refuses to leave his back, so his

new role adheres to his nature, corrupting his good intentions, turning him into a crazed tyrant whose rabid behavior can only be halted by killing him. The lesson is not so much that power corrupts as that a role inappropriate to one's inborn station in life leads to an irreconcilable inner conflict; life is a stage on which one must play one's assigned role, rather than usurping that of another. The unnatural garb he forces upon the nobility, women, and priests—short robes or pants beneath which no weapons can be hidden—reflects the inappropriateness of his revolution as an emblem of the resultant social and moral anarchy. The masquerades of the clown Allegro also reinforce this theme. He cleverly changes clothes, and thus roles, in order to serve his best material interests of the moment, now joining the revolutionaries, now the nobility. When the revolution is over, he happily returns to his natural and original role, that of the parasite who entertains for his dinner, as his lines in the finale indicate. A comedy from this early period of Weise's dramatic oeuvre, *Vom niederländischen Bauer* [The Peasant from the Netherlands, 1681], explores the theme in a complementary tale of a peasant who is dressed up as king for one day before being shunted back to his former role and station.

A theme which receives relatively minor treatment in *Masaniello,* the proper behavior of politicians, is central in the comedy *Bäurischer Machiavellus* [Village Machiavelli, 1679]. Like the *Irenaromachia,* this play operates on two levels, one involving pagan gods and personifications of qualities set on Parnassus, the other dealing with the smalltown politics of the citizens of Querlequitsch. Machiavelli, author of the infamous textbook of political expediency, is being tried on Parnassus for causing all the evil in the world, but in his own defense he claims that amoral politics existed before his book appeared and still exists in places where no one has read the book or heard of him. To judge his claim, Eusebius and Politicus (Religion and Wise Politics) are sent to earth to observe the election of a new Pickelhering in Querlequitsch. Each of three candidates acquires powerful backers, and when one must be selected, the other two are given equally remunerative and useless benefices fabricated at taxpayer expense in order to accommodate all three. Appalled by the bribery, hypocrisy, and blackmail involved, the heavenly emissaries return and partially exonerate Machiavelli. The actual cause of evil, Antiquus (Oldest Evil, the Devil), is convicted of the crime and hauled away in chains at the end.

In contrast to Rist's plays, the *Zwischenspiel* among the low characters usurps the thematic burden, as well as occupying the greater number of lines, relegating the Parnassus plot to an interpretative interlude like Stieler's mythological masque in *Der Vermeinte Printz* (in spite of Weise's reversed terminology). The Parnassus characters appear in the first act as a kind of *Vorspiel,* followed by two much longer acts in Querlequitsch. They return in the very brief fourth act and again after the fifth act in the short *Schluß-Handlung* ("end act") in the function of a commentator or chorus. Meanwhile, the Querlequitsch election forms the basis of a satirical comedy not greatly different from Gryphius's *Horribilicribrifax* or *Peter Squentz* in terms of humor, language, or theatricality. The traditional comic types make their appearance: the pretentious schoolmaster with his wildly inappropriate Latin, the meek man with his shrewish wife, the fathers anxious to get their daughters married off at any cost. The three candidates and their political allies provide in their scurrilous behavior a political satire aimed at corrupt government at every level. Weise's verse prologue addressed to *Nemini* ("Nobody") satirizes the refusal of his audiences to see themselves in the vices depicted—his barbs are aimed at Nobody, since Nobody is guilty of all the evil. He even laughs at his own slavish use of the tradition of Latin nomenclature for personifications (e.g., Simplex, Candidus, Fidelis, Innocens all appear in the Parnassus plot) by giving his small-town citizens irrelevant Latin names (e.g., grammatical terms like Adjectivus, Vocativus, Accusativus).

The comedy ends with an apotheosis of the city of Zittau, lauded by the denizens of Parnassus as the residence of virtue and decency in political matters. Eusebius and Politicus, with their spouses, Urania (Heavenly orientation) and Civilis (Good government), decide to make Zittau henceforth their abode. All join in an aria praising the reign of the ultimate Prince of Peace, Jesus Christ, for its freedom from war and foreign domination, its security, and its just ruler. The aria ends with a prayer for protection from vice and from Machiavellian politics. Weise may be trying to win the approval of the powers that be through flattery, although it is more likely that this ending expresses his heartfelt love for his hometown, to which he had only recently returned after studies and positions abroad. But the pedagogue in Weise also has a didactic purpose in mind, for this praise demands that Zittau live up to the billing. Thus Weise affects his audience through the purging laughter of satire, through providing *exempla* of bad politics and adages governing good politics, and through a "prophecy" which will, he hopes, fulfill itself in local government. Meanwhile, his schoolboys have learned moral behavior through ridicule of vices, *exemplum,* and adage, but they have also, as Rist states, improved their public-speaking abilities, exercised their memories, and learned appropriate social graces.

Chapter Eight

Conclusion

By the end of the seventeenth century, no more high tragedies were being written, although new editions indicate their continuing popularity. Christian Weise turned from the satirical comedy to the italianate comedy of love and intrigue in his late plays (e.g., *Ungleich und gleich gepaarte Liebes-Alliance,* 1703), but a new dramatist, Christian Reuter, applied his pen to the creation of several satirical comedies during the last five years of the century when he was a student in Leipzig. The most famous of these, *Die Ehrliche Frau von Plißane,* while it satirizes such disparate vices as drunkenness among women, the vanity of girls, and the heartlessness of landladies, actually constitutes retaliation against Reuter's own landlady for turning him out when he could not pay his rent. The resulting lawsuits, jail term, and expulsion from the university elicited a whole series of satirical writings directed at the landlady and her family, but their quick popularity did not gain permanent fame or success for their author. The influence of the French comedy of Molière is apparent in the abandonment of the usual German comic types, as well as in the fiction that the play is a translation from the French. Yet the play is slow-moving and redundant, too involved in its scurrilous misogyny to recognize and imitate Molière's keen witticisms.

The watered-down foreign and native dramas of the itinerant stage, increasingly dominated by the clown Hans Wurst, ruled the theatrical scene until 1730, when Johann Christoph Gottsched (1700–1766) chased the clown from the stage and proposed emulation of French Neoclassicism in his *Versuch einer critischen Dichtkunst vor die Deutschen* (Attempt at a Critical Poetics for the Germans). Baroque "Schwulst" (excessive ornamentation and convoluted mannerism of style) is rejected in favor of "reason" and "good taste"; the wild formlessness, as Gottsched perceived it, is replaced by rules such as the classical unities; the love of mystification and multiple meanings is forced to give way to unadorned clarity. But this rejection of the Baroque is not permanent, for in their discovery of Shakespeare later in the eighteenth century, German dramatists rediscovered some of the positive characteristics of their own dramatic heritage. Remnants of the Baroque in dusty corners of libraries may have to account for signs of influence from Baroque drama in the works of Goethe, Schiller, and Kleist in middle and northern Germany, but in Vienna the Baroque drama retained an unbroken theatrical tradition which manifested itself in such works as Mozart's *Die Zauberflöte* (The Magic Flute, 1790), Grillparzer's tragedies, the comedies of Raimund and Nestroy in the nineteenth century, and the libretti and dramas of Hugo von Hofmannsthal in this century. Baroque literature, including drama, experienced revivals of interest, resulting in new editions, in the periods of Romanticism and Expressionism due to certain perceived relevancies to current taste. Yet the dominant reaction since 1730 has been a negative one which has long colored scholarly response to it, an attitude which is once again giving way, one hopes permanently, in recent years.

This study has taken the point of view that the nature of the drama of the literary Baroque is allegorical; that is, Baroque tragedy and most Baroque comedy tend to conceal a religious or political significance beneath the cloak of historical or romantic detail. These hidden meanings are conveyed to the audience/reader by means of clues: biblical allusions, analogies to biblical or political events, emblematic references and structures. Sigmund von Birken makes analogies to biblical events the central creative mechanism in his *Teutsche Rede-Bind- und Dicht-Kunst,* as he himself states: "Der Vorsatz in diesem Buch ist/ allemal ein geistliches Beispiel zu geben" (The intent of this book is to give a spiritual example for each literary genre, 201). Thus a poem wishing someone a happy birthday is to be modeled on celebrations of Christ's birth, literary works in honor of a wedding should emulate the marriage of Christ and the soul portrayed in the Song of Songs, poems honoring victories should imitate the commemorations of Christ's victory over the Devil. The hidden universal schema gives increased importance both to the drama and to the event or occasion for which it may have been designed to be performed. Any political polemic it may contain is effectively conveyed to the receptive audience "sugar-coated and gold-plated," to use Stieler's words. In addition, most dramas contain a more easily perceived moral lesson, often conveyed via commentary of the choruses, adages, or *exempla* (models for behavior). The best Baroque dramas also express universal metaphysical truths and deal with the problematical nature of the human condition.

Such meanings are accessible to the perceptive reader, but dramas were not designed to be read. A performance in a theater, which sets up an interchange among text, actors, and audience, transcends rational exegesis and analysis. A reconstruction of the experience of a performance, based on information in Baroque poetics coupled with our own experiences in modern performances of plays of any period, adds another dimension to interpretation of Baroque drama. The audience, through viewing the imitation of a pathetic action, is purged of vices and/or excessive emotions by means of empathy with the tragic character and fear of a similar fate, an experience shared by the schoolboy actors who usually played the roles. Through viewing the imitation of a ridiculous action, the audience is purged of similar pretensions and vices in themselves by means of laughter. And through viewing the imitation of potentially pathetic actions with happy outcomes, the audience is purged of its sorrow and fear by the arousal of joy and hope. These purgative effects—constituent parts of a Baroque theory of catharsis—cause alterations in the future behavior of the audience members and the actors which no text alone could accomplish, for as Aristotle perceived, the bodily imitation of an action has the potential for a far greater effect than the mere description of it. And this effect was compounded in the seventeenth century, when life itself was just a stage and its personages merely players.

Notes and References

Chapter One

1. Ernst Robert Curtius, *Europäische Literatur und Lateinisches Mittelalter* (Bern: Francke, 1948); H. Hartmann, "Barock oder Manierismus? Eignen sich kunsthistorische Termini für die Kennzeichnung der deutschen Literatur des 17. Jahrhunderts?" *Weimarer Beiträge* 7 (1961):46–60.

2. For a survey and criticism of the discussion, see Manfred Brauneck, "Deutsche Literatur des 17. Jahrhunderts—Revision eines Epochenbildes: Ein Forschungsbericht, 1945–1970," *Deutsche Vierteljahrsschrift,* Sonderheft 1971, pp. 389–434.

3. Curtius, *Europäische Literatur.*

4. E.g., W. Weisbach, *Der Barock als Kunst der Gegenreformation* (Berlin: Cassirer, 1921); H. Hatzfeld, "A Clarification of the Baroque Problem in the Romance Literatures," *Comparative Literature* 1 (1949):113–39.

5. Fritz Strich, "Der europäische Barock," in his *Der Dichter und die Zeit* (Bern: Francke, 1947), pp. 71–131.

6. René Wellek, "The Concept of Baroque in Literary Scholarship," *Journal of Aesthetics and Art Criticism* 5 (1946–47):77–109.

7. Brauneck, "Deutsche Literatur," p. 434.

8. Albrecht Schöne, "Postfigurale Gestaltung," in *Säkularisation als sprachbildende Kraft: Studien zur Dichtung deutscher Pfarrersöhne,* Palaestra, no. 226 (Göttingen: Vandenhoeck and Ruprecht, 1958), p. 166.

9. Herbert Cysarz, *Deutsche Barockdichtung: Renaissance, Barock, Rokoko* (Leipzig, 1924), p. 40; Irene Wanner, *Die Allegorie im bayerischen Barockdrama des 17. Jahrhunderts,* diss. Munich 1941, pp. 8–9. Other scholars who stress allegory in their discussions of Baroque literature are Walter Benjamin, *Ursprung des deutschen Trauerspiels,* Wissenschaftliche Sonderausgabe (Frankfurt am Main, 1963), pp. 174–243; Paul Hankamer, *Deutsche Gegenreformation und deutsches Barock: Die deutsche Literatur im Zeitraum des 17. Jahrhunderts* (Stuttgart, 1935), pp. 301–303; Paul Böckmann, *Formgeschichte der deutschen Dichtung* (Hamburg: Hoffmann and Campe, 1949), pp. 430 ff.

10. Hartmann, "Barock."

Chapter Two

1. Hans Heinrich Borcherdt, "Geschichte des deutschen Theaters," in *Deutsche Philologie im Aufriß,* ed. W. Stammler, vol. 3 (Berlin: Schmidt, 1962), cols. 1099–1103, feels that these traditions lead into medieval German drama, while Eduard Hartl, "Das Drama des Mittelalters," in the same work, vol. 2, cols. 1949 ff, discounts their importance.

2. The major work on medieval drama is Karl Young, *The Drama of the Medieval Church* (Oxford, 1951), which includes texts of most of the short liturgical dramas, as well as analyses and attempts at periodization. Other important works on medieval religious drama used in this survey are Julius Schwietering, "Über den liturgischen Ursprung des mittelalterlichen geistlichen Spiels," *Zeitschrift für deutsches Altertum und deutsche Literatur* 62 (1925):1–21, and Eduard Hartl, "Das Drama." A recent survey by David Brett-Evans, *Von Hrotsvit bis Folz und Gengenbach: Eine Geschichte des mittelalterlichen deutschen Dramas,* Grundlagen der Germanistik, no. 15 (Berlin, 1975), 2 vols., helps to clarify the development, but is largely derivative without giving credit to the earlier works.

3. David Brett-Evans, *Von Hrotsvit,* discusses the morality play type, pp. 46–49.

4. E.g., Brett-Evans, *Von Hrotsvit,* p. 74.

5. The major work used for this brief survey of *Fastnachtspiele* is Eckehard Catholy, *Fastnachtspiel,* Sammlung Metzler (Stuttgart, 1966), which surveys previous scholarship and presents Catholy's theory about their genesis in the *Fastnacht* context. Brett-Evans's work also deals with the *Fastnachtspiel.*

6. In the absence of a basic work on German Humanist drama, I have consulted the following works in the construction of this survey: Friedrich Gaede, *Humanismus, Barock, Aufklärung: Geschichte der deutschen Literatur vom 16. bis zum 18. Jahrhundert,* Handbuch der deutschen Literaturgeschichte, Darstellungen, vol. 2 (Bern/Munich, 1971); Hans Rupprich, *Die deutsche Literatur vom späten Mittelalter bis zum Barock: Erster Teil, Das ausgehende Mittelalter, Humanismus und Renaissance, 1370–1520,* Geschichte der deutschen Literatur von den Anfängen bis zur Gegenwart, ed. De Boor/ Newald, vol. 4, part 1 (Munich, 1970); Wolfgang Stammler, *Von der Mystik zum Barock: 1400–1600* (Stuttgart, 1950); Gunther Müller, *Deutsche Dichtung von der Renaissance bis zum Ausgang des Barock,* Handbuch der Literaturwissenschaft (Darmstadt, 1957); Derek van Abbé, *Drama in Renaissance Germany and Switzerland* (London, 1961); and Willi Flemming, "Formen der Humanistenbühne," *Maske und Kothurn* 6 (1960):33–52.

7. Protestant biblical drama is discussed in most of the above works, and in Brett-Evans, *Von Hrotsvit.* In addition, the article by Klaus Ziegler, "Das

deutsche Drama der Neuzeit," in *Deutsche Philologie im Aufriß,* vol. 2, cols. 1997 ff, was used for this survey.

8. E.g., Van Abbé, *Drama in Renaissance Germany,* pp. 20–21, who quotes Luther on drama in full.

9. Willi Flemming, *Geschichte des Jesuitentheaters in den Landen deutscher Zunge,* Schriften der Gesellschaft für Theatergeschichte, no. 32 (Berlin, 1923), p. 1. Other works primarily used for this brief survey are Willi Flemming, "Einführung," *Barockdrama: Das Ordensdrama* (Hildesheim, 1965), pp. 7 ff; Johannes Müller, S.J., *Das Jesuitendrama in den Ländern deutscher Zunge vom Anfang (1555) bis zum Hochbarock (1665),* Schriften zur deutschen Literatur für die Görresgesellschaft, no. 7 (Augsburg, 1930), 2 vols.; Elida Maria Szarota, *Geschichte, Politik und Gesellschaft im Drama des 17. Jahrhunderts* (Bern/Munich, 1976); and her two articles on Jesuit drama related to chapters in this book which were published in *Daphnis* in 1974 and 1975. To date, so far as English-language surveys are concerned, there exists only a recent article on early German Jesuit drama: Richard G. Dimler, "A Geographic and Genetic Survey of Jesuit Drama in German-speaking Territories from 1555–1602," *Archivium historicum Societatis Jesu* 43 (1974):133–46.

10. It was reported that at the first performance of Bidermann's *Cenodoxus* in Munich in 1602, fourteen high-ranking courtiers traded their worldly glory for a monk's robes, according to Richard Newald, *Die deutsche Literatur vom Späthumanismus zur Empfindsamkeit, 1570–1750,* Geschichte der deutschen Literatur von den Anfängen bis zur Gegenwart (Munich, 1960), 5:102. Another Jesuit play of the early seventeenth century so affected the audience that the loud sobbing actually forced a pause in the action (Flemming, *Ordensdrama,* 25).

11. E.g., Szarota, *Geschichte, Politik und Gesellschaft,* p. 7.

12. Ibid., pp. 53–54.

13. E.g., Müller, *Das Jesuitendrama,* pp. 60 ff. This dual nature of Jesuit drama is described by the contemporary theorist Jakob Masen in an excerpt from his *Palaestra eloquentiae ligatae* quoted in Werner Eggers, *Wirklichkeit und Wahrheit im Trauerspiel von Andreas Gryphius* (Heidelberg: Winter, 1967), pp. 160–61.

14. Szarota, for example, ignores important dramas which do not coincide with her theory of periodization. Her generalizations are nonetheless useful for illuminating certain tendencies in the choice of subject matter over the history of the Jesuit drama in Germany.

15. A monograph on Bidermann exists in English: Thomas W. Best, *Jacob Bidermann,* Twayne World Authors Series, no. 314 (Boston, 1975). It contains a selected bibliography of the relatively vast material available on this author.

16. Avancini remains relatively unstudied. The introductions to his works in Flemming's *Geschichte des Jesuitentheaters,* pp. 9–13, and Müller's *Das Jesuitendrama,* pp. 89–96, are useful. An unpublished dissertation is the only monographic study: Angela Kabiersch, *Nikolaus Avancini, S.J. und das Wiener Jesuitentheater (1640–1685),* diss., Vienna, 1972.

17. It continued to exist side by side with the Italian opera in Vienna after the erection of the opera house in 1666, partly due to the theatrical genius of Avancini, but was relegated once again to the domain of the schools in Munich with the establishment of opera in the court theater in 1648 (Flemming, *Ordensdrama,* 26).

18. The two major works on the English Comedians and the *Wanderbühne* are Willi Flemming, "Einführung," in *Barockdrama: Das Schauspiel der Wanderbühne* (1931; 2nd revised ed. Hildesheim, 1965), and Anna Baesecke, *Das Schauspiel der englischen Komödianten in Deutschland: Seine dramatische Form und seine Entwicklung,* Studien zur englischen Philologie, no. 87 (Halle, 1935). The two form the basis for this survey.

19. A contemporary letter containing such a judgment has been published in Flemming's collection, pp. 71–72. The letter describes activities during the two weeks before Lent, 1608, in Graz (Austria), including performances of ten plays by a troupe of English comedians and two Jesuit plays.

20. Flemming, *Wanderbühne,* p. 17.

21. Flemming, *Wanderbühne,* pp. 6 ff, devotes several pages to the financial situation of the troupes.

22. Appearances of English troupes at the Saxon court in 1585 and 1587 do not seem to have constituted dramatic performances, but rather a mixture of comedy routine, acrobatics, and music (Baesecke, *Das Schauspiel,* 73).

23. In the opinion of Roy Pascal, *German Literature in the 16th and 17th Centuries: Renaissance—Reformation—Baroque,* Introductions to German Literature (New York, 1968), 2:68. Ayrer's plays retain the traditional German *Knittelvers* meter, while Heinrich Julius initiated prose, in imitation of the English Comedians, in his plays.

24. Stammler, *Von der Mystik zum Barock,* p. 481.

25. Baesecke, *Das Schauspiel,* p. 103; Flemming, *Wanderbühne,* p. 18.

26. The collections have recently been reprinted in *Spieltexte der Wanderbühne* (see bibliography), while the latter two plays have long been available in the *Barockdrama* series, ed. Willi Flemming, vol. 3: *Das Schauspiel der Wanderbühne.*

27. The first record of an actress in an English or German *Wanderbühne* troupe dates from 1654, according to Baesecke, *Das Schauspiel,* p. 115. Actresses were generally wives of important troupe members. The Italian

commedia dell'arte and opera troupes apparently brought actresses and female sopranos much earlier, but only to Austria and Southern Germany.

28. A. H. J. Knight, *Heinrich Julius, Duke of Brunswick* (Oxford, 1948), p. 10. In addition to this monograph, this survey relies on a monograph by Ingrid Werner, *Zwischen Mittelalter und Neuzeit: Heinrich Julius von Braunschweig als Dramatiker der Übergangszeit,* Europäische Hochschulschriften, Reihe 1: Deutsche Literatur und Germanistik, no. 160 (Frankfurt am Main/Bern, 1976). Knight's study, although plagued by subjective judgment, provides a valuable survey, while Werner's work offers much in the way of penetrating interpretative insight, in spite of a tendency to overgeneralize periodization.

29. Newald, *Späthumanismus,* pp. 88–90.

30. Knight, *Heinrich Julius,* pp. 100 ff, inquires into the German sources, after refuting earlier claims of influence from or upon Shakespeare.

31. Werner, *Zwischen Mittelalter,* pp. 5, 44–50; she notes on p. 114 that his tragedies, with one exception, would qualify as *bürgerliche Trauerspiele* ("bourgeois tragedies")—a genre which reemerges a century and a half later in Lessing's *Miss Sara Sampson,* much to the astonishment of a public long accustomed to the rule that tragedy concerns the fall of high personages, while comedy is the proper vehicle for the concerns of characters of lower social class.

32. Flemming, *Wanderbühne,* p. 50.

33. Newald, *Späthumanismus,* p. 88.

Chapter Three

1. The best works on Martin Opitz are Marian Szyrocki, *Martin Opitz* (Munich, 1974), and Richard Alewyn, *Vorbarocker Klassizismus und griechische Tragödie: Analyse der 'Antigone'-Übersetzung des Martin Opitz* (1926; rpt. Darmstadt, 1962). Also used for this survey was Hugo Max, *Martin Opitz als geistlicher Dichter,* Beiträge zur neueren Literaturgeschichte, no. 17 (Heidelberg: Winter, 1931). Bernard Ulmer has provided an English introduction to his life and work in this series: *Martin Opitz,* TWAS, no. 140 (New York, 1971).

2. The alexandrine verse, as used and promoted by Opitz, is a line composed of six stressed syllables, each paired with unstressed syllables in iambic or trochaic feet, broken in the center with a caesura (pause), and ending with either masculine or feminine rhyme:

$$\acute{}-/\acute{}-/\acute{}-//\acute{}-/\acute{}-/\acute{}-/ \qquad \text{or} \qquad -\acute{}/-\acute{}/-\acute{}//-\acute{}/-\acute{}/-\acute{}/$$

Unlike the French model, which counts the total number of syllables, or the Latin hexameter, which counts syllable length, Opitz's new German verse follows the natural character of the German language in counting stressed syllables.

3. The madrigal verse form, whether used in short poems or in dramas, is characterized by rhyming lines of irregular length ranging from six to twelve syllables. It is the form chosen by Giovanni Battista Guarini for his famous *Il Pastor fido* (1589). Opitz was the first German to use this freer versification.

4. It was not set to music until 1646 (seven years after Opitz's death), when Apelles von Löwenstern wrote the score for a performance in Thorn. It was performed again in Breslau in 1651 in this form.

5. Stichomythia is dialogue in which each speaker makes his point in one line, to be countered by the other in the next.

6. Dedicatory poem, *Dafne,* in *Weltliche Poemata,* Teil 1, 1644, rpt. 1967, p. 106.

7. The tradition of allegorizing Ovid's *Metamorphoses* begins with the French *Ovide Moralisé,* although this was not the first instance of Christian allegorization of pagan myth by any means, and culminates in the seventeenth century in an essay dated 1668 by Sigmund von Birken called "Programma Poeticarum," which he appended to his treatise on poetics, *Teutsche Rede-Bind- und Dicht-Kunst* (Nuremberg: Riegel, 1679). Birken uses the myth of Apollo and Daphne as a model for modern poets to use allegorization in their works. For a summary of this tradition in Germany, see my *The Mission of Rome in the Dramas of Daniel Casper von Lohenstein: Historical Tragedy as Prophecy and Polemic,* Stuttgarter Arbeiten zur Germanistik, no. 21 (Stuttgart, 1976), pp. 29–32.

8. This useful term, which signifies that a contemporary person, event, or institution is modeled on or runs parallel with an event from the Bible, is coined (in German) by Albrecht Schöne, "Postfigurale Gestaltung," in *Die Dramen des Andreas Gryphius: Eine Sammlung von Einzelinterpretationen,* ed. Gerhard Kaiser (Stuttgart, 1968), pp. 117–69. The idea of marriage as a postfiguration of the love of Christ and the human soul derives from the traditional exegesis of the Song of Songs, which can be found, for example, in Martin Opitz's preface of his own *Hohelied* translation.

9. Among the papers Gryphius left at his death, but now lost, was an unfinished Gibeoniter play of his own. Two of his royal "martyrs," Leo Armenius and Carolus Stuardus, exhibit some of the characteristics of the fall of the great, and certainly the idea of the transience of worldly glory is as important in these plays as martyrdom modeled on the passion of Christ. In *Papinian,* the tyrant receives a great deal of attention, so that his fall is as much the center of interest as Papinian's constancy to virtue.

10. Five of Lohenstein's six tragedies belong to this category. The exception is *Ibrahim Bassa* (1650), his earliest dramatic effort, a martyr play modeled on those of Gryphius.

11. See Werner Richter, *Liebeskampf 1630 und Schaubühne 1670: Ein Beitrag zur deutschen Theatergeschichte des siebzehnten Jahrhunderts,* Palaestra, no. 78 (Berlin, 1910), pp. 12–25, for an extensive analysis of this stage translation. As Richter demonstrates, the *Liebeskampf* version of the *Aminta* has more theatrical value, perhaps, but less literary merit; the madrigal verse is abandoned for prose; and the requisite "comic person" of the itinerant theater is added. Richter theorizes that the German text may be a translation from a French intermediary, rather than a direct translation from the Italian. A new translation in 1642 by Michael Schneider, also in prose, can only be described as pedantic (see Richter, *Liebeskampf 1630,* 20).

12. Two German translations of the seventeenth century precede Hofmannswaldau's: the first, by Eilgerus Mannlich in *Knittelvers,* appeared in 1619; the second, by Statius Ackermann in 1636, was in prose. On the German translations see my article "Guarini's *Il Pastor fido* in Germany: Allegorical and Figural Aspects," *Studi Germanici* 2 (1978), which also contains a discussion of previous secondary treatments.

13. Joachim Schulze, essay in *Die Dramen des Andreas Gryphius: Eine Sammlung von Einzelinterpretationen,* pp. 339–62.

Chapter Four

1. Jacobus Pontanus, *Institutio Poetica* (Ingolstadt: Sartorius, 1597); Martin Opitz, *Buch von der deutschen Poeterey* (Breslau: Müller, 1624); Georg Phillip Harsdörffer, *Poetischer Trichter/ Die Teutsche Dicht- und Reimkunst/ ohne Behuf der Lateinischen Sprache/ in VI. Stunden einzugiessen* (Nuremberg: Endter, 1648–53); August Buchner (d. 1661), *Anleitung zur deutschen Poeterey* (Wittenberg: Wenden, 1665); Jakob Masen, *Palaestra Eloquentiae ligatae* (Cologne: Busaeum, 1664; first edition 1654–57); Sigmund von Birken, *Teutsche Rede-bind- und Dicht-Kunst* (Nuremberg: Riegel, 1679).

2. David E. R. George, *Deutsche Tragödientheorien vom Mittelalter bis zu Lessing: Texte und Kommentare* (Munich, 1972), p. 100. This work has been used for the survey of the theories of Pontanus and, to a lesser extent, those of the other theorists discussed here.

3. Birken, *Teutsche Rede-bind- und Dicht-Kunst,* p. 323.

4. Authors of poetical treatises and Aristotelian scholars alike have, until recently, adhered to some variant of the idea (gleaned from Aristotle's *Politics* rather than from his *Poetics*) that Aristotle uses the term "catharsis" in the sense of a therapeutic purgation of emotions brought about as a result of viewing imitations of tragic actions which arouse pity and fear in the

beholder. While Gerald F. Else has challenged this assumption in his book *Aristotle's Poetics: The Argument* (Cambridge, Mass.: Harvard University, 1957) on the basis of a close reading of the *Poetics* alone, I find his conclusion—that catharsis is a peripheral rather than central concept to Aristotelian theory of tragedy and that it has nothing to do with an end effect upon the audience—less useful for any discussion of tragic drama than those "less accurate" ones of his predecessors. And since Baroque theoreticians, without exception, are interested in the effect of tragedy upon the audience, it will be assumed that catharsis refers to some sort of therapeutic process of purgation in the viewer, here to be further defined in Baroque terms by the new poetics themselves. The usual terminology corresponding to Aristotle's "pathos" (*misericordia* and *Mitleid*), although defined in dictionaries as "compassion," usually seems (like Aristotle's own term) to connote some kind of identification with the sufferer which in English is usually rendered as "empathy," in German with "sich einfühlen." I have used the term "empathy" when this sense is more appropriate to the context than "pity."

5. Opitz, *Die Trojanerinnen*, in *Weltliche Poemata*, "An den Leser," p. 315.

6. Harsdörffer, *Poetischer Trichter*, Part 2, pp. 83–84. George, *Deutsche Tragödientheorien*, pp. 115–16, has a different interpretation of the passage.

7. See the bibliography for the edition of this play used in quotations, and all other dramas discussed in the text. References will only be given by act and line or page number inserted in the text.

8. Albrecht Schöne, "Ermordete Majestät: Oder Carolus Stuardus König von Groß Britannien," in *Die Dramen des Andreas Gryphius: Eine Sammlung von Einzelinterpretationen*, pp. 117–69, especially pp. 151–56.

9. Simon's Leo is an iconoclast who destroys sacred images and thus—in this Jesuit perspective—a parallel to the Lutheran destruction of the venerated images of saints. Gryphius has eliminated this aspect.

10. See Young, *Drama of the Medieval Church*, 1:252. A famous German version, in the "Innsbrucker Osterspiel," can stand for many. The participants turn to the audience/congregation at the end and announce the resurrection:

> Nu hort, vil lyben lute . . .
> Sollen wir loben den heiligen Christ,
> der von dem tode erstanden ist.
>
> (Now listen, very dear people.
> We should praise the holy Christ
> Who has risen from the dead.)

11. Young, *Drama of the Medieval Church,* 1:209.

12. Walter Benjamin, *Ursprung des deutschen Trauerspiels,* in *Schriften,* 1:187.

13. See Friedrich Ohly, "Vom geistigen Sinn des Wortes im Mittelalter," *Zeitschrift für deutsches Altertum* 89 (1959):6–7.

14. See Albrecht Schöne, *Emblematik und Drama* (Munich, 1964), pp. 104–105.

15. See Schöne, *Emblematik und Drama,* p. 102; used by Antonius himself to describe his situation, 1:945.

16. Giovanni Battista Comazzi, *Morales des Princes,* trans. anon. (Paris, 1754), pp. 85–88. Comazzi was the official court historian of emperor Leopold I; the original, which was not available to me, was written in Italian.

17. This widely used interpretation is contained, for example, in the famous letter by Dante on application of biblical exegesis to literature, *Dantis Aligherii Epistolae/ The Letters of Dante,* ed. and trans. Paget Toynbee (Oxford: Oxford University, 1966), pp. 173–74.

18. Lohenstein's note to this passage refers to Suetonius's biography of Augustus, yet this source is not adequate to explain the entire passage, for Suetonius does not mention that this closure was the third (in his account it was in fact the first). This use of half-truth in references to sources had the same purpose in Gryphius's *Carolus Stuardus* (see above): history can be altered to bring facts into accord with the internal logic of *Heilsgeschichte* and Christian truths.

19. In the poem "In ein Stambuch" from *Poetische Wälder,* Book 2, published in Fleming's *Teutsche Poemata* (Lübeck: Jauchen, 1642), p. 56, line 12.

20. This idea was worked out in a seminar paper by Julie Kunke, University of Iowa, Fall 1979, titled "Messianic Meanings in Hallmann's *Mariamne.*" This paper includes a detailed comparison of Mariamne's trial with rabbinical analyses of Judaic principles of justice as they applied to Christ's trial.

21. See the introduction by Robert R. Heitner to the modern reprint of the play, Nachdrucke deutscher Literatur des 17. Jahrhunderts (Bern and Frankfurt am Main, 1974), pp. 31–32.

22. Ibid., p. 12.

Chapter Five

1. Harsdörffer, *Poetischen Trichters Zweyter Theil,* pp. 71 ff.

2. The terms "satire" and "satyr" have divergent etymologies ("satire" from *satira* or *satura,* Lat., "medley"; "satyr" from *satyros,* Gr., "lascivious

demi-god"), but the two were already connected by ancient authors in a false etymology. All German Baroque authors who use the terms "Satyrspiel" or "Satyra" assume that the comic Satyr plays following a Greek tragedy were satirical—as, indeed, the only complete extant Satyr play, Euripides's *Cyclops,* can be seen to be.

3. Buchner, *Anleitung zur Deutschen Poeterey,* pp. 8–12.

4. Birken, *Teutsche Rede-bind- und Dicht-Kunst,* pp. 323–24.

5. Daniel Georg Morhof, *Unterricht von Der Teutschen Sprache und Poesie* (Kiel: Reumann, 1682), in the exerpt reprinted in *Poetik des Barock,* ed. Marian Szyrocki, Rowohlts Klassiker der Literatur und der Wissenschaft, Deutsche Literatur, no. 23 (Hamburg: Rowohlt, 1968), pp. 188–93.

6. Caspar Stieler, *Dichtkunst des Spaten 1685,* ed. Herbert Zeman, Wiener Neudrucke, no. 5 (Vienna: Österreichischer Bundesverlag, 1975); the parts used in this discussion all also appear in Johannes Bolte, "Dichtkunst: Eine Ungedruckte Poetik Stielers," *Sitzungsberichte der Preussischen Akademie der Wissenschaften*; page numbers will derive from this edition, but line numbers will also be included.

7. G. P. Harsdörffer, *Frauenzimmer Gesprächspiele,* 6. Theil, ed. Irmgard Böttcher, Deutsche Neudrucke, Reihe Barock, no. 18. (1644 ff; rpt. Tübingen: Niemeyer, 1969), 6:163–64.

8. Richard Alewyn, "Der Geist des Barocktheaters," in *Weltliteratur: Festgabe für Fritz Strich zum 70. Geburtstag,* ed. Walter Muschg and Emil Staiger (Bern, 1952), pp. 32–33.

9. See Gerhard Kaiser, "Peter Squentz," in *Die Dramen des Andreas Gryphius,* pp. 222–23.

10. Suggested by Herbert Cysarz, "Motive, Komik und Text des 'Peter Squentz,'" in his edition of the play, Reclam Universalbücherei, no. 917 (Stuttgart: Reclam, 1954), p. 4; the preface to the 1657 edition indicates that it was performed with a tragedy, but does not indicate which one.

11. In this case a mother rivaling her daughter; the story of Don Carlos and his father, Philip II of Spain, was already popular in the seventeenth century, although it received dramatization only in Jesuit theater before Schiller's tragedy *Don Carlos* (1787).

12. He wrote the pastoral *Silvia* to be performed with his translation of Masen's *Androfilo.*

13. Kaiser, "Verlibtes Gespenste—Die gelibte Dornrose," in *Die Dramen des Andreas Gryphius,* pp. 256–84, demonstrates this interpretation at length, although he avoids use of the term "allegory."

14. Birken, *Teutsche Rede-Bind- und Dicht-Kunst,* p. 208.

15. Discussed in Chapter 3.

16. Birken, *Teutsche Rede-Bind- und Dicht-Kunst,* p. 324.

Chapter Six

1. On the variety of nonliterary court performances and entertainments, see two works containing numerous contemporary illustrations, Margarete Baur-Heinhold, *Theater des Barock: Festliches Bühnenspiel im 17. und 18. Jahrhundert* (Munich: Callwey, 1966); and Eberhard Fähler, *Feuerwerke des Barock: Studien zum öffentlichen Fest und seiner literarischen Deutung vom 16. bis zum 18. Jahrhundert* (Stuttgart: Metzler, 1974).

2. As Dietrich Walter Jöns has demonstrated in his essay in *Die Dramen des Andreas Gryphius*, pp. 285–301; he points out that the coronation itself took place not in May, but in June, thus indicating that Maytime had a symbolic significance so strong that it remained in the play in spite of a schedule change.

3. The description of the *Festspiel* of Eucharius Gottlieb Rinck can be found in his *Leopolds des Großen Röm. Kaysers Wunderwürdiges Leben und Thaten* (Leipzig: Fritsch, 1708), 2:124–25. See also H. Seifert, "Die Festlichkeiten zur ersten Hochzeit Kaiser Leopolds I," *Österreichische Monatsschrift* 29 (1974):6–16.

4. *Emblemata: Handbuch zur Sinnbildkunst des XVI. und XVII. Jahrhunderts*, ed. Arthur Henckel and Albrecht Schöne (Stuttgart: Metzler, 1967), col. 1633.

5. See Georges Dontrepont, "Jason et Gedeon, patrons de la Toison d'Or," *Melanges Godefroid Kurth* (Liège/Paris: Champion, 1908), 2:191–208; Gert Pinkernell, introduction to Raoul Le Fèvre, *L'Histoire de Jason: Ein Roman aus dem 15. Jahrhundert* (Frankfurt am Main: Athenäum, 1971), pp. 36 ff.

6. D. W. Jöns, in *Die Dramen des Andreas Gryphius*, pp. 297–98.

7. K. G. Just, "Das Opernlibretto als literarisches Problem," in *Marginalien: Probleme und Gestalten der Literatur* (Bern/Munich: Francke, 1976), pp. 30 ff. Opera scholars assure me he is not exaggerating. On Baroque opera see also John D. Lindberg, "The German Baroque Opera Libretto: A Forgotten Genre," in *The German Baroque: Literature, Music, Art,* ed. George Schulz-Behrend (Austin: University of Texas, 1972), pp. 89–122.

8. Galeazzo Gualdo Priorato, *Ragguaglio di quanto e seguito nel Terzo Matrimonio di Su Maestá Cesarea, Anno 1676, 1677* (Vienna, 1677).

9. In 1669. It exists in the original manuscript in Weimar.

10. Anon., *Der Schütz- und Schatten-reich ausgebreitete Kaisers-Adler/ Oder: Das Glor-grünende Römische Reichs-Zepter/ unsers Allergroßmächtigsten Augusti LEOPOLDI Des Ersten* (Augsburg, 1690), pp. 29–30.

11. Published in *Barockdrama*, 5:125–79.

12. Ibid., pp. 180–97.

13. Flemming, "Einführung," *Barockdrama*, 6:7–26.

14. Ibid., pp. 14–15.

Chapter Seven

1. D. G. Morhof, *Unterricht von Der Teutschen Sprache und Poesie*, p. 739.

2. As the dedicatory preface indicates. He did obtain a position as a clergyman in nearby Wedel the following ·year.

3. The idea that tragedy should contribute to the development of a stoic attitude in the audience, central to Opitz's theory, is ignored here. See Eberhard Mannack, "Johann Rists 'Perseus' und das Drama des Barock," *Daphnis* 1 (1972):141–49.

4. Ibid., p. 147.

5. Marianne Kaiser, *Mitternacht, Zeidler, Weise: Das protestantische Schultheater nach 1648 im Kampf gegen höfische Kultur und absolutistisches Regiment*, Palaestra, no. 259 (Göttingen, 1972), p. 182, lists those she has located, beginning with the *Herodes* by the schoolman Christian Rose, subtitled *in einem lustigen SchauSpiel Zur andern Probe der Rhetorischen MutterSprache vorgestellet* ("presented in a comic play as another example of the rhetorical native tongue," Hamburg, 1649). Kaiser notes the influence of Rist's dramas on this genre and defines its rhetorical nature. I do not agree with her interpretation of the "cavalier" theme and am not convinced that the dramas of the genre were conceived of as antiabsolutist.

6. Kaiser, *Mitternacht*, p. 72, views this defense as a subterfuge and credits him with political intentions.

7. They have been superficially and subjectively discussed by Hans Schauer, "Christian Weises biblische Dramen" (diss., Leipzig, 1921).

8. This theme is discussed by Heinz Otto Burger, "Das Barock im Spiegel von Jacob Bidermanns 'Philemon Martyr' und Christian Weises 'Masaniello,'" in his *Dasein heißt eine Rolle spielen: Studien zur deutschen Literaturgeschichte* (Munich, 1963), pp. 80–93.

Selected Bibliography

PRIMARY SOURCES

1. Drama Editions Used: Collections

Barockdrama. Edited by Willi Flemming. 6 vols. 1931 ff. 2nd revised edition, Hildesheim: Olms, 1965.

Microfilm Series of the German Baroque Literature collection of the Yale University Library, available in many American and European libraries. Catalogue: Curt von Faber du Faur. *German Baroque Literature.* New Haven: Yale University, 1958.

Spieltexte der Wanderbühne. Edited by Manfred Brauneck. 4 vols. Ausgaben deutscher Literatur des 15. bis 18. Jahrhunderts. Berlin: De Gruyter, 1970–1975.

2. Drama Editions Used: Individual Authors

Avancini, Nikolaus. *Pietas Victrix.* In *Barockdrama,* vol. 2 (*Das Ordensdrama*).

Bidermann, Jakob. *Ludi Theatrales Sacri.* Edited by Rolf Tarot. Vol. 1. Deutsche Neudrucke, no. 6. Tübingen: Niemeyer, 1963.

Birken, Sigmund Von, trans. *Androfilo Oder die Wunder Liebe.* Wolfenbüttel: Biszmarck, 1656. Faber du Faur microfilm, reel 125, no. 535.

Gryphius, Andreas. *Gesamtausgabe der deutschsprachigen Werke.* Edited by Marian Szyrocki and Hugh Powell. Neudrucke deutscher Literaturwerke, Neue Folge. Göttingen and Tübingen: Niemeyer, 1963 ff. Vols. 4–8.

Hallmann, Johann Christian. *Sämtliche Werke.* Ausgaben deutscher Literatur des 15. bis 18. Jahrhunderts. Berlin: De Gruyter, 1975. Vol. 1: *Theodoricus* and *Mariamne.*

———. *Trauer- Freuden- und Schäffer-Spiele.* Breslau: Fellgiebel, 1684. (*Urania* and *Adonis und Rosibella.*) Faber du Faur microfilm, reel 155, no. 649.

Harsdörffer, Georg Philipp. *Seelewig.* In *Barockdrama,* vol. 5 (*Die Oper*).

Haugwitz, August Adolf Von. *Prodromus Poeticus/ Oder: Poetischer Vortrab bestehende aus unterschiedenen Trauer- und Lust-Spielen/ Sonetten/ Oden/*

Elegien. Dresden: Bergen, 1684. *(Soliman.)* Faber du Faur microfilm, reel 155, no. 653.

————. *Schuldige Unschuld oder Maria Stuarda.* Edited by Robert R. Heitner. Neudrucke der deutschen Literatur des 17. Jahrhunderts, no. 1. Bern: Lang, 1971.

Heinrich Julius Von Braunschweig. *Vincentius Ladislaus.* In *Barockdrama,* vol. 4 *(Komödie).*

Hofmann Von Hofmannswaldau, Christian, trans. *Der Getreue Schäfer.* In his *Deutsche Übersetzungen und Getichte.* Breslau: Fellgibel, 1679. Faber du Faur microfilm, reel 399, no. 1281.

Klaj, Johann. *Redeoratorien und "Lobrede der Teutschen Poeterey."* Edited by Conrad Wiedemann. Deutsche Neudrucke, Barock. Tübingen: Niemeyer, 1965.

Lohenstein, Daniel Casper Von. *Afrikanische Trauerspiele: Cleopatra, Sophonisbe.* Edited by Klaus Günther Just. Bibliothek des Literarischen Vereins Stuttgart, no. 294. Stuttgart: Hiersemann, 1957.

————. *Großmüthiger Feldherr Arminius oder Hermann Als Ein tapfferer Beschirmer der deutschen Freyheit/ Nebst seiner Durchlauchtigen Thußnelda In einer sinnreichen Staats- Liebes- und Helden-Geschichte.* 1689–1690; rpt. ed. Elida Maria Szarota. Nachdrucke deutscher Literatur des 17. Jahrhunderts. Vol 2, pp. 483–512. Bern: Lang, 1973.

————. *Römische Trauerspiele: Agrippina, Epicharis.* Edited by Klaus Günther Just. Bibliothek des Literarischen Vereins Stuttgart, no. 293. Stuttgart: Hiersemann, 1955.

————. *Türkische Trauerspiele: Ibrahim Bassa, Ibrahim Sultan.* Edited by Klaus Günther Just. Bibliothek des Literarischen Vereins Stuttgart, no. 292. Stuttgart: Hiersemann, 1953.

Mitternacht, Johann Sebastian. *Dramen 1662/1667.* Edited by Marianne Kaiser. Deutsche Neudrucke, Reihe Barock, no. 22. Tübingen: Niemeyer, 1972.

Opitz, Martin. *Geistliche Poemata (1638).* Edited by Erich Trunz. Deutsche Neudrucke, Reihe Barock, no. 1. Tübingen: Niemeyer, 1966. *(Judith.)*

————. *Weltliche Poemata Erster Teil (1644).* Edited by Erich Trunz. Deutsche Neudrucke, Reihe Barock, no. 2. Tübingen: Niemeyer, 1967. *(Antigone, Die Trojanerinnen,* and *Dafne.)*

Reuter, Christian. *Die Ehrliche Frau von Plißine.* In *Barockdrama,* vol. 4 *(Komödie).*

Rist, Johann. *Sämtliche Werke.* Edited by Eberhard Mannack. Vol. 1. Berlin: De Gruyter, 1967.

Stieler, Caspar. *Basilene.* Rudolstadt: Freyschmidt, 1667.

————. *Bellemperie.* Jena: Nisio, 1680. Faber du Faur microfilm, reel 69, no. 348.

————. *Der betrogene Betrug.* Rudolstadt: Freyschmidt, 1667.

————. *Die erfreuete Unschuld.* Rudolstadt: Freyschmidt, 1666. Faber du Faur microfilm, reel 68, no. 345.

————. *Ernelinde/ Oder die Viermahl Braut.* Rudolstadt: Freyschmidt, 1665.

————. *Der Vermeinte Printz.* Rudolstadt: Freyschmidt, 1665. Faber du Faur microfilm, reel 67, no. 343.

————. *Willmut.* Jena: Nisio, 1680. Faber du Faur microfilm, reel 69, no. 348.

————. *Die Wittekinden.* Jena: Neuenhahn, 1666. In *Barockdrama,* vol. 6 (*Oratorium/Festspiel*). Also in Faber du Faur microfilm, reel 67, no. 344.

Weise, Christian. *Sämtliche Werke.* Edited by John D. Lindberg. Vol. 1 (*Masaniello*) and vol. 11 (*Bäurischer Machiavellus*). Berlin: De Gruyter, 1971 ff.

SECONDARY SOURCES

1. Bibliographies and Annotated Bibliographical Essays

Asmuth, Bernhard. *Daniel Casper von Lohenstein.* Sammlung Metzler. Stuttgart: Metzler, 1971. Succinct summary of Lohenstein scholarship to 1971, with selected bibliography. Needs updating.

Brauneck, Manfred. "Deutsche Literatur des 17. Jahrhunderts: Revision eines Epochenbildes: Forschungsbericht, 1945–1970." *Deutsche Vierteljahrsschrift* 45 (1971):378–468. Because Brauneck not only selects and annotates the important scholarly literature, but also analyzes strengths, weaknesses, and lacunae, this is the most useful bibliography of Baroque scholarship to 1970.

Dünnhaupt, Gerhard. *Bibliographisches Handbuch der Barockliteratur: Hundert Personalbibliographien deutscher Autoren des 17. Jahrhunderts.* 3 vols. Hiersemanns bibliographische Handbücher, vol. 2:1–3. Stuttgart: Anton Hiersemann, 1979–1981. An ambitious undertaking which aspires to be a complete bibliography of known literary works by the most important authors of the seventeenth century, with locations of copies of seventeenth-century editions.

Gabel, Gernot Uwe. *Drama und Theater des deutschen Barock: Eine Handbibliographie der Sekundärliteratur.* Hamburg: Gabel, 1974. A fairly complete bibliography of secondary works on drama and theater to 1973, organized by subject, without annotation.

Habersetzer, Karl-Heinz. *Bibliographie der deutschen Barockliteratur: Ausgaben und Reprints, 1945–1976.* Dokumente des Internationalen Arbeitskreises für Barockliterature, vol. 5. Hamburg: Hauswedell, 1978.

Useful bibliography of those many Baroque works made available in new editions between 1945 and 1976.

Mannack, Eberhard. *Andreas Gryphius.* Sammlung Metzler. Stuttgart: Metzler, 1968. Succinct summary of Gryphius scholarship to 1968, with selected bibliography. Needs updating.

Merkel, Ingrid. *Barock.* Handbuch der deutschen Literaturgeschichte, Abt. Bibliographien, no. 5. Bern/Munich: Francke, 1971. A selected bibliography of Baroque scholarship to 1967 organized by subject, without annotations.

Neumeister, Erdmann. *De Poetis germanicis.* 1695. Edited by Franz Heiduck. Rpt. Deutsche Barock-Literatur. Bern: Francke, 1978. Reprint and translation of late Baroque dictionary of *literati,* with extensive accompanying bio- and bibliographical notes by the editor for each author.

Tarot, Rolf. "Literatur zum deutschen Drama und Theater des 16. und 17. Jahrhunderts: Ein Forschungsbericht (1945–1962)." *Euphorion* 57 (1963):411–53. A survey of scholarship on Baroque drama.

2. Basic and Recent Studies: General

Alewyn, Richard. "Der Geist des Barocktheaters." In *Weltliteratur: Festgabe für Fritz Strich zum 70. Geburtstag.* Edited by Walter Muschg and Emil Staiger. Bern: Francke, 1952. Penetrating essay which sees the nature of Baroque drama and theater in the theatrical metaphor for life and the perception of all activities as role-playing.

Baesecke, Anna. *Das Schauspiel der englischen Komödianten in Deutschland (Seine dramatische Form und seine Entwicklung).* Studien zur englischen Philologie, no. 87. Halle: Niemeyer, 1935. Useful analysis of the offerings of the itinerant stage as published in the two important collections of 1630 and 1670.

Benjamin, Walter. *Ursprung des deutschen Trauerspiels.* Frankfurt am Main: Suhrkamp, 1963. Written in 1928, this long essay offered the first insights into the allegorical nature of Baroque tragedy.

Catholy, Eckehard. *Das deutsche Lustspiel.* Vol. 1. Stuttgart: Kohlhammer, 1969. Survey of German comedy. Section on Baroque comedy excludes romantic (heroic) comedy from consideration, but contains excellent analysis of social function of satirical comedy.

Cysarz, Herbert. *Deutsche Barockdichtung: Renaissance, Barock, Rococo.* Leipzig: Haessel, 1924. A good example of *Geistesgeschichte,* this work is thought-provoking, but lacks the material proof (e.g. concrete examples, quotations, or footnotes) scholarship expects today.

Flemming, Willi. Introduction ("Einführung") of each volume. *Barockdrama.* Hildesheim: Olms, 1965. These introductions by one of the great Baroque scholars, when taken together, constitute the only survey of Baroque drama. Written in the 1930s, all are still basic to the field.

Gaede, Friedrich. *Humanismus—Barock—Aufklärung.* Handbuch der deutschen Literaturgeschichte, Abt. Darstellungen, no. 2. Bern/ Munich: Francke, 1971. The most readable of recent surveys of the period. But its brevity means that only major genres and major works of major authors find a place within it. It belongs to the group of studies of the early 1970s which view the Baroque as a stepping stone to the Enlightenment.

George, David. *Deutsche Tragödientheorien vom Mittelalter bis zu Lessing: Texte und Kommentare.* Munich: Beck, 1972. This useful work pairs exerpts from many of the most important drama theorists with descriptions and analyses.

Hankamer, Paul. *Deutsche Gegenreformation und Deutsches Barock.* Stuttgart: Metzler, 1935. Still the basic survey of Baroque literature. This study, perhaps more than any other, served to canonize certain works and consign others to relative oblivion, thus largely determining his own and subsequent overviews of the period.

Hinck, Walter. *Das deutsche Lustspiel des 17. und 18. Jahrhunderts und die italienische Komödie.* Germanistische Abhandlungen, no. 8. Stuttgart: Metzler, 1965. One of the few studies to recognize the importance of Italian theater for German Baroque drama. A useful survey and perceptive analysis which resurrects many key plays ignored by Hankamer, Catholy, and others.

Kirchner, Gottfried. *Fortuna in Dichtung und Emblematik des Barock: Tradition und Bedeutungswandel eines Motifs.* Stuttgart: Metzler, 1970. Excellent study of a motif which not only demonstrates the religious basis for concepts of luck and destiny, but also serves as a perceptive overview of sixteenth- and seventeenth-century literature from a very fruitful perspective.

Lunding, Eric. *Das schlesische Kunstdrama.* Copenhagen: Haase, 1940. On Gryphius, Lohenstein, Hallmann, Haugwitz. Sees Gryphius's plays as religious and metaphysical, those of his later countrymen as secularized political drama.

Müller, Günther. *Deutsche Dichtung von der Renaissance bis zum Ausgang des Barock.* 1927. Rpt. Darmstadt: Wissenschaftliche Buchgesellschaft, 1957. An older survey which still has value.

Newald, Richard. *Die deutsche Literatur vom Späthumanismus zur Empfindsamkeit, 1570–1750.* Vol. 5 of *Geschichte der deutschen Literatur von den Anfängen bis zur Gegenwart.* Munich: Beck, 1960. A detailed survey which does not ignore "minor" works or writers, but which rarely surmounts the fragmentation and superficiality of a description of all known literary phenomena of the period.

Pascal, Roy. *German Literature in the Sixteenth and Seventeenth Centuries: Renaissance, Reformation, Baroque.* Vol. 2 of *Introductions to German Literature.* New York: Barnes & Noble, 1968. Straightforward introduction to the concept and literature of the German Baroque. Useful appendix of major authors, with brief biographical and bibliographical material on each. Only survey in English.

Reichelt, Klaus. *Barockdrama und Absolutismus: Studien zum deutschen Drama zwischen 1650 und 1700.* Europäische Hochschulschriften, Reihe 1, vol. 387. Frankfurt: Peter Lang, 1981. Another productive survey of Baroque literature from a single perspective: Baroque drama and the rising absolutistic political system. Perhaps stresses minor dramatists at the expense of major figures.

Richter, Werner. *Liebeskampf 1630 und Schaubühne 1670: Ein Beitrag zur deutschen Theatergeschichte des 17. Jahrhunderts.* Palaestra, no. 78. Berlin: Mayer and Müller, 1910. Positivistic survey of the offerings of the itinerant stage.

Rupprich, Hans. *Die deutsche Literatur vom späten Mittelalter bis zum Barock.* Vol. 4 of *Geschichte der deutschen Literatur von den Anfängen bis zur Gegenwart.* 2 parts. Munich: Beck, 1970. A basic survey of sixteenth-century literature.

Schöne, Albrecht. *Emblematik und Drama im Zeitalter des Barock.* 2nd rev. ed. Munich: Beck, 1968. The most exciting approach yet to Baroque drama, a groundbreaking effort which has already borne much fruit and which dominates current scholarship.

Stammler, Wolfgang. *Von der Mystik zum Barock: 1400–1600.* Stuttgart: Metzler, 1950. Still one of the basic surveys of the period. Less detailed than Rupprich, but more perceptive.

Szarota, Elida Maria. *Geschichte, Politik und Gesellschaft im Drama des 17. Jahrhunderts.* Bern/Munich: Francke, 1976. Major reanalysis of the political ideas to be found in Baroque drama based on extensive readings in contemporary political theory, historiography, and popular thought.

3. Drama before Opitz

Brett-Evans, David. *Von Hrotsvit bis Folz und Gengenbach: Eine Geschichte des mittelalterlichen deutschen Dramas.* Grundlagen der Germanistik, no. 15. 2 vols. Berlin: Erich Schmidt, 1975. Best survey of medieval German drama, including early *Fastnachtspiel.*

Catholy, Eckehard. *Fastnachtspiel.* Sammlung Metzler. Stuttgart: Metzler, 1966. Excellent succinct introduction to the carneval farces, combining survey and annotated bibliography.

Van Abbé, Derek. *Drama in Renaissance Germany and Switzerland.* Parkville: Melbourne University, 1961. The only survey in English on German sixteenth-century drama.

Young, Karl. *The Drama of the Medieval Church.* 2 vols. Oxford: Oxford University Press, 1951. Most important work on medieval drama in any language. Includes most of the important short liturgical texts in their entirety, as well as survey, analysis, and periodization.

4. Gryphius

Flemming, Willi. *Andreas Gryphius: Eine Monographie.* Sprache und Literatur, no. 26. Stuttgart: Kohlhammer, 1965. One of the basic monographs.

Hillen, Gerd. *Andreas Gryphius' Cardenio und Celinde: Zur Erscheinungsform und Funktion der Allegorie in den Gryphischen Trauerspielen.* De Proprietatibus Litterarum, Series Practica, no. 45. The Hague: Mouton, 1971. Demonstrates the approach of the allegorical exegete to a sample drama text.

Hinck, Walter. "Gryphius und die italienische Komödie: Untersuchung zum *Horribilicribrifax."* *Germanisch-Romanisch Monatsschrift,* n.s., 13 (1963):120–46. Applies his italianate perspective to this very relevant comedy of contemporary German soldiers of fortune at war's end.

Jöns, Dietrich Walter. *Das "Sinnen-bild": Studien zur allegorischen Bildlichkeit bei Andreas Gryphius.* Stuttgart: Metzler, 1966. One of the basic monographs on Gryphius. The first massive use of traditional symbols and allegories as a key to the works of Gryphius. Contains a useful bibliography of sourcebooks of such traditional imagery.

Kaiser, Gerhard, ed. *Die Dramen des Andreas Gryphius: Eine Sammlung von Einzelinterpretationen.* Stuttgart: Metzler, 1968. Collection of essays on each of Gryphius's dramatic works. Many are still the definitive studies.

Schings, Hans-Jürgen. *Die patristische und stoische Tradition bei Andreas Gryphius: Untersuchungen zu den Dissertationes funebres und Trauerspielen.* Kölner Germanistische Studien, no. 2. Cologne: Böhlau, 1966. One of the basic monographs. Reveals religious meaning in Gryphius's works through another source: patristic and stoic traditions. Invaluable partner to the work of Jöns. Useful bibliography of these materials.

Steinhagen, Harald. *Wirklichkeit und Handeln im barocken Drama: Historisch-ästhetische Studien zum Trauerspiel des Andreas Gryphius.* Studien zur deutschen Literatur, no. 51. Tübingen: Niemeyer, 1977. Recent study of Gryphius's tragedies.

5. Heinrich Julius von Braunschweig

Knight, A. H. J. *Heinrich Julius, Duke of Brunswick.* Oxford: Oxford

University Press, 1948. In English. Although plagued by subjective judgments, it provides a valuable survey.

Werner, Ingrid. *Zwischen Mittelalter und Neuzeit: Heinrich Julius von Braunschweig als Dramatiker der Übergangszeit.* Europäische Hochschulschriften, 1, no. 160. Bern: Lang, 1976. Recent survey, offers penetrating interpretative insights.

6. Jesuit Drama

Best, Thomas W. *Jacob Bidermann.* TWAS. New York: Twayne, 1974. English monograph on Bidermann.

Flemming, Willi. *Geschichte des Jesuitentheaters in den Landen deutscher Zunge.* Berlin: Gesellschaft für Theatergeschichte, 1923. One of the two older surveys, still valuable.

Müller, Johannes. *Das Jesuitendrama in den Ländern deutscher Zunge vom Anfang (1555) bis zum Hochbarock (1665).* 2 vols. Augsburg: Filser, 1930. Other older survey, still useful.

Szarota, Elida Maria. "Das Jesuitendrama als Vorläufer der modernen Massenmedien." *Daphnis* 4 (1975):129–43. An audience-oriented presentation of the intentions of Jesuit drama.

————. *Das Jesuitendrama im deutschen Sprachgebiet: Eine Periochen-Edition, Texte und Kommentare.* Munich: Fink, 1979 ff. One of the two very recent surveys. It consists both of texts and of a final presentation of Szarota's recent studies in the area.

————. "Versuch einer neuen Periodisierung des Jesuitendramas." *Daphnis* 3 (1974):158–77. Presents a reinterpretation of chronological groupings of Jesuit plays by subject matter rather than by stylistic similarities to secular drama.

Valentin, Jean-Marie. *Le Théâtre des Jesuites dans les pays de langue allemande (1554–1680): Salut des âmes et ordre des cités.* 3 vols. Berner Beiträge zur Barockgermanistik, vol. 3. Bern: Lang, 1978. Important new study. In French.

7. Lohenstein

Aikin, Judith P. *The Mission of Rome in the Dramas of Daniel Casper von Lohenstein: Historical Tragedy as Prophecy and Polemic.* Stuttgarter Arbeiten zur Germanistik, no. 21. Stuttgart: Akademischer Verlag Hans-Dieter Heinz, 1976. Views the plays from a single perspective: the traditional religious interpretation of the significance of the Holy Roman Empire in universal history.

Gillespie, Gerald. *Daniel Casper von Lohenstein's Historical Tragedies.* Columbus: Ohio State University, 1965. Only survey in English. Interprets Lohenstein's plays as universally understandable texts of world literature, ignoring traditional imagery and traditional attitudes toward morality and politics.

Juretzka, Joerg C. *Zur Dramatik Daniel Caspers von Lohenstein: 'Cleopatra' 1661 und 1680.* Deutsche Studien, no. 18. Meisenheim: Hain, 1976. Comparison of the two versions of *Cleopatra* yields conclusions about Lohenstein's creative process and concerns.

Just, Klaus Günther. *Die Trauerspiele Lohensteins: Versuch einer Interpretation.* Philologische Studien und Quellen, no. 9. Berlin: Schmidt, 1961. Basic study of Lohenstein's tragedies by the editor of the critical edition. Stresses exoticism, pragmatic politics, and erotic forces.

Spellerberg, Gerhard. *Verhängnis und Geschichte: Untersuchungen zu den Trauerspielen und dem 'Arminius'-Roman Daniel Caspers von Lohenstein.* Berlin/Zurich: Gehlen, 1970. One of the basic monographs on Lohenstein. He sees a secular and autonomous historical process as the core of Lohenstein's works.

Tarot, Rolf. "Zu Lohensteins *Sophonisbe.*" *Euphorion* 59 (1965): 72–96. He criticizes earlier secular approaches to this play.

8. The Nuremberg School

Franz, Albin. *Johann Klaj: Ein Beitrag zur deutschen Literaturgeschichte des 17. Jahrhunderts.* Beiträge zur deutschen Literaturwissenschaft, no. 6. Marburg: Elwert, 1908. Only monograph on Klaj.

Gärtner, H. "*Seelewig*: Ein Nürnberger Singspiel: Deutschlands ältestes Operndokument." *Frankenspiegel* 2, no. 5 (1951):10–14. On Harsdörffer's opera libretto.

Heitner, Robert R. "Johann Klaj's Popularizations of Neo-Latin Drama." *Daphnis* 6 (1977):313–25. On Klaj's oratorios.

Tittmann, Julius. *Die Nürnberger Dichterschule: Harsdörffer, Klaj, Birken: Ein Beitrag zur deutschen Literatur- und Kulturgeschichte des 17. Jahrhunderts.* 1847; rpt. Wiesbaden: Sändig, 1965. Only survey of the Nürnberg School.

9. Opitz

Alewyn, Richard. *Vorbarocker Klassizismus und griechische Tragödie: Analyse der 'Antigone'-Übersetzung des Martin Opitz.* Heidelberg, 1926; rpt. Darmstadt: Wissenschaftliche Buchgesellschaft, 1962. Penetrating comparison of Opitz's Antigone translation with the original.

Szyrocki, Marian. *Martin Opitz.* 2nd revised edition. Munich: Beck, 1974. Best monograph on Opitz. Much attention to his political role and political stands.

Ulmer, Bernhard. *Martin Opitz.* TWAS. New York: Twayne, 1971. Only study in English.

10. Stieler

Höfer, Conrad. *Die Rudolstädter Festspiele aus den Jahren 1665–1667 und ihr Dichter: Eine literarhistorische Studie.* Leipzig: Voigtländer, 1904. Useful positivistic study of the plays which, following Köster's lead, identifies the mysterious "Filidor" as Caspar Stieler, and provides stylistic, dialect, and source studies of the texts.

Zeman, Herbert. *Kaspar Stieler, Versuch einer Monographie und 'Die Dichtkunst des Spaten 1685.'* Diss. Vienna, 1965. Only monograph on Stieler, containing major breakthroughs in biography and documentation. Superficial treatment of the dramas.

11. Weise and the Rhetorical Drama

Burger, Heinz Otto. "Dasein heißt eine Rolle spielen: Das Barock im Spiegel von Jacob Bidermanns *Philemon Martyr* und Christian Weises *Masaniello.*" In *Dasein heißt eine Rolle spielen.* Munich: Hanser, 1963, pp. 80–93. Compares Weise's play with the Latin Jesuit play in terms of a common theme—role-playing. Result undermines recent tendency to see Masaniello as an admirable revolutionary.

Kaiser, Marianne. *Mitternacht, Zeidler, Weise: das protestantische Schultheater nach 1648 im Kampf gegen höfische Kultur und absolutistisches Regiment.* Palaestra, no. 259. Göttingen: Vandenhoeck & Ruprecht, 1972. Basic Marxist study of seventeenth-century protestant prose school theater.

Mannack, Eberhard. "Johann Rists 'Perseus' und das Drama des Barock." *Daphnis* 1 (1972):141–49. Sees influence of itinerant theater in deviations of this play from Opitzian drama theory.

Sorg, Norbert. *Restauration und Rebellion, die deutschen Dramen Johann Sebastian Mitternacht's: ein Beitrag zur Geschichte des protestantischen Schuldramas im 17. Jahrhundert.* Hochschulsammlung Philosophie: Literaturwissenschaft, vol. 5. Freiburg: Hochschulverlag, 1980. Recent study, unavailable to me at press time.

Index

179

03